FOR SAMUEL

TRADE UNIONISTS AGAINST TERROR

TRADE
GUATEMALA
UNIONISTS
CITY
AGAINST
1954–1985
TERROR

THE UNIVERSITY OF
NORTH CAROLINA PRESS
CHAPEL HILL AND LONDON

DEBORAH LEVENSON-ESTRADA

© 1994 The University of North Carolina Press

All rights reserved

Manufactured in the United States of America

Library of Congress Cataloging-in-Publication Data

Levenson-Estrada, Deborah.
Trade unionists against terror : Guatemala City, 1954–
1985 / by Deborah Levenson-Estrada.
p.   cm.
Includes bibliographical references and index.
ISBN 0-8078-2131-4 (cloth : alk. paper). — ISBN
0-8078-4440-3 (pbk. : alk. paper)
1. Trade-unions—Guatemala—Guatemala—Political
activity—History—20th century.   2. Working class—
Guatemala—Guatemala—History—20th century.
3. Guatemala—History—1945–1985.   4. Violence—
Guatemala—Guatemala—History—20th century.
I. Title.
HD6548.5.L48   1994
322'.2'097281—dc20

                                    93-32054
                                         CIP

The paper in this book meets the guidelines for permanence
and durability of the Committee on Production Guidelines
for Book Longevity of the Council on Library Resources.

Deborah Levenson-Estrada is associate professor of history
at Columbia University.

98 97 96 95 94   5 4 3 2 1

Contents

Illustrations

Acknowledgments

My biggest debt is to past and present Guatemalan trade unionists. From the bottom of my heart I thank many women and men for their time, interest, trust, and, in some cases, friendship. Wisdom, however, dictates that I not acknowledge them here by name.

I thank Myrna Mack Chang, assassinated on September 11, 1990, for the warm and witty encouragement that she gave me, and that my memories of her continue to provide me.

For varied kinds of generous support, I am grateful to Emily Berg, Edna Coleman, Marilee Crocker, Barbara Fields, Judith Fleisher, Ted Joyce, Herb Klein, and Karen Nelson. Warren Dean's confidence in me—as well as his unfailing insight and generosity—has been very important to this work and to my life as a historian. Clara Arenas, Betsy Blackmar, Joshua Freeman, Jim Handy, Marcie Mersky, Barbara Weinstein, and Peter Winn read drafts of the manuscript and gave me excellent advice, most of which I took. Stevie Champion was a wonderful and sensitive copyeditor. I also appreciate the efforts of David Perry at the University of North Carolina Press.

It is a pleasure to record in print that my little daughters Ana and Jasmin have brought me great joy, and that time and again while I was writing this book they saved my sense of humor and of perspective.

Finally, I especially thank my best critic, my husband Samuel Estrada, for his candor, intelligence, and love, and for his power to be compassionate.

Abbreviations

A-DAT	Archivo, Dirección Administrativo de Trabajo
AFL	American Federation of Labor
AGA	General Association of Farm Owners
AGAE	Association of Nurses' Aides
AID	Agency for International Development
AIFLD	American Institute for Free Labor Development (AFL-CIO)
ATRG	Association of Telegraph and Radio-telegraph Operators
CACIF	Coordinating Committee of Agricultural, Commercial, Industrial, and Financial Associations
CACM	Central American Common Market
CAVISA	Central American Glass Industry
CDIC	Centro de Documentación, Inforpress Centroamérica
CETE	Emergency Committee of State Workers
CGTG	General Confederation of Guatemalan Workers
CIDASA	Atlantic Industrial Company
CIO	Congress of Industrial Organizations
CLAT	Latin American Confederation of Workers
CNDCC	Committee for the National Defense Against Communism
CNRS	National Committee of Trade Union Reorganization
CNT	National Central of Workers
CNUS	National Committee on Trade Union Unity

COJUCO	Legal Aid for Workers and Peasants
CONSIGUA	Confederation of Guatemalan Unions
CONTRAGUA	Confederation of Guatemalan Workers
CRN	Committee on National Reconstruction
CSG	Guatemalan Trade Union Council (ORIT affiliate)
CTC	Confederation of Cuban Workers
CTF	Central of Federated Workers
CUC	Committee of Campesino Unity
EGP	Guerrilla Army of the Poor
EGSA	Coca-Cola Bottling Company of Guatemala
FAR	Rebel Armed Forces
FASGUA	Autonomous Federation of Guatemalan Unions
FCG	Guatemalan Federation of Peasants
FDCR	United Front Against Repression
FECETRAG	Central Federation of Guatemalan Workers
FEGUA	Company of Guatemalan Railroads
FENOT	National Federation of Transport Workers
FESEB	Bank Workers' Federation
FETULIA	Sugar Workers' Federation
FTC	Christian Workers' Front
FTG	Federation of Guatemalan Workers
FUR	United Revolutionary Front
ICA	Associated Civil Engineers
ICCR	Interfaith Center on Corporate Responsibility
ICFTU	International Conference of Federated Trade Unions
IDESAC	Institute for the Economic and Social Development of Central America
IGSS	Guatemalan Institute of Social Security
IRCA	International Railways of Central America
IUF	International Union of Food and Allied Workers' Associations
JOC	Young Catholic Worker
MLN	Movement for National Liberation

MONAP	National Movement of Pobladores
MR-13	Revolutionary Movement of November 13
ORIT	Inter-American Regional Organization of Workers (AFL-CIO)
ORPA	Revolutionary Organization of the People in Arms
PAR	Revolutionary Action party
PDC	Christian Democratic party
PGT	Guatemalan Labor party
PID	Party for Institutionalized Democracy
PR	Revolutionary party
PSD	Social Democratic party
SAG	Union of Graphic Arts
SAMF	Railroad Workers' Mutual Aid Union
SPAS	Union of Automobile Pilots
STECSA	Union of Workers at Embotelladora Central SA
STEG	Union of Guatemalan Educational Workers
STEGAC	Coca-Cola Bottling Company Workers' Union
UFCO	United Fruit Company

Introduction:
Facing the Devil

During May and June 1980, when his union at the Coca-Cola Bottling Plant in Guatemala City suffered the worst of its violent history, delivery truck driver Marco Tulio Loza had the following recurrent dream: "I'm driving through the city and at each corner the devil is waiting for me and he tries to stop me and seize me. He has horns and a mangled, bloody body and at every corner I accelerate and go on, but he is always at the next corner, waiting. Finally I decide to stop and confront him. Then I wake up." Twenty-six-year-old Loza explained to me that his dream was "about life. It means you cannot run away from reality. You must confront it. Why do I wake up before the fight? Maybe because I'm afraid I might lose. But if I don't fight, definitely I'll lose. The devil never goes away on his own."[1] Five of Loza's fellow trade unionists had been murdered in a five-week period; two of them were tortured to death. At a time when many workers were leaving the union, Loza did not. Decisiveness, solitude, and power—the devil's and Loza's—pervaded a dream that encapsulates the drama of the Guatemalan labor movement, a small movement persistently battling extreme violence in order to survive.

Unlike most states in twentieth-century Latin America, the Guatemalan state has seldom attempted to ally or negotiate with organized labor. From the time of a 1954 coup that destroyed Guatemala's decade-long, sole experiment in democratic government, the state began repressing trade unionists with as much brutality as its functionaries could imagine inflicting. The representation of the devil in Loza's dream is a haunting one: it suggests Catholic images of evil and suffering, a torturer, and a tortured body, the ubiquitous figure of pain and annihilation in Guatemala. That the devil's "mangled, bloody body" was not weak but vigorous and ready to stop Loza's vehicle and "seize" him is emblematic of the frightening proposition that the torturer and the tortured body constitute the strength of the Guatemalan state. It is hardly surprising that Loza might think that.[2]

The nuanced forms of capitalist control of labor to which readers in the United States are accustomed have not existed in recent Guatemalan history. Without the aid or cushion of reformism or populism, the industrial development of the 1960s occurred under the auspices of a terrorist state. This state did not try to win legitimacy through the production of meanings and values that create a consensus about the distribution of power in society. Perhaps because of this, foreign and national capitalists did not establish a subtle means to subdue struggle within the workplace. Violence simplified the politics of production for owners and managers. Asked, "How does one respond to a bothersome labor leader?," a businessman replied, "Shoot him or eliminate him. Assassinate him. Murder him. Whichever word is applicable."[3] A worker recalled this experience in a modern textile plant:

> We tried to organize a union once and the death squad people came and beat up a worker with the sound of the machinery covering his screams. And then someone was taken away and did not reappear. And then another one was taken. They took him blindfolded to an unknown place and removed the blindfold and there was the man who had been kidnapped before he was, hanging still alive, his body in shreds, completely cut up, wounded. And they said to the second man, "Do you still want to be a trade unionist?" Well . . . with that, the first attempt to start a union ended. I left soon afterwards. I didn't want to work in a place like that.[4]

Just as Guatemalans had to take this terrorism into account while they went about their lives, the historian must consider the thoughts and feelings of people living in such a society. On one level, Guatemalan workers unionized for the same reasons their counterparts did elsewhere, but in post-1954 Guatemala the quest for dignity and a decent life translated into an unusual labor movement. Preoccupied with questions of being, its members often conceptualized in existentialist terms. One trade unionist said: "You question yourself, whether you call life one thing which is not life, and whether you prefer to be a human being for a short time or a vegetable for a long time. You know that by choosing to be a human being for a short time you point the way for others to live as humans. I think this is the process most workers go through when they are in the labor movement—not all, but many."[5]

Trade unionism transformed lives in the few workplaces where it flourished. Before a union existed at the Coca-Cola Bottling Plant in Guatemala City, workers barely knew one another, generally did not dare to lift their heads in front of managers, and received the lowest wages paid in the beverage industry. As of 1985, after a decade of trade unionism, the Coca-Cola workers were self-confident, proud, and outspoken; they earned among the highest factory wages in the city; and they understood one another, the company, their country, the law, and the state's extralegalism. They attended union-sponsored seminars, spread trade unionism as best they could, and brought their families to union-sponsored cultural events. When they became trade unionists, these workers started to assume identities and take actions that negated an inadequate existence. Cast as maimed, they acted in their own image of health.

Trade Unionists' Views of History

Four union officers, including General Secretary Rodolfo Robles, of the Coca-Cola Bottling Company Workers' Union (STEGAC) were sitting in the union office, located on the plant grounds, in the late evening of February 17, 1984, when management informed them, "This piece of shit [the plant] is closed." Instead of leaving the premises as ordered, they rounded up thirty more workers and began to occupy the plant that night. "That was our decision," explained Robles. By the following afternoon the four-hundred-person work force had joined them. The workers stayed inside the plant for a year, at which point the company conceded and reopened. The shutdown was management's most recent attempt to destroy STEGAC. Battling for nine years to root it out, Coca-Cola finally decided to give up the plant rather than accept a union. And then even that maneuver failed.

At the time of the occupation, the country was under a state of siege. Outside of a few unions operating almost as secret societies, no labor movement existed. The most important urban labor confederations of the 1954–80 period had been destroyed. In addition, the Marxist parties that had played roles of varying intensity in the labor movement were disconnected from it as a result of an unusually effective urban counterinsurgency that had begun in mid-1978 and was still operating. On the first full day of the Coca-Cola occupation, a trade unionist in a neighboring factory suspected of revolutionary sympathies was kidnapped.

Despite the state of siege, and without a labor confederation, labor lawyers, or Marxist cadres, the union won. Its capacity to sustain a yearlong occupation under these conditions grew out of its history. The union was stronger in 1984 than it had ever been and even stronger a year later. The success of the occupation vindicated the workers' sense of their own capacity to change and grow. Robles, comparing himself and other STEGAC leaders with the organizers of labor associations that had been destroyed by the repression in 1980, commented, "We are the same generation, but with different ideas."[6]

Guatemalan trade unionists had strong convictions about how their history was made. Julio Arriaza, a member of a textile workers' union, discussed theories of history in literature one night with a group of trade unionists and myself. He observed that he loved Mario Benedetti and disliked Gabriel García Márquez because "García Márquez's characters are like animals tied up during a storm which drowns them. In Benedetti the characters have space. You see the choices they face, you watch them decide, you watch them dealing with the consequences of that."[7] Literature was scarce in Guatemala and few in the room had heard of Benedetti or García Márquez, but the idea of finding a way rather than, as Arriaza portrayed García Márquez, being overwhelmed by colorfully described obstacles, appealed to all. Guatemalan trade unionists strongly opposed notions of victimization, predestination, or determinism, yet they did not think that "the people make history." They believed that some people make history because they decide to. Necessity and exploitation were the sine qua non of trade unionism, but not all workers became trade unionists. Unions existed because some workers decided to make them happen, and their decision and consciousness were central to such action as well as to their subsequent behavior. These two words—*decision* and *consciousness*—were the key words of Guatemalan trade unionism and part of its magnetism. The ideas most commonly expressed in the labor movement were that workers could intervene in situations not of their own making and change them, and that the labor movement at every point reflected the ideas of workers.

As of 1986, when a civilian government came to power after the civil war of the early 1980s peaked and as a new urban labor confederation was gaining momentum, trade unionists felt even more sure that if they were committed, if they understood their strengths and weaknesses, and if they understood their era, they could advance. They could be labeled complete idealists and voluntarists, but whatever the ultimate truth of their view of historical agency, or its roots, *is* it not the case that the way people think history is made, the way they understand historical agency, has much to do with how they make history? If they had not believed in their own power to effect change, if they had not been voluntaristic, jumping in where only "fools" dared to tread, they could not have built unions. The incessant struggle of unions to exist given a terrorist state and antiunion companies has seemed Sisyphean at times, but some members of the collective keep reaching the top of the next mountain.

What has been written by Guatemalans about the labor movement has been part of this self-conscious attempt to push against the grain. Before he went into exile in the late 1970s, Carlos Figueroa Ibarra wrote of the political contradictions of the artisanal circle that had helped defeat President Manuel Estrada Cabrera in 1920 in order to point out the pitfalls of alliances in his own time. The year before he was shot to death in 1977, labor lawyer Mario López Larrave wrote *Breve historia del movimiento sindical guatemalteco* so that workers could have in hand a brief outline of the century's significant organizations and strikes. A similar work, warning against apoliticism, was produced by Guadalupe Navas in 1978, two years before her assassination by poisoning. In exile in the early 1980s, labor leader Miguel Angel Albizures began the work of

The May First rally in front of the National Palace in downtown Guatemala City, 1988. In the foreground stands a union leader who lost his leg as a result of an assassination attempt in the early 1980s. (Photograph by Derrill Bazzy)

self-appraisal in his *Tiempo de sudor y lucha*.[8] All of these volumes were written by serious activists for people who needed more information and broadened perspectives.

Inspired by these authors, and by the labor movement, I want to communicate my knowledge of the Guatemalan labor movement to the English language reader. I hope that this book will encourage the reader to realize that it is possible to "blast open the continuum of history."[9]

In addition, it is my wish to provide insight into a historically important debate in Guatemala and elsewhere about left-wing philosophy and practice. I take issue with vanguard parties' conception of trade unions as organizations that are braked by economism (or ignorance) unless middle-class intellectuals give them ideological leadership.[10] This view presumes that workers are not thinkers and activists who seek more in life than material goods and who do more on their own, without being told to, than eat, work, play, and rest.[11] Workers are never isolated from the people and ideas of other social classes, and even of other countries. Their own views and daily lives are informed from both outside and within their own class. Like anyone, they need all the knowledge they can obtain; the point is simply that they can deliberate theories and information without constant paternalistic mediation.

Vanguard parties in Guatemala have asked basically one question about unions: what role do they play in revolution? The answer has varied depending on the party's view of revolution. The conception that unions have historical significance only insofar as they aid schemes for large-scale social change obscures the role that they have played in working-class life to protect the sanity, dignity, identity, and good sense of workers, all of which relate to the function of unions as defenders of material well-being. In Guatemala urban unions have produced a space in which democracy, egalitarianism, and honesty have been at least valued, if not always practiced. Unions have resisted authoritarianism, hierarchical notions of intelligence and importance, and the devaluation of truth telling. They have resisted the alienation from self, feelings, community, and thought that is at the heart of the dominant culture in Guatemala, and they have sharpened the sense of alienation inherent in exploitation in the workplace. How can we presume to change the world if we are not sensitive to the importance of this?

The Dimensions of Trade Unionism in Guatemala

The history of Guatemalan trade unionism from 1954 to 1985 stands in contrast to the "patient, silent struggles" celebrated by James Scott in his discussion of everyday resistance against repression and oppression in rural communities.[12] Explicit, political, and impatient, trade unionists in Guatemala City even won some concessions. Although the degree and the duration of state terrorism distinguished Guatemala from other Latin American countries living under military dictatorships in the 1970s and early 1980s, trade unionists in Guatemala and in countries such as Brazil and Chile often employed forms of struggle that were more open and frontal than one might imagine given the forms of repression.[13]

The years covered in this study, 1954 to 1985, were framed by the coup against reformist government in 1954 and, at the other end, by both the army's temporary defeat of revolutionary movements and the successful conclusion of the yearlong factory occupation by a few hundred Coca-Cola workers to protect their jobs and union in 1985. In the intervening years modernization and state politics generated social upheaval.

After the 1954 coup, which brought to power a series of repressive regimes, capitalist development surged in the late 1950s, 1960s, and early 1970s as export agriculture rapidly expanded in the countryside, displacing thousands from their land and driving many into the country's only important urban center, Guatemala City. In Guatemala City, bustling with migrants, industry developed on a significant scale for the first time in national history under the Central American Common Market (CACM).[14] This industrialization spawned trade unions that by the late 1970s led a mass movement in the city, while guerrilla groups also gained strength nationally.

In 1980, by which time industrialization had slithered into crisis after regional war and revolution had undermined CACM, massive kidnappings of leaders and members effectively halted the urban labor movement, and the revolutionary struggle came to overwhelm all others.[15] Still, a few unions, such as the Coca-Cola workers' union, weathered the military juntas and the counterinsurgency of the early 1980s, when war raged throughout the country. In that war, which lasted until 1985, 440 villages were destroyed, over 70,000 people were killed, and as many as 1 million were driven from their homes.[16] In 1986 the military returned the nation to constitutional rule and civilian presidents came to preside over a land controlled by the army. By 1986 the country and its economy were in ruins. In the city a de-proletarianization of the existing industrial work force had begun. The only new industries spawned during the "lost decade" of the 1980s were foreign-owned *maquiladoras* employing young women new to the urban proletariat and, as of this writing, yet to unionize.

Because of violence, Guatemala since 1954 has had the lowest percentage of unionized workers in Latin America—between 1.2 and 3 percent of the industrial work force. Probably at the labor movement's height in the mid-1970s, no more than a few thousand workers regularly participated in unions, although

Table 1 Number of Active* Unions, 1954–1983

1954	34	1971	208
1955–58	51	1972	188
1959	53	1973	213
1960	58	1974	251
1961	60	1975	251
1962	62	1976	237
1963	69	1977	244
1964	79	1978	228
1965	104	1979	205
1966	147	1980	146
1967	175	1981	114
1968	189	1982	83
1969	218	1983	46
1970	236		

Source: Calculated from registers, Guatemala, Archivo, Dirección Administrativo de Trabajo.

*According to the Guatemalan Labor Code, an active union is one that has twenty-one members and elects leaders who pass certain requirements, such as literacy, every two years. A union can be legal and inactive, but only active ones can bargain.

far more were involved in the major actions of organized labor; in 1977, for example, some 70,000 workers went on strike.

Between 1954 and 1980 the Labor Ministry legalized 623 unions. In any given year far less than that actually functioned (held meetings, elected officers, filed grievances, negotiated contracts), depending on the level of state violence (see Table 1). The majority, 466, of these unions were located outside of Guatemala City. This figure is deceptive, however, because at least one-fourth of the so-called unions in the rural areas were not unions but cooperatives of peasants listed as unions by the Labor Ministry. Their growth in the mid-1960s, when development agencies from the United States encouraged them, explains the increase of unions between 1965 and 1970.

In Guatemala City, 157 unions were granted legal status between 1954 and 1980 and 75 of these were in factories. No more than two dozen of the 75 remained active for more than ten years, and they formed the heart of the labor movement by the mid-1970s. These unions were located primarily in the large, modern, and often foreign-owned firms producing consumer goods and employing over two hundred workers. Among others were the unions at Philip Morris's TACASA cigarette plant, the Coca-Cola Bottling Company, Kern's canning company (a division of Riviana Foods), the Japanese-owned ACRICASA textile plant, and the Guatemalan-owned INCATECU shoe and CAVISA glass factories. Membership in these unions varied from the legal minimum of twenty-one employees to almost the entire work force, depending on the national situation.

Almost every other formal sector of the wage-earning work force had a few unions. Between 1954 and 1985 there existed (sometimes only for brief periods) various unions of bus drivers; electrical, railroad, hotel, university, construction, and bank workers; and shoeshiners, private guards, shoemakers, bakers, musicians, photographers, and printers. In addition, state workers, barred from unionizing, formed important associations in hospitals, schools, and other state institutions that led job actions, despite their extralegality. By 1985 the state workers' associations had been destroyed and approximately fourteen unions of private sector workers still had "active" status in the city.

The Structure and Sources of This Book

The first chapter of this study discusses how Communists as well as labor organizers supported by the American Federation of Labor–Congress of Industrial Organizations (AFL-CIO) attempted, with limited success, to rebuild the labor movement in Guatemala City in the 1950s and early 1960s after it was destroyed by the 1954 coup. The second chapter describes the growth of the city and industry in the 1960s and the economic, social, and cultural milieu in which an industrial labor movement was eventually constructed in that decade by former members of the Young Catholic Worker (JOC). How young workers interpreted JOC precepts—"See, Judge, Act"—and went on to become union activists is the topic of the third chapter. The fourth and fifth chapters deal with the rapid development of the citywide labor union movement in the 1970s, its unique methods and values, and its demise by 1980 as a consequence of state terrorism. The final chapter chronicles the history of the Coca-Cola Bottling Company Workers' Union, an exceptional union that survived and even prevailed from the mid-1970s and into the war-torn 1980s.

I give more attention to the Coca-Cola workers' union, STEGAC, for several reasons. In the first place, because it won concessions from a notoriously antiunion multinational company, STEGAC assumed a leadership position among other unions. Second, the union's success depended on its connection with international labor organizations, and it was therefore easier to research. The Coca-Cola workers were eager to talk to me in the 1980s because they were building international support for themselves at a time when other trade unionists were in hiding. Finally, the relationship between a small union in a small Central American country and a world labor movement is its own important and encouraging story in today's global economy, where unionism is on the defensive everywhere and not just in Guatemala.[17] If the mobilization of international labor could help defend workers in this one particularly difficult case, surely it can do so in other struggles in other places.

It is hard to study labor history in Guatemala. The National Archive and the National Hemeroteca have kept few documents pertaining to trade unionism. I had limited access to Labor Ministry archives, which in any case are incomplete, and it was a piece of good luck that I saw anything there. Above all, I relied on oral testimonies. These were rich and usually the only sources. I interviewed over one hundred trade unionists and tape-recorded forty life histories. Many of these interviews took place inside the Coca-Cola Bottling Plant when it was occupied by workers in 1984–85. Other interviews were held elsewhere in Guatemala City, as well as in Costa Rica, Mexico, and the United States. Informants were often speaking of events that were ongoing, such as the 1984 occupation, or in the recent past. Mercedes Gómez's description in the sixth chapter of his not dying twice in one day and the murder of three friends on the same day was tape-recorded inside the occupied Coca-Cola plant, where he faced similar dangers, and only four years after the incidents that he described took place.

Oral testimonies present problems. They are subjective, their form is the spoken word, the particular present from which informants speak colors their memory and their presentation of the past, what is remembered and what is forgotten abound with meaning, informants have their own reasons for telling their stories, and they speak to a visible audience which is evocative. However, I do not think that the authority of oral sources is qualitatively different from that of other sources. Any source is subjective, after all is said and done, and charged with absence and presence. Each has a form and special problems arising therein. Many sources come into being at one particular time about another time and are complicated by the politics of memory. All are informed by the present from within which they are created, and every source is produced for reasons, purposes, and persons, as are scholarly works based on primary sources. Like oral histories, primary sources and scholarly works are part of a complex set of generative social relations.

Bearing in mind these limitations, I have tried to use my sources judiciously. I have employed oral testimonies in two ways: as documents that I checked against and used in conjunction with other testimonies, newspapers, leaflets, and other archival material; and as windows onto workers' subjectivity. In the text I have sometimes utilized workers' words instead of my own to communicate their perceptions of what happened. Mercedes Gómez's own narrative of his not dying and others' deaths presents both his memory of the facts and of how events stung him. Oral histories offer the special opportunity to gather insights into what historical reconstruction, self-perception, and self-construction have to do with the making of history.[18]

The workers' own accounts also made clear that activists wove trade unionism from the multiplicity of their lives, and not only in response to their workplaces. When workers spoke of trade unionism they talked as well of families, schooling, neighborhoods, religious beliefs, personal loyalties, and so forth. Religious ideas, characters, and dramas, for example, were vital to the urban poor. Many trade unionists stated that they would have retreated had it not been for their religious convictions and the comforting thought that a supreme being was on their side. As activists they felt they could genuinely fulfill the demands of being Christian, as they interpreted those demands. Trade unionists' conceptions of male and female also colored their movement: union militancy was usually represented as masculine even though many women belonged to unions; this and the way in which individual women and men contested or accommodated gender ideologies marked a trade unionism wherein nonconformity and conformity coexisted. The diverse strands of trade unionism were apparent in the complexity of the stories workers narrated. Guatemalan trade unionists often portrayed themselves as social nonconformists, rebels against a life-denying society. Simultaneously, and perhaps making it possible to live as dissidents close to the "subversive," many saw themselves and acted as defenders of their own brand of Christian morality, of Guatemalan constitutional rights, and of conservative patriarchal family life.

Like anyone else, wage earners are people with specific histories, relationships, and concerns. The use of the term *worker* in this and other labor studies communicates powerful truths and, at the same time, is a simplified, one-dimensional identification. This point is underscored by the men and women in factories in Guatemala City who protested the devaluation of work and workers, *and* at the same time rebelled against the reduction of their entire being to worker. No one who works in a factory is properly understood by that one fact or without it. To comprehend workers as workers offers much, but to leave it at that diminishes the power of the cultural configuration within which they live and which they help create. To explain their consciousness as simply one of class is an underestimation of the intricacy of their material, intellectual, and emotional lives. To attribute their "good" acts to class consciousness and their "bad" behavior—racism, sexism, or virulent nationalism—to something else (such as religion or television) is to do an injustice not only to the complexity of the construction of ways of being in history but also to workers' power to choose among alternatives, however limited these may be.

1

Legacies and New Beginnings, 1944–1960s

Guatemalan states and elites have plagued the laboring population for centuries. During the colonial period, a state existed in large part to
forcefully collect and distribute indigenous labor, a task at which it did not
always succeed. The newly named Indians proved difficult to transform into
a passive labor force; as late as the eighteenth century colonial officials had to
chase down and whip Maya Indians to ensure the state's and hacienda owners'
repartimiento labor.[1] By the late nineteenth century, no sizable rural proletariat had emerged, and no widespread, nonviolent, stable manner of securing
labor existed. To meet the demands of coffee growers experiencing a boom in
world market prices in the 1870s, Liberal party president Justo Rufino Barrios
(1871–85) reinstituted the colonial form of forced labor, and until 1944 much
large-scale agriculture depended on compulsory labor. Except for a period of
political turmoil in the 1920s, Guatemala spent the first part of the twentieth
century under the long Liberal party dictatorships of Manuel Estrada Cabrera
(1898–1920) and Jorge Ubico (1931–44), who protected labor systems based
on forms of extraeconomic coercion such as vagrancy laws.[2]

The ascendancy of a free labor market did not occur until recently. Even by
the middle of the twentieth century, money was an important part of life, but it
had not become holy or almighty. Money appeared in rural tales of the period
as the provenance of tall white strangers from whom villagers obtained it only
at the cost of trouble, and in the oral tradition of the lower-class barrios of

Guatemala City, it had a fiendish quality.[3] By the 1940s, in Guatemala City—with a population of 170,000 and the country's sole political, commercial, cultural, and financial center—several thousand artisans in over seven hundred small and medium-sized workshops dominated manufacturing.[4] Modern industry was there but it was scarce: a few factories produced textiles, rubber shoes, soft drinks, beer, and cement. At the same time that large-scale capitalist relations of production based on wage labor were present in both the city and the countryside, they had not come to dominate life and they were not recognized as right, natural, or necessary.

By mid-century no cultural hegemony existed. The ruling Liberals of the late nineteenth and early twentieth centuries had not formulated a national discourse that articulated the enormous distinctions of class and culture into a relatively coherent whole. Guatemala was (and is) comprised of impoverished Maya Indians who were a majority speaking twenty-three languages, impoverished *ladinos* (non-Indians although often of mixed heritage), a small ladino middle class, and a wealthy minority that described itself in several different ways, including *blanco*, *ladino*, and *español*.[5] Oligarchic Liberal party leaders such as Justo Rufino Barrios and Manuel Estrada Cabrera, the latter immortalized as the archetypal Latin American dictator in Miguel Angel Asturias's *El Señor President*, believed in science, private property, progress, and individual achievement. The Liberals gave currency to notions of citizens' rights and then constructed a despotic state that negated the liberties of which the Liberals spoke. Simultaneously nationalist and ardently North Atlantic–centric, the Liberals planned to re-create the Guatemalan population by "civilizing"—as they understood that—ladinos and Maya Indians through an extensive school system and by importing Europeans. But their educational projects and their schemes to attract European immigrants were implemented only minimally.[6] Indians and lower-class ladinos remained as the majority, without cultural reformation and without developing a sense of cohesion with the urban and rural elites. The Liberals increased the state's strength dramatically between the 1870s and the 1920s, but they did not legitimize it to most Guatemalans and they were inattentive to awakening grass roots democratic sentiment.

Although the Liberals courted urban artisans, an intellectual and mobilized group that articulated its views through brotherhoods, cooperatives, and mutual aid societies, they ultimately refused to incorporate artisans into national political life.[7] Adopting aspects of Liberal ideology, these artisans were patriotic democrats who thought that "the working classes" should have rights; they were also Catholic militants who hated Liberal party anticlericalism. Disappointed in the Liberals, they organized against President Estrada Cabrera in the late 1910s to protest inflation and periodic forced urban labor on public works; as a teenager and already a carpenter, Antonio Obando Sánchez recalled being snatched off the street, "kidnapped" to dig graves and bury the dead in the city's General Cemetery. Led by tailor Silverio Ortíz, artisans formed the Workers' League and allied with the conservative, prochurch Unionist party in 1920 to overthrow Estrada Cabrera three years after an earthquake had devastated the city.[8] Obando Sánchez fought with a Remington rifle alongside hundreds of young men and women from the urban popular classes. Artisans felt empowered by the 1920 uprising; Obando Sánchez remembered that "after what we did, there was not going to be this lowering of brows and taking off hats when we walk down the street and pass a señor . . . because now we are equals!" And a few years later, disillusioned by the Unionists and dismayed that "misery and poverty remained common and unchanged," he and other artisans such as Antonio Cumes had enough freedom in the post–Estrada Cabrera 1920s to form the Guatemalan section of the Central American Communist party. Small, vocal, and very active, the party's life ended in late 1931 after Liberal Jorge Ubico took power. Obando Sánchez and many others were jailed, unions and parties were abolished, most newspapers were closed, and even particular words, such as *strike* and *worker*, were banned.[9]

Obando Sánchez got out of jail in Guatemala City in July 1944, freed by uprisings that led to a popular revolution in October 1944 as the Allies were triumphantly ending World War II. He felt confidant of the victory of democratic capitalists and Communists over tyranny everywhere on earth, and he thought that humanity, armed with conscience and science, would soon "end forever war, hatred, prejudice, poverty, injustice and disease."[10] Consumed by the power of this promise, he spent the next forty years trying to make it come true in Guatemala, but he could not.

The 1944–1954 Period: Artisans and Communists

Large-scale capitalist relations of production became more extensive after the 1944 October Revolution. The governments of Juan José Arévalo (1945–51) and Jacobo Arbenz (1951–54) abolished forced labor and debt peonage, encouraged modern industry, and oversaw the rapid expansion and diversification of export agriculture. During what became known as the "ten years of springtime in the land of eternal dictatorship," the government granted civil liberties, extended the vote to more Guatemalans (but not to illiterate women), expanded education, and created social services. A labor code passed in 1947 granted all urban and some rural workers the right to unionize. This singular attempt to modernize the economy within a political system of bourgeois democracy was short-lived, and economic transformation was incipient; a land reform had only eighteen months of life before it was halted by the 1954 coup.[11]

Artisans, teachers, and railroad workers were critical to the 1944 revolution, and during the next ten years they built a dynamic urban labor movement that vigorously advocated broad social change.[12] A euphoric spirit of being in the forefront of a heroic epoch pervaded the urban unions. "*Brothers*: Your work is the art of printing *life*!," read a line of poetry in a printer's newspaper.[13] Urban trade unionists were visionary modernists calling for industrial development and spending their Sundays in the countryside exhorting peasants to agitate for land reform. They fought for and achieved much, including higher wages, social security, minimal day-care, a working-class press, cultural circles, and a fair degree of organization; trade unionism flourished as never before or since. By 1954 10 percent of the urban and rural labor force was unionized and belonged to a national alliance, the General Confederation of Guatemalan Workers (CGTG), established in 1951. Forming the backbone of the confederation were unions of tailors, printers, barbers, bakers, textile workers, carpenters, and shoemakers; teachers in the Union of Guatemalan Educational Workers (STEG); and railroad workers organized in the Railroad Workers' Mutual Aid Union (SAMF).[14] The achievement of a unified central signaled the victory of members of a new Guatemalan Communist party and independent

Salvadoran shoemaker Miguel Mármol and Guatemalan carpenter Antonio Obando Sánchez, founders of the Guatemalan urban labor movement and the Communist Guatemalan Labor party, in San Salvador, El Salvador, 1993. (Courtesy of Miguel Angel Albizures)

militants over a less effective group of openly anticommunist union leaders, who were primarily from the railroad workers' SAMF, the only urban union where Communist participation in leadership was seriously contested.[15]

The Communist party, named the Guatemalan Labor party (PGT), evolved from a closely woven milieu of artisans and intellectuals drawn to the task of elaborating a just society and an authentic national culture. Its leaders included writer Huberto Alvarado (immersed in literary circles, he was the son of a printer involved in the 1920 overthrow of Estrada Cabrera and in the 1944 revolution), journalist and law student José Manuel Fortuny, printer José Alberto Cardoza, university student Bernardo Alvarado Monzón, schoolteacher Víctor Manuel Gutiérrez, who became the party's most prominent spokesperson, and Salvadoran Communists living in Guatemala City such as feminist trade unionist Graciela García and shoemaker Miguel Mármol. After lengthy debates over the nature of the Arévalo government and of progress, they constituted the party in 1949.[16]

PGT, like Communist parties elsewhere in Latin America, identified feudalism and not capitalism as the principal cause of poverty and stagnation, and it supported an alliance with the native bourgeoisie to construct nationally owned capitalism; land reform would destroy the "feudal" landed oligarchy, create an internal market, and thus "open the path to industrialization of the country, prosperity, and national economic independence."[17] In line with world Communist thinking in the post–World War II years, PGT at times projected national capitalism as a good means for reaching socialism and at times as simply good. In either case, it did not propagandize for workers' power over production or for the abolition of wage labor. Nevertheless, constantly red-baited and violently attacked because it demanded benefits and higher wages for workers and land reform for peasants, PGT protected itself by building a consensus in the labor movement and among many government officials that anticommunism was a weapon against nationalism and democracy. Belittling anticommunism—and not an awareness of, or interest in, an alternative to capitalism—emerged as a major theme in cartoons and articles in the over forty newspapers published in this brief era by unions and by groups of students, artists, women, and peasants.[18]

It is necessary to recognize the importance of Communists, especially in the Arbenz years (1951–54). The Guatemalan Labor party enthusiastically generated support for Arbenz through organizations such as unions and peasant leagues, and PGT intellectuals became vanguard planners of national capitalist growth; they coauthored the Land Reform of 1952 and read about Soviet agriculture to help them develop small-scale capitalist farming in the Guatemalan countryside.[19] The robust, influential artists and writers in Saker-Ti, the period's main cultural group, were usually also members of PGT or, if not, independent Marxists.[20] No ideology was as explanatory, nationalistic, developmentalistic, optimistic, or emotionally powerful as world Marxism in mid-century Guatemala, even though, and in part because, it was not decidedly anticapitalistic. But as vital as PGT was and as much leadership as it gave, it did not single-handedly direct unions (no one did), and, in any case, it gave no clear directions about how to reconcile supporting capitalist growth and defending workers.

To a certain extent the urban unions were captivated by the logic of the Communists' dramatic strategy of promoting national capitalism as a road to social justice. Many labor activists saw the modern world, from Franklin D. Roosevelt's United States to Joseph Stalin's Soviet Union, as a promising one of gains and rights for workers, one that abolished everything that was "backward." The General Confederation of Guatemalan Workers confirmed that "a pact or agreement must be made between the organized proletariat of Guatemala and the progressive capitalist classes to develop a plan of industrialization which will bring economic independence to the country, economic development and the national and cultural elevation of the masses of workers."[21] Wage labor was theorized as progressive, and artisans portrayed artisans in their own union press as "belonging to the Middle Ages because they do not accept the introduction of machines and become reactionary in the face of progress."[22] With notions of development common to Communists and reformers alike, trade unionists upheld the call to create a new Guatemala. The remarkable artisans who were an essential part of the urban labor movement's leadership could write about artisans as retrograde, and they imagined a better world as one without them. Inhibited by the social relations that surrounded them, these artisans wished to burst loose and achieve something new, and watching the way the new sometimes fell out, they fought to retain what they had and remain artisans.

No progressive bourgeoisie rallied to the cause of bourgeois democracy: Guatemalan industrialists, such as the Novella family which owned the city's oldest factory, Cementos Novella y Cía, and the Abularach family, which threatened to close its textile factory, Nueva York, when a union began there in 1953, turned out to be among reformism's worst enemies. And no matter what it said, the labor movement did not try to do away with artisans. Craft unions defended artisans against machines and aspired to accommodate machines as well, struggling with self-defense and the promotion of a paradigm of progress. In this context artisans often gave land reform and industrialization greater thought than did many government functionaries. When the Guatemalan-owned INCATECU rubber shoe factory won the right to import machinery to produce leather shoes in 1946, the shoemakers' union successfully opposed the ruling on the grounds that thousands of artisans would lose their jobs. Salvadoran Communist shoemaker Miguel Mármol, a leader of the shoemakers' union in Guatemala City, recalled:

> Arévalo intervened and stated that our position did not seem correct because it contradicted the basic national need of industrial development. And looking at the thing superficially, it would be easy to say that the government was right, that it was progressive and we were regressive. Our union responded to Arévalo by saying what the moment demanded in terms of industrial progress was the Agrarian Reform. . . . While the peasant masses had no capacity to consume, we said in our manifesto, industry had no possibility to develop because it depended on too small a market. What could you hope for from a market where only 6 percent of the population wore shoes?[23]

Mármol defended artisans and industrial development reasonably enough: ideally no contradiction had to exist between craft and industrial production. "Nothing but sophistry," stated the union; "with agrarian reform there would be a market for both artisans and industrialists."[24]

Things did not work out so smoothly. It soon became clear that machines could hurt, if not artisans, then wage workers. When workers in the Mishanco textile factory struck in 1952 against layoffs caused by state-of-the-art machines whose introduction the government had encouraged, a union newspaper editorialized:

> The development of capitalism and the protection that the state must give industrialists is often spoken about in Guatemala. . . . In principle we are for this, and we support it with total sincerity, especially when it is oriented against feudalism. . . . But there are those who think that capitalism must come about at the expense of workers and that it is unpatriotic to seek demands for workers at this point in Guatemalan history

so as not to create problems for president Arbenz. . . . The labor movement must insist that new machinery should not be introduced without
an agreement that the number of workers remain constant. . . . Capitalism
signifies an overcoming of the conditions of feudalism, but this progress
does not seem what its ideologues announce. . . . Workers must demand
an end to layoffs caused by machinery.[25]

By the early 1950s the concept of a progressive capitalism that would not
"come about at the expense of workers" seemed a fragile one. Wishing and
straining to support national capitalist development, labor activists, including
many individual Communists, often ended up defending both artisans and
industrial workers against it, without reexamining their theory of progressive
capitalist development.

Organized labor's relation to the government hovered between independence and dependence. Arévalo and Arbenz allowed many unions to exist, but
unions were created by workers and not by the government.[26] This was first
unintentional and later by choice. The hundreds of unions that arose immediately after the October Revolution formed without government promotion,
and they remained unprotected until the 1947 Labor Code was passed. When
the government proposed that unionization in urban areas be made obligatory
and state regulated, the labor movement successfully opposed the proposal,
explaining that "this would be a way to control the movement. . . . Voluntary
unionization is the only way to win the working people on the basis of their
consciousness. In the system of voluntary unionization, the union is a class-
room, it demonstrates, teaches, and gives culture, [sic] that raises the political
and revolutionary level of the worker."[27]

On the one hand, urban unions rarely sacrificed their needs to satisfy the
government's. Initially labor leaders yielded to Arévalo's anxiety that strikes
would provoke a coup and in 1945 they discouraged some, but they soon abandoned this position. Even though according to the strictures of the 1947 Labor
Code many strikes were illegal, unions and confederations supported them
and tried to amend the code. When Arbenz attempted to stop strikes of rail-

road and United Fruit Company (UFCO) workers in fear of straining relations with the United States, the General Confederation of Guatemalan Workers supported the workers. Clearly unions and the government did not cooperate harmoniously. Populism was even discussed in the labor movement, dismissed as co-optive, and attacked in the union press. Peronismo was described as a "fog" enveloping the Argentine proletariat, Haya de la Torre's Aprismo in Peru as a "bourgeois manipulation," and Juan Perón's Latin American labor federation, ATLAS, as "fascist."[28]

On the other hand, the labor movement fervently supported the government in the name of progress and its own survival. The October Revolution was the midwife of unionization, and to ensure its own existence the labor movement endeavored to prevent the government from failing. For this reason, the General Confederation of Guatemalan Workers organized Committees for the Defense of the Revolution and participated in electoral politics. In 1949 trade unions formed political action committees and gave these a national structure, the National Political Committee of Workers, to support Arbenz's presidential bid. Unions created these groups precisely to back Arbenz without being assimilated into his Revolutionary Action party (PAR) and hence to maintain labor's independence.[29] They also chose committees as an organizational form because they did not want to start a labor party to compete with PAR, in effect leaving the political arena to PAR. The labor movement did not depend on the reformist government to create unions, but the movement relied on and implored it to handle politics.

By June 1954, shortly before the coup, the General Confederation of Guatemalan Workers had assembled—against the army's wishes—350,000 people in Committees for the Defense of the Revolution. The committees asked Arbenz for arms. Communist printer José Alberto Cardoza recalled:

President Arbenz vacillated in giving us arms when we asked for them. . . . He trusted the "honor of the national army," his class army. He asked us not to insist because we would "only sow mistrust." When finally he decided to give some arms in view of the obvious betrayal of his principal "friends and companions," the heads of the Armed Forces, it was too late, it was 24 hours away from his demoralizing resignation speech [faced with the coup threat, Arbenz resigned on June 23, 1954]. In response to Arbenz's request that we be given arms, the Military Chiefs took us to march in the Maya Golf Club, as if we were preparing for a military parade.[30]

Communist tailor Miguel Valdés remembered how little the Communists or the trade union confederation could do in these critical moments:

We kept marching around thinking they would give us arms to defend the government, but the military just kept us all day marching on the golf course. We told them it was not the moment to learn to march, but to learn to use weapons. They were already involved in betrayal. We were running around in cars throughout the capital telling the people over loudspeakers that the victory was ours, we did not even know that Arbenz had already resigned. The night of the resignation speech, we were on guard at the Confederation building, more than a thousand men, waiting for the order to arm, but this order never came. What came was the resignation speech. We cried when we heard it and people started to disband. The next day some were still in the Confederation building. I came to get some direction from the leaders. The only leader I found was Víctor Manuel Gutiérrez [of PGT and the teachers' union]. A little later we realized that the anticommunists were going to attack the building and we had to leave. . . . We left just in time because they came and broke into the building and we would have been hung. After that no one tried anything. . . . It was total panic.[31]

Valdés went into the Mexican embassy a few days after the invasion. Víctor Manuel Gutiérrez hid for a month before he sought refuge in the Argentine embassy, only to be later jailed in Argentina along with Antonio Obando Sánchez and dozens of other Guatemalans exiled in Buenos Aires. Most returned secretly: Huberto Alvarado, Valdés, Gutiérrez, and Obando Sánchez were back in Guatemala City by the end of the 1950s. In the following years these Communists, as well as many other activists, saw in the 1944–54 era Guatemala's only possible future.

The Liberation

A U.S.-organized military force, which received partial support from the Guatemalan army, brought Colonel Carlos Castillo Armas to power in June 1954.[32] His years of rule, known as the Liberation, would end with his assassination in 1957, after which elections were held under a new 1956 constitution. This was a transition to shaky elite electoral politics and not to bourgeois democracy, which was by then shattered: within weeks of the coup the Liberation massacred over 9,000 Guatemalans, jailed 7,000, and commanded the firing of over 18,000, including hundreds of banana and railroad workers, thousands of schoolteachers, and every inspector in the Ministry of Labor. Responsible for much of this repression was the Committee for the National Defense Against Communism (CNDCC), dedicated to eradicating "sovietism."[33] The Liberation dissolved the political parties and the labor confederations of the 1944–54 period, and it temporarily suspended unions and simultaneously forbade them from using the color red.[34] Literary journals, books, and union newspapers disappeared in huge street bonfires, and prominent trade unionists, political leaders, and progressive intellectuals who did not flee were imprisoned, if not tortured and killed.

Few forgot the devastating experience of rapid, frenetic destruction after ten years of energetic social construction. A Coca-Cola worker in the late 1970s, Carlos Escobar worked on a state-managed coffee estate before the 1954 coup. He was startled to earn enough in 1953 at age fifteen to be able to leave the *finca* and take his mother to the capital, where he wanted to attend school, thus demonstrating the sort of behavior elites feared would erode their labor supply in the reform era. He was in Guatemala City studying, as none of his relatives ever had, when "the Liberation burned whole houses with people inside and machine-gunned one-half the world. They killed whomever they pleased. According to the archbishop everything was OK and would be normal, but son of a bitch!—you saw dead people everywhere, even in rivers. They said they had been killed by the Arbenz regime, but a dead person starts to decompose after a few days and these were appearing fresh every day."[35] Escobar's description and the unspecific "they" encapsulates the sense of terror, confusion, and mystery that the Liberation tried to create.

The Liberation did not seriously attempt to build a pro-Liberation consensus among people from whom it was retracting rights and benefits, but it presented its own version of reality. It justified the coup as a God-given struggle against atheistic communism, terms that might have meaning in a Catholic country. Immediately after the coup, the pro-Liberation press ran photographs of mutilated bodies over captions such as "tortured beyond recognition by the godless communists." A "communist torture chamber" was uncovered where "anticommunist freedom fighters jailed under Arbenz were submerged in water and had scratched out with their bloody fingernails a drawing of Christ on the Cross."[36]

The new regime labeled itself anticommunist as if that fully described a system of governing, a way of living and thinking, and a type of person. Castillo Armas was the "Anti-Communist Hero," and no person or institution supporting the Liberation bothered to define a program beyond anticommunism. An antidevil by definition must be holy; the negation of the "imposed" (communism) would liberate the "natural" (religion, family, law, order, inequality of wealth). The Liberation's messages were hysterical and superficial, and they could not accommodate common sense, such as Carlos Escobar's deduction about who was killing whom given the speed at which bodies decompose. As Castillo Armas was restoring the United Fruit Company's expropriated properties and U.S. union organizers were arriving to reform a labor movement, the Liberation, itself financed by a foreign power, condemned Arbenz as pro-foreign and gave that term an ominous sound. As military roadblocks were set up throughout the country and people had to present passes issued by the police to move about, an article in the pro-Liberation press, entitled "Why Aren't There Bicycles in the USSR?," explained: "Why on earth would Russians want bicycles? Where would they go? It is impossible to move from one place to another without the permission of the police."[37] Everything horrific was "communist," even if it patently was not. Yes, it was true that now bodies floated in the rivers. Yes, there were curfews, searches, and roadblocks, but this was the fault of the Communists, even if they were no longer there. Facts became part of a fiction, experience was at once mystified and denied, and violence was exalted in the name of Christianity.

Typical of press articles published in the weeks following the coup was a government report appearing under the headline, "Female Vampires Are Instruments of Communist Terror," concerning three women who, upon being accused of being Communists, had left the country. The report stated: "God deems that the evil beast of communism not return and if it does that it will be smashed without hesitation. If the red vampires return, they shall receive the exemplary punishment their crime merits. Their insides will be made sterile."[38] Such glorification and moralization of whatever sadistic means it took to destroy the myriad forms of reformist activity that the Liberation called Communist has remained to this day a pillar of state ideology. In the immediate postcoup period, the state did not sterilize "subversive" women, but it threatened to do so and argued that such treatment was acceptable; later it did far worse. In late 1954 live bodies were not ripped apart on the vast scale that they would be in the next decade, but society was shattered as the 1944–54 reforms were dismantled or altered, mass organizations were destroyed, the workweek was lengthened, and wages were cut drastically everywhere and as much as 50 percent in the countryside.[39]

Workers' rights were reduced further when the 1947 Labor Code was amended in 1956. The new code explicitly prohibited union participation in politics (which the 1947 code had expressly encouraged), limited legal grievances to economic ones, severely curtailed rural organization, and made it illegal for state employees to form or join labor unions. Urban workers in the private sector retained the right to unionize, but the new code mandated procedures for unionization and contract negotiation that were so perilous as to be just barely worth risking. To win a union legal status, twenty-one workers had to petition the Labor Ministry, which was required to accept or reject the petition within sixty days. However, if the company fired any of the twenty-one workers during that period, the petition was automatically invalid. Companies often did fire workers who signed such petitions, and this is one important reason why between 1956 and 1985 few unions—approximately 623—actually gained legal status.[40] The code specified that unions that finally won legal standing could vote to strike if no contract had been executed with their employer after eight months of negotiating. A strike was legal if three-fourths of the work force—both union and nonunion workers—voted in favor of it. Once a union struck legally, the court had to rule the strike "just" or "unjust"; a strike was just only when the union proved, based on the company's books, that the company was able to meet the strikers' demands. If the union failed to make its case and the strike was declared unjust, workers legally but not justly striking could be laid off. This procedure gave companies tremendous advantages; between 1954 and 1985 only one strike was ever declared both legal and just. Over the years hundreds of union members were legally fired for striking and then had to pay the extralegal penalty of being effectively blacklisted or worse.

The 1956 Labor Code was key to the subsequent labor movement. Unlike twentieth-century labor law in most Latin American countries, the Guatemalan code did not ennoble the role of the state as a neutral mediator between labor and management. Although the revised code sought to impose apoliticism and economism, it rendered the struggle for wages and benefits so fraught as to make politics and economics virtually inseparable. To win the smallest economic demands in the coming years, workers ended up in bitter and overdrawn conflicts with employers and the state. But above all and despite all, this code did not return Guatemala to the pre-1944 era; it represented a revised code, not one that had been abolished. Trade unionism was still lawful for many workers, and dozens of the 1947 provisions regulating conditions of work in favor of the worker remained. The state enforced almost nothing, but by incorporating some of the language of modernization and labor rights, which it could not avoid doing in the international context of the 1950s, it made trade unionism possible.

It was at this juncture of the immediate post-1954 reorganization of society that bankers, merchants, and factory owners, as well as sugar, coffee, and cotton planters and other large landowners, formed what would become the most powerful owners' association of the twentieth century, the Coordinating

Committee of Agricultural, Commercial, Industrial, and Financial Associations (CACIF). CACIF assembled all groups in private enterprise to cooperate when necessary, to conciliate diverse interests, and to advise government. Many of its member groups had formed in the 1944–54 period with government encouragement for national private enterprise and in response to the growing unionization. CACIF reflected the tenor of the postcoup years. Born in a fanatical anticommunism that far surpassed the U.S. cold war McCarthyism that inspired it, CACIF was less interested in nationalistic capitalism than it was in capitalist success. It sought the support of U.S. capitalists, and it opposed trade unionism and any form of government that promoted popular organization. In the post-1954 years, CACIF never altered its view of trade unions. It never came around to the position, as did its counterparts in many Latin American countries, that institutionalized unions could stabilize society and legitimatize political power.

By ridiculing and red-baiting any owners' group that expressed a pre-1954 nationalism or a willingness to accept democratic pluralism, CACIF imposed conservatism among business people who offered few objections or alternatives. As one scholar has observed, a "psychotic fear of communism" possessed Guatemalan elites that had been traumatized by the sight of workers and peasants organizing themselves and winning a land reform after centuries of latifundia.[41] The post-1954 state was not imported from the United States—though U.S. government agencies helped construct it—and it was not an independent variable, a ghastly apparatus glued onto society by a single coup. Rather, it was rooted both in the authoritarian legacy of late nineteenth- and early twentieth-century Liberalism and in the social conflict of the reform period, and it had the support of the upper classes.

The Official Reconstitution of the Urban Labor Movement, 1954–1960s

Labor reorganization began immediately after the 1954 coup under the auspices of international and national pro-Liberation organizations and individuals. Shortly before the coup the American Federation of Labor, through its

Latin American Inter-American Regional Organization of Workers (ORIT), had established an organization in Mexico called the "Union of Guatemalan Workers in Exile," which was led by a Guatemalan named Rubén Villatoro.[42] Within ten days of the coup, Villatoro arrived in Guatemala City with Serafino Romualdi, the AFL's ambassador to Latin America, Daniel Benedict of the Congress of Industrial Organizations, and Raul Valdivia from the pro-Batista Confederation of Cuban Workers (CTC). Their mission was, in Romualdi's words, to "counter the false news appearing in the U.S. that with the fall of communism had come the fall of trade unionism. We consider it our duty to be here, to develop this work, to help the anticommunists maintain and retake their positions. The immediate task is to build a movement without communists in it. We are here to fill the space left by the communists." A few days later Villatoro opened the new AFL-ORIT–affiliated National Committee of Trade Union Reorganization (CNRS) in the General Confederation of Guatemalan Workers' old headquarters after painting over the radical slogans on the walls.[43]

CNRS and Romualdi opposed what they considered to be "excessive" repression against trade unions—the inclusion of the railroad workers' union, SAMF, on a list of Communist front groups and the jailing of important railroad leaders who were not Communists.[44] Image and reputation were at stake; as Romualdi pointed out, "Other nations are upset because of the apparent lack of trade union rights in Guatemala."[45] The AFL and ORIT had openly encouraged the overthrow of Arbenz (a coup vigorously protested throughout Latin America), and neither wanted to undermine further their standing on the continent. A second issue was containing discontent within observable and controllable bounds. Romualdi explained this clearly in a 1954 press conference in Guatemala City: "With free trade unionism, the problem of communism will be reduced; without any unions, the problem will only grow."[46]

The AFL—by 1955 the AFL-CIO—and ORIT were nevertheless ineffective in part because their call for mild trade unionism as a vital form of social control did not receive support from the Guatemalan state or from capitalists, foreign or national. After CNRS collapsed in 1955, when Villatoro, an arch anticommunist, was accused of promoting communism by the frenetic Committee for the National Defense Against Communism, ORIT representative Andrew McClellan and bank worker Mauro Monterroso started another ORIT affiliate, the Guatemalan Trade Union Council (CSG).[47] CSG concentrated on cultivating ties with workers in U.S.-owned companies such as W. R. Grace and the United Fruit Company. UFCO successfully resisted CSG efforts to make inroads on the company-controlled worker associations it had started on its plantations after the coup, and it fought CSG's attempt to unionize its radio station, Tropical Radio. When UFCO refused to bargain at Tropical Radio, Romualdi, anxious to prove that an ORIT affiliate could win, personally took the case to the new labor minister. The minister and UFCO were outraged, and United Fruit accused Romualdi of "empire building." Tropical Radio offered a wage increase to any worker who signed an antiunion contract, and the union lost its bid for recognition.[48] CSG did unionize workers at W. R. Grace's National Maritime Agency in Puerto San José, but the company refused to sign a contract.[49] Perhaps more predictably, CSG could not make headway with Guatemalan urban and rural capitalists. CSG and ORIT—in its own name—attempted to embarrass a landowner infamous even by post-1954 standards into paying his field laborers the minimum wage but could not.[50] In 1956 a frustrated Romualdi, in and out of Guatemala in those years, criticized many parts of the revised Labor Code for making unionization difficult for many workers and impossible for state employees, harangued against the lengthening of the forty-five-hour workweek to forty-eight hours, and berated "Guatemalan owners, including some from the United States, newspapers, high government advisers, and government officials for not recognizing the absolute necessity of a labor movement."[51] This critical stance never became a combative one.

Well-funded U.S. labor organizers and their Guatemalan associates could not build a substantial union structure or establish roots in the working class. CSG sent hundreds of workers to ORIT or AFL-CIO training schools, where they studied accounting, editing, parliamentary procedure, and the "indoctrination techniques of totalitarianism" without producing an effective core of working-class leaders.[52] Labor leaders who associated with the AFL-CIO/ORIT relied on state and company flexibility and on cultivating ties with elite parties and politicians to win victories for their followers, and these were weak tactics. Andrew McClellan helped textile worker Leticia Najarro form a textile workers' federation, which remained insignificant and small. Najarro found a degree of power only as a confidante of Castillo Armas's successor, General Miguel Ydígoras (1958–63). When Najarro was able to save a clothing factory from bankruptcy by winning it an army contract to make uniforms, she considered it a milestone in the federation's history.[53] When the army took power in 1963, junta head Colonel Enrique Peralta Azurdia convinced Mauro Monterroso, general secretary of CSG, to join his right-wing Party for Institutionalized Democracy (PID), and with that CSG faded. An ex-CSG leader, Jaime Monge Donís, started yet another ORIT affiliate, the Confederation of Guatemalan Workers (CONTRAGUA), and a year later a Monge Donís rival began a second ORIT affiliate, the Confederation of Guatemalan Unions (CONSIGUA). Pressured by the AFL-CIO and ORIT, these groups soon united. In 1965 they became an arm of the right-center Revolutionary party (PR), but this link to the PR did not protect CONTRAGUA/CONSIGUA members from the death squad violence that flourished after PR presidential candidate Julio César Méndez Montenegro won office in 1966: at the worst of death squad activity in 1967, four of its activists were kidnapped in a two-day period alone.[54] A pressed CONTRAGUA/CONSIGUA temporarily allied with a Communist labor group to call for the protection of 1944–54 legal rights and to protest violence, which it blamed on the far right, explaining that the attacks on it were due to "our [CONTRAGUA/CONSIGUA] attitude of increasing good relations between bosses, the state, labor authorities and workers."[55]

CONTRAGUA/CONSIGUA's biggest success in "increasing good relations" was with the railroad workers' union, SAMF, the country's largest union; it had thousands of members in 1954, when hundreds of them were fired, imprisoned, or killed. Fiercely anti-Liberation (notwithstanding their history of ambivalence toward the Communist PGT), railroad workers refused to regain their union's "active" status by electing a pro-Liberation slate, and it was not until after Castillo Armas's death that SAMF became active under anti-Liberation, non-PGT leadership, which, politically undefined and looking for refuge, eventually affiliated with the AFL-CIO's CONTRAGUA/CONSIGUA.[56] The militant rank and file, ever critical of their own leaders without ever deposing them, waged unsuccessful wildcat strikes against layoffs, pay cuts, and the lengthened workday in the 1950s and into the 1960s as their leaders and many members came under attack from the state and from death squads.[57] When the United Fruit Company's International Railways of Central America (IRCA) claimed bankruptcy in 1967, CONTRAGUA/CONSIGUA obtained a loan from the state for IRCA in order to pay back wages and then supported the nationalization of the company in 1968. This was hailed by CONTRAGUA/ CONSIGUA as a triumph because at least workers were paid, but as state employees in the renamed Company of Guatemalan Railroads (FEGUA), they lost the right to unionize. To prevent SAMF leaders' loss of whatever even weak power they had over a notoriously angry and ill-organized rank and file, the Ministry of Labor allowed SAMF to continue, but when it presented grievances, the company simply pointed out that the union had no legal status.[58] The rank and file, by then reduced to a few hundred, contested this state of affairs through meetings, demonstrations, and wildcats over a four-year-period, but in 1974 they were unable to prevent an "employee's association" from finally replacing SAMF, a state maneuver that the AFL-CIO allied confederation did not oppose.[59]

By that time the AFL-CIO had structured a new organization in Latin America, the American Institute for Free Labor Development (AIFLD). Started in 1962, AIFLD was financed by the U.S. State Department's Agency for International Development (AID) to combat the influence of Marxists in Latin American unions as well as to rival the new Christian Democratic Latin American Confederation of Workers (CLAT) for leadership of anticommunist unions. AIFLD introduced a different strategy into the AFL-CIO's work in Guatemala: it organized rural cooperatives of peasants instead of unions of workers. AIFLD called these cooperatives "unions," and the Labor Ministry registered them accordingly, thereby inflating the number of unions officially active. Shifting the work of CONTRAGUA/CONSIGUA in the mid-1960s away from the growing city and its new factories to the countryside, AIFLD funded urban trade unionists to aid cooperatives. These cooperatives, in turn, were supported by the Alliance for Progress programs that were building rural infrastructure linking peasants to the world market. AIFLD promoted an image for CONTRAGUA/CONSIGUA trade unionists as sophisticated nation builders uniting with politicians in the leadership task of civilizing a backward peasantry. This had some glamour; under AIFLD's tutelage urban CONTRAGUA/CONSIGUA members even met with Nelson Rockefeller to discuss Alliance for Progress programs in the countryside.[60]

But AID and AIFLD projects for involving urban trade unionists in the task of modernizing the Guatemalan peasantry had serious limitations. Of the two most important elite parties, the presumably reformist PR only weakly supported the cooperative movement and the army's political arm, PID, opposed it. As apolitical as cooperatives seemed, they strengthened the peasantry and drained the rural wage labor pool. Because of this, and because CONTRAGUA/CONSIGUA—by 1970 renamed the Central of Federated Workers (CTF)—demanded an accelerated colonization of the isolated jungles of the Petén, where army officers had started to control land for cattle ranching and export crop development, CTF leaders were attacked and many were killed. PID promoted Leticia Najarro instead of CTF leaders, rewarding her with a position as head of the new Workers' Bank in exchange for her support of PID candidate Colonel Arana Osorio in the 1970 elections. Without political party patronage, CTF, the last AFL-CIO group formed before 1985, could not hold the little ground it had. Its few member organizations, such as the sugar workers' federation, would follow the leadership of the radical labor centrals that dominated in the 1970s.

The Discreet Reconstitution of the Labor Movement, 1954–1960s

In the months after the 1954 coup few workers were as outspoken as the shoeshiners in the Central Park facing the National Palace who petitioned Castillo Armas, "since you are such a nice guy," to simply give them cloth to make clothing "so that the public will not realize that we are starving to death."[61] But some workers quickly took advantage of the official reconstitution of unions to recompose their forces. In 1954 the Liberation had abolished the 1944–54 federations and confederations on the grounds that they were Communist

fronts, but it did not annul individual 1944–54 unions. Instead, the junta's Decree of July 21, 1954, declared the 532 pre-June trade unions suspended and
"inactive," and it mandated that they elect leaders approved by the Committee
of National Defense Against Communism to resume an "active" status. Within
days of the coup, Luis Felipe Balcárcel, an anticommunist trade unionist isolated in the 1944–54 period, and José García Bauer, a pro-Liberation lawyer,
started a federation that came to be called the Autonomous Federation of Guatemalan Unions (FASGUA). Their hope was that precoup unions purged of
Communists would affiliate with FASGUA, which could then fill the vacuum
created by the destruction of the 1944–54 confederations. FASGUA's stated
purpose was "to banish forever from the working class all Marxist influence
and in its stead, create religion."[62] Its failure was dramatic; a FASGUA activist of the late 1960s who was unaware of the federation's genesis laughed when
he read the preceding quote.

A fervent believer in the philosophy of Social Christian Action as expounded
by Pope Leo XIII in the 1891 *Rerum Novarum* and a supporter of the Catholic
Action groups founded in Guatemala in the 1940s, García Bauer was an exceptional national politician who had repeatedly urged the church to organize
Christian and anticommunist unions during the 1944–54 period.[63] He had no
success, in part because Arévalo and Arbenz curtailed the church's powers in
secular life, but after the coup he took up the task with the help of Catholic
Action groups, such as the Young Catholic Worker (JOC). More thoughtful
than most anticommunist ideologues, García Bauer saw unions as a means
whereby workers could eventually obtain certain rights from, and achieve harmony with, their employers. He was not unlike the AFL's Serafino Romualdi,
with whom he maintained good relations, except that his labor organization
was religious and nationalist. FASGUA started well enough: Archbishop Mon-
seigneur Rossell y Arellano blessed its new office in July 1954, Liberation head
Castillo Armas indicated his support, and for months García Bauer vigorously
defended trade unionists not in the Communist PGT from persecution. On
the first May First after the coup, FASGUA organized a demonstration that the
Liberation endorsed and where Romualdi read a message from George Meany
("six million workers in the USA support unions in Guatemala"), Balcárcel and

others spoke, and JOC youth attended under a banner depicting Christ nailed to the cross.[64]

Within weeks of the coup, however, clandestine Communist PGT members and other militants took advantage of the status the Liberation allowed precoup unions to reconstruct their own organizations within the shelter FASGUA provided. Entering a federation that the Liberation supported was not official PGT policy until 1955; however, individual workers in the party and other labor activists did so as soon as the opportunity arose. Twenty-one members of the Communist-led Union of Graphic Arts (SAG), for example, walked into the FASGUA office at the end of July 1954, immediately after the Liberation declared all unions suspended pending clearance of their leadership by the Committee for the National Defense Against Communism and within days of FASGUA's formation. The printers joined FASGUA and, in accordance with the state's edict, elected a new leadership, except that the winners were 1944–54 militants. SAG sent the list to CNDCC, which declared the union's new secretary general, Jesús Santiago, "inappropriate in view of our proofs that situated him in a political position counterproductive to the new political orientation of the country."[65] Ignoring this, SAG resumed normal functions. It was several months after the CNDCC ruling that the Labor Ministry received an angry letter from the print shop owners' association, one that had formed in the 1944–54 years to oppose unionization. It was "appalled" that Santiago had turned up representing SAG at a meeting when "his active collaboration with Communist leaders during the Arbenz regime is well known." The owners' association also contacted CNDCC, which informed the Labor Ministry that not only was Santiago a signer of PGT's constitution, but also three of the other new SAG representatives were "tainted"—one for working in a literacy campaign.[66] SAG did not reelect Santiago (who went underground), but it retained the three other suspected Communists. Lacking proof that these three representatives were in fact Communists, CNDCC approved the union's new slate. With or without Santiago in the leadership, old union members stayed together and the union retained its precoup political outlook.

In a similar manner, other unions with leftist precoup antecedents joined FASGUA and then sought and eventually received clearance. Within a year

and a half of the coup, while FASGUA's leadership remained fanatically conservative, nine of the thirteen unions affiliated with it were led by clandestine
PGT members or sympathizers.[67] Obviously CNDCC was not as astute or as repressive as state mechanisms would be in later years; tenacious activists tested
again and again the limits set by the state and were able to overcome some of
them. Communist tailor Miguel Valdés spent a few months in jail after returning from exile in Mexico, but by 1956 he was again in the thick of the fray
of his old tailors' union, which was now an active member of the new FAS-
GUA. Communist bus driver Carlos Osorio Zecena spent six months in jail in
1954, then returned to his job and to the reconstituted 1944–54 citywide bus
workers' federation in 1959, after CNDCC had been dissolved.[68]

By then the political orientation of FASGUA's membership was not secret.
In 1956 a FASGUA General Assembly had even refused to allow the AFL-CIO's
Serafino Romualdi to speak and voted down a proposal by Balcárcel, still FAS-
GUA's secretary general, to affiliate with ORIT. The rank and file loudly ap-
plauded Miguel Valdés when he accused Romualdi of being an "agent of US
Imperialism, of breaking up the union movement and forcing thousands to
eat the bitter bread of exile."[69] As it became clear that precoup activists were
continuing to play a leading role inside unions, state repression increased. Bus
driver Osorio Zecena was one of several union members killed by the death
squads in the 1960s. But in the time it took for state planners to realize their
ineffectiveness in purging the labor movement of radicals and to reorganize to
meet new challenges, FASGUA had been rebuilt along antigovernment lines.
It is remarkable that immediately following the 1954 coup an organization
earnestly struggling to extirpate Marxism among workers was simultaneously
being appropriated by Communists.

Once having reconstituted the labor movement, what did the Communists
do? FASGUA became the left of the urban labor politics spectrum in the
late 1950s and in the early 1960s in good measure because it projected itself
through daring, boisterous May First demonstrations, which for a time became its hallmark. FASGUA made May First—introduced in Guatemala City
by Communists in the 1920s, later legitimatized by the 1944–54 governments,
and then expropriated as a national procoup holiday by the Liberation—a tra-

ditional day of antigovernment protest. In 1956 FASGUA's members and the rank and file of SAMF led thirty thousand workers and peasants in ripping up official May First signs prepared by its sponsoring groups, the AFL-CIO's Guatemalan Trade Union Council and the conservative leadership of FAS-GUA, and replacing them with banners denouncing changes in the 1947 Labor Code. The thousands of demonstrators halted the official speakers, including Serafino Romualdi, with "uninterrupted screams, shouts and whistles" until "a smiling worker with dark skin and dark glasses walked toward the speakers' platform, climbed up with the help of many friends and pronounced a fiery speech which began 'Dignified and valiant workers.'" He exalted May First and the heroes of Haymarket, the eight-hour day, and the revolution of 1944; condemned the new government; and ended by shouting, "For a free Guatemala!" He was followed by other workers while Romualdi and others sat wordlessly on the platform.[70] In 1957 this scene repeated itself except that a leather worker from FASGUA seized the microphone (last year's "smiling worker with dark skin," a railroad employee, had been kidnapped) after the minister of labor was shouted down, and CSG did not participate for fear of embarrassing itself again by being on the wrong side of the speakers' platform.[71] In 1958 progovernment groups withdrew their sponsorship, and FASGUA and members of SAMF led a demonstration that emphasized "National Reconciliation," amnesty for exiles, and a return to the 1947 Labor Code and the 1952 Land Reform.

At the May First demonstration in 1959 (while several SAMF, FASGUA, and even JOC members were attending one in Havana), a message from underground Communist leader Víctor Manuel Gutiérrez urging workers to "retake lost positions" was read to thundering applause, and banners supporting Arbenz, Arévalo, and Fidel Castro were abundant; similar demonstrations were held in 1960 and in 1961, when a member of the underground Guatemalan Labor party actually spoke.[72] Political turmoil led to the cancellation of May First in 1962 and again in 1963 shortly after Gutiérrez and Antonio Obando Sánchez were arrested at a FASGUA meeting while planning the May First rally. Still, in the 1960s FASGUA kept its profile high through leaflets and other publications, conferences, and occasional May First marches, such as one in 1966 in which FASGUA actually joined with the AFL-CIO affiliate

CONTRAGUA/CONSIGUA to oppose the escalating violence. FASGUA and CONTRAGUA/CONSIGUA demanded the legal protections of the 1944–54 era amid "vivas" to the incoming president, Julio César Méndez Montenegro.[73]

These demonstrations, always well publicized by the media and by FASGUA, kept alive the ardor and the representation of working-class oppositional politics, even if the real political messages appeared increasingly moderate as the notion of "revolutionary" started to shift from the politics of 1944–54 to something not yet well defined, but clearly different, that was unfolding in the city and the countryside. But perhaps more detrimental to FASGUA than a political line that did not fully endorse armed struggle was its size. The federation did not grow significantly in the city in the 1950s and 1960s, despite its May First marches and the many concrete services it provided, such as legal aid and a mimeograph machine. In 1959 thirteen unions belonged to FASGUA, and by 1968, after key years of industrial growth, only about fifteen unions were affiliated, in addition to the bus workers' federation. Of these, four were in the countryside, to which FASGUA's work had expanded, eight were craft unions, and one was industrial.[74]

FASGUA's problems were not so different from those of the railroad workers and the AFL-CIO's supporters in Guatemala. State repression damaged the federation, and its militants' own understanding of power restricted their range of activities and their ability to organize. Obviously the left (FASGUA) and the right (the AFL-CIO affiliates) of the labor movement were poles apart, yet their similarities are striking. Both were obsessed with state power in a way that diminished their interest in workers' power on the shop floor or in neighborhoods. Both put forward an analysis that constructed a far right within the state as the explanation for underdevelopment and the lack of civil rights and predicted the emergence of a countervailing reformist sector, which they saw as their only hope. In their view of historical causality, elite power was what ultimately mattered; after all was said and done, states, not workers, were the vital agents of labor history. Often hailing one politician or another as a harbinger of new times, the Communists, like the AFL-CIO affiliates, constantly scrutinized formal politics for allies. They did not look with the same intensity and passion at what urban wage earners were thinking or doing to see how their power could be mobilized. Fragile at the point of production, where the Communists represented a reduced number of their precoup base of craft workers in small shops, they did not offset this vulnerability by building a constituency that included industrial workers or a patchwork of grass roots alliances.

Bereft of the reformist governments of the 1944–54 years, the Communists no longer tried to be in the forefront of organizing labor by the 1960s, when industry grew. Waiting for the state to shift its policies even if ever so slightly, they did not embark on a campaign to organize industrial workers. Workers in the one industrial union affiliated with FASGUA sought out the federation and not vice versa. These were young workers from the new Central American Glass Industry (CAVISA). Opened in 1964 by the Guatemalan Castillo Sinibaldi clan, CAVISA was suddenly Guatemala's largest factory, gigantic by national standards; its 1,500 workers daily produced thousands of glass bottles on new machinery to supply the Central American Common Market. Eager to affiliate with a federation, CAVISA's organized workers joined FASGUA in 1966 precisely because of its radical reputation. In 1967, at the height of death squad terror, the glass workers' union won its first demand—for a supervisor's dismissal—by illegally walking off the job on May 1 and attending the annual FASGUA march. Shortly afterward, following a series of illegal slowdown strikes and with the assistance of law professor Mario López Larrave, the union negotiated one of the few contracts to be won in a factory since 1954. Subsequently, when the contract was violated, workers struck, again illegally, for one day in 1969. CAVISA's owners called the police and fired thirty-eight workers, but on the steps of the National Palace union members staged a highly visible hunger strike, which eventually won the workers' reinstatement. FASGUA, however, distanced itself from this action. The glass workers criticized FASGUA: the union noted angrily that young people from Young Catholic Worker had leafleted the public in support of CAVISA's workers but FASGUA had not.[75]

The CAVISA union introduced a different sort of trade unionism based on illegal and collective direct action, the effectiveness of which depended on the size of the work force. In the context of FASGUA, the glass workers at CAVISA seemed hotheaded and rough, and the language they used in their newspaper, entitled *DECISION*, reeked of voluntarism. The federation and the union argued about the need for, and the efficacy of, illegal direct action, militancy, and organized mass support. The CAVISA union proposed, in the words of one glass worker, "to really MOVE things, to go out elsewhere and find out about other struggles and build support for our struggle among other workers and for theirs among CAVISA workers," and FASGUA's leaders did not do this. "We were the mainstay of FASGUA," he continued, "but FASGUA did not take us seriously. We were industrial, we brought in the most dues, we bought the stencils and paper, we were the best, most equipped union and the most class-conscious. We always had disagreements with FASGUA because it was not strengthening the union movement. There was a certain egotism, a fear of letting the movement go into the hands of a new generation and we were that new generation."[76]

The older generation consisted of many of the same artisans who had boldly led a movement for national social change in the 1944–54 period and now did not. After reforming their union in late 1954, for example, the pro-Communist tailors could find no way to organize more tailors or to engage their members in shop floor or other struggles. For seven years the Labor Ministry found every possible reason to deny the tailors' union its active status while the union petitioned and repetitioned until 1962, when it received recognition. Once legally active, the tailors spent three years petitioning the ministry to inspect the shops of several employers who violated standards of working conditions established in the 1956 code. The ministry never responded to any of the union's many letters. The tailors breathed a sigh of relief when the Revolutionary party candidate, Julio César Méndez Montenegro, won the 1965 presidential election: "Now with the Third Government of the Revolution," read the minutes of what turned out to be the tailors' last meeting, "it is hoped more activities can be developed."[77] By then reduced to sixty discouraged members, the union was decimated by the death squads that flourished under the same Méndez Montenegro in whom the tailors had placed such hope and during whose presidency the CAVISA workers managed to win a contract.

In the 1960s guerrilla organizations and death squads became the dominant forces shaping Guatemalan political life. This tranformation had its roots in the previous decade, when several new parties emerged. The most important of these groups was the conservative Movement for National Liberation (MLN), which described itself as the "party of organized violence" and to which the wealthiest and most influential Guatemalan families adhered. A second group was the Christian Democratic party (PDC), legally inscribed in 1955 when it espoused anticommunism, anti-Liberalism, and a "Third Path" to national development.[78] Non-PGT ex-government officials of the 1944–54 years formed a third cluster, the Revolutionary party, which advertised support for a "return to the revolutionary path of 1944–1954." Finally, a handful of professionals and businessmen founded the Redemption party to challenge MLN as the leading party of the industrial and agrarian elite, although in fact the Redemption party had few substantial disagreements with MLN.

All four parties had candidates in the 1957 presidential election. The Redemption party ran an old Ubiquista, General Miguel Ydígoras, on a platform that was mildly critical of the Liberation. The Communists, who first used their broad influence to build support for the presumably reformist Revolutionary party, told their followers to vote for Ydígoras on the assumption that he had a chance against the party that PGT understood to be the real danger, MLN. When Ydígoras polled a plurality, the MLN-controlled electoral tribunal announced the MLN candidate the winner. With Communist backing, thousands then poured into the streets and railroad workers struck. As a result, the election was reheld and Ydígoras took office in early 1958.

Ydígoras was an underhanded conservative who did not have support from the army, many of whose officers had not reconciled their own nationalist feelings with the 1954 coup, which they had not designed. Ydígoras's day-to-day corruption and his subservience to the United States, most dramatically expressed in his willingness to allow U.S. mercenaries to use Guatemala as a training ground for an invasion of Cuba, led officers who had come of age in the reform era to attempt their own coup on November 13, 1960. Many supported that coup, which was nevertheless squashed. Taking advantage of a general amnesty, most of the over one hundred implicated officers went back to their barracks, while several, including Marcos Antonio Yon Sosa and Luis Turcios Lima, decided to continue the fight from the countryside. Politically amorphous reformists and nationalists, they made contact with the Revolutionary party, and tried to keep ties with their military friends. They camped in the rural east, an area of unrest where the 1952 Land Reform had been effective and the 1954 counterrevolution had been severe. According to Yon Sosa, government persecution, rejection by the PR, and the experience of living as outlaws among the angry rural dispossessed radicalized the military officers.[79] In early 1961, with verbal support from PGT, which had endorsed "all forms of struggle" at its Third Congress in 1960, they initiated armed actions under the name of the Revolutionary Movement of November 13 (MR-13) and thus launched the guerrilla movement that lasted in its various permutations into the 1990s, one born from the military and one of the most important in Latin America.[80]

In the meantime, antagonisms between the political parties and the government became especially intense when President Ydígoras's Redemption party manipulated the municipal election in December 1961 and leaders of MNL, PDC, and PR all took to the streets in protest, despite their divergent politics. That demonstration, open warfare in the east in early 1962, massive discontent with postcoup conditions, and the sense of possibility awakened by the Cuban Revolution led to a popular urban uprising in March and April, a revolt sparked by high school students protesting the dismissal of progressive staff from the public schools.[81] For two months city residents fought the police while railroad, social security, electrical, and municipal workers, artisans, and bus drivers pressed separate demands and struck intermittently. Dozens were killed, including members of FASGUA and SAMF, and hundreds were arrested. As the insurrection dwindled in late April 1962, students, railroad workers, and artisans formed a coalition, which included FASGUA and SAMF, to demand that Ydígoras resign. Ineffective, the coalition faded and in its aftermath a number of radicalized workers and students, including many from high schools, organized a second guerrilla group, the April 12 Movement, and PGT started its own, the Twentieth of October Movement. In late 1962 these two organizations joined the military officers' guerrilla group to form the Rebel Armed Forces (FAR), which then opened three fronts in the eastern region of the country.

Because the civilian parties had been unable to prevent urban unrest or to check the growth of the guerrilla movement, the army, now purged of progressive nationalists, decided to temporarily take power in 1963. During Colonel Peralta Azurdia's junta (1963–66) Guatemala City remained under a state of siege and repression increased. By late 1965 many underground PGT and FAS-GUA members had been kidnapped, and in early 1966, immediately before the army restored constitutional rule, twenty-seven PGT leaders, including Víctor Manuel Gutiérrez, were kidnapped and never seen again. Subsequently, Julio César Méndez Montenegro of the Revolutionary party won the election pledging to construct the "Third Government of the [1944] Revolution." The tailors' union was still around, waiting for the Labor Ministry to act on its petitions and anxiously anticipating Méndez Montenegro's ascension to the presidency. According to the Communist PGT, PR represented the electoral path to a new Guatemala. The Guatemalan Labor party had even sent its guerrillas down from the mountains to vote for Méndez Montenegro.

FAR's guerrillas were torn by the issue of elections and embittered by what they understood as an astonishing duality on PGT's part. Within the guerrilla movement the Guatemalan Labor party had no concrete approach to armed struggle, and inside and outside of the armed struggle, it endorsed the centrist Revolutionary party. Its critics in the Rebel Armed Forces accused PGT of politically maneuvering for successive displacements of conservative groups in government until a combination of forces came to power that would allow PGT to participate in the state, as it had in the 1944–54 period.[82] The critique within FAR of PGT's use of violence as a pressure tactic and not as a strategy led the Rebel Armed Forces to split from the Guatemalan Labor party in 1968, when FAR declared that it sought socialism through revolutionary war, not the ballot. With this, FAR became one of many "revolutionary left" groups in the world that divided itself from the "revisionist left." No longer in the ideological void of being influenced by PGT without actually having their own politics, the leaders of FAR were inspired by their interpretations of revolutionary movements in Cuba and Vietnam, as well as by their experiences with the Communists of PGT and with PR.[83]

As it turned out, President Méndez Montenegro's "revolutionary" language was an attempt to steal the guerrillas' thunder, and his realpolitik aimed to destroy them. Upon taking office he signed a secret pact with the military guaranteeing it autonomy, and a major counteroffensive against the Rebel Armed Forces, directed by Colonel Carlos Arana Osorio and financed by the United States, began in the east. The limited reforms that were implemented never went beyond those required by a constricted modernization. Cooperatives to stimulate peasant production geared to the international market were promoted by international agencies, and under a small land reform program a number of families colonized in the rough terrain of the Petén.

Of greater importance than these reforms in the years of the first self-proclaimed progressive government since 1954 was the organization of nineteen death squads that transformed Guatemalan life. At the height of death squad activity during Méndez Montenegro's presidency, some forty-three persons were killed and/or kidnapped every week, actually every five days because death squad members did not work on weekends.[84] By late 1967 there were daily press announcements of kidnappings; these were accompanied by an urgent family plea appearing under a solemn school graduation photograph or a blurry smiling snapshot.

Guatemalans were taken off buses and from street corners, pulled from restaurants, classrooms, cars, workplaces, or their homes, and hustled away by the proverbial "unknown armed men" into expensive cars without license plates, never to appear again or to appear dead and disfigured by torture—as the press put it, "signs of torture"—without hands or feet, without breasts or skin on large areas of the body, with torn limbs and marks from burnings. Most commonly the eyes, tongue, and ears were ripped away from the body. In the 1960s such mutilated bodies and faded photographs of absent people became the unofficial official images of the laboring poor. This is the way they were (and continue to be) most commonly represented: absent or on the side of some dirt path blind, deaf, mute, and dead.

The death squads were not an occasional phenomenon. Waves of state-directed violence, and the fear that violence provoked, constituted a system of social control that ruled, and still rules, Guatemala, a system that the business community has not opposed.[85] The first wave of state terror lasted from 1966 until 1973, when death squad activities declined after the army won its war against the guerrillas in the east. A second and even more violent episode occurred under the government of General Romero Lucas García from 1978 to 1981, the year the army supplanted the death squads with open war against the renewed guerrilla movement of the late 1970s and early 1980s.

The death squad system of disciplining society, which since 1986 has returned to Guatemala, is peculiarly pernicious. Its target has always been members of peasant groups, trade unionists, intellectuals, artists, students, revolutionaries, and above all the population in general. The majority of its victims have been "innocent," that is, neither members of mass organizations nor self-declared enemies of the state. By being at once discriminate and indiscriminate, death squad terrorism aims to paralyze the will and induce self-censorship plagued by doubt about what the rules are. Laws and law enforcement agents exist but what they signify remains obscure; the perpetrators of state terrorism are not apparent, yet clearly they are everywhere with their spies, tape recorders, telephone taps, and specially hired thugs disguised as street vendors or waiters or students or anyone.

This system is remote and intimate, transparent and opaque. Everyone sees the well-defined shadows and confronts the concrete reality of mystery, of an unfathomable sphere that everybody knows but cannot know the state designs and controls. No social mechanism to find truth has existed; the mechanism of violence has gone on, steadily, professionally. Somewhere files are kept up to date, names put on computers, victims chosen, dates fixed. In the death squad system there is only terrible punishment, the disappearance and the maiming of the body in life and death and in secrecy, without previous accusations, investigations, trials, and means of defense; without, it would seem, a crime except life itself.

In the middle and late 1960s terror infiltrated all aspects of Guatemalan life to one degree or another, and it transformed the way life was understood and negotiated. It bred extreme caution in all relationships and in all communications, and it made trade unionism a life-and-death struggle. When its tenor intensified between 1966 and 1973 and between 1978 and the 1980s, trade unionism declined, and when it declined trade unionism increased. But what is astounding is that trade unionism never completely stopped dead in its tracks. Perhaps because random state terrorism made all living so risky it made trade unionism worth the risk, and perhaps the random negation of life made defiance seem to be a natural part of living. In any case, the urban and rural poor were not completely paralyzed by fear. In the 1960s, when the death squad system made its debut on a grand scale, three simple facts suggest that its effectiveness had limits in that decade: a new labor federation, the National Central of Workers (CNT), was formed in 1968; FASGUA, the federation of Guatemalan unions, however unable to lead a sustained revival of working-class activism, was especially hard hit by the squads and it survived them (although two of its member unions did not); and labor militancy continued. The CAVISA glass factory workers unionized, walked off the job, and held a hunger strike during the years of constant kidnapping and murder. They were not alone in their overt activism during the 1960s, for in that decade workers unionized at other new factories such as the Kern's canning plant of Riviana Foods and Goodyear's Ginsa tire factory.

The men and women who were Communists must be given the credit for the existence of an oppositional trade unionism in the years following the 1954 coup, and thus for a major accomplishment. They altered what would have been an otherwise utterly barren landscape for workers, they foiled one of the coup's aims—the destruction of a language of class among workers—and they protected the legacy of the 1944–54 era. Who else in those years would have taken the risks Communists took? Yet because they linked their ability to build a movement to changes in state institutions and lacked a means to encourage workers to be empowered despite a hostile state, Communists could not cultivate the labor activism they had sown.

Without growing beyond a few more unions scattered throughout the city, and without ever organizing large masses of people, FASGUA enjoyed a public life until 1980, when an even greater state repression than that of the 1960s first drove it underground and then, finally, destroyed it as the country exploded into war. During the federation's long lifetime its offices were repeatedly ransacked and closed down, and at one time or another most of its activists were either killed or forced into exile. Nervy, committed people such as tailor Miguel Valdés—murdered in the street in 1978—and carpenter Antonio Obando Sánchez—who miraculously survived in clandestinity and remained a Communist into the 1980s, when, at age eighty-five, he was jailed and robbed of the tools of his trade—were extraordinary sons of the urban working class. They left their mark even if their debates and activities as Communists were often distant from the everyday lives of the city's wage earners for whom they sought a just and safe world.

2

City Life:
The Labor Movement's Crucible

Rodolfo Robles, a union leader of the 1980s, remembered the section of Guatemala City where he grew up as a "neighborhood typical in all respects—most people stay poor, very few finish high school, and many die under strange circumstances." He was born in 1949 in La Parroquia, Zone 6, Guatemala City, near one of the city's oldest factories, the turn-of-the-century Cementos Novella y Cía, where his father worked. Everyone called the factory a finca because it had extensive lands on which it housed workers, allotted them garden plots, and built a church. In the 1950s and early 1960s it was still common to grow corn and other vegetables, gather wild greens and herbs, and pasture animals in the city, which is not to imply that Robles's memories are idyllic ones. Whether life was worse or better then he cannot say, but the daily struggle to make ends meet wrecked his nerves, and sudden explosive challenges to the status quo redoubled tensions. Robles recalled vividly the mass urban uprising of March–April 1962, when three high school students were shot to death against a wall next to his mother's small house, and the assassinations of neighborhood sons and daughters who joined the guerrillas during Julio César Méndez Montenegro's presidency (1966–70).[1]

By then the city had changed and Robles had already worked in a print shop, an ice factory, and a bakery. A few more higher-than-three-story buildings marked the colonial downtown, new shantytowns expanded the city's limits, and space seemed scarce. Whatever paternalism and payment in kind that had existed in the city faded; Cementos Novella y Cía no longer provided housing or land. Robles's future employer, the Coca-Cola Bottling Company of Guatemala, had begun operations in 1941 under the franchise of a U.S. pilot named Matt Fleming; the plant was located in a small building accommodating fifty workers, who hand-capped bottles that were delivered from mule-drawn carts. By the late 1960s the plant employed hundreds in a large compound on an avenue that was under construction in the new industrial area on the southern edge of the city.

By the time Méndez Montenegro assumed office in 1966, industrial growth was under way. The 1944–54 governments had attempted to promote industrialization based on national capital and the creation of an internal market generated by land reform. When the Liberation came to power in 1954, it replaced this development strategy with one that relied on foreign capital, dismissed land reform, and sought little expansion of the internal market. The economy became cash-based, but for workers it was still cash-short. After 1954 workers were not paid the sort of wages that could make them modern consumers, and the modernization built by their labor only taunted them, offering abundance and then giving them almost nothing except the repression that sheltered it. Junta head Colonel Enrique Peralta Azurdia made that clear to workers when the army took over in 1963, as new factories producing such goods as Colgate Palmolive toothpaste, Goodyear rubber tires, Kellogg cereals, Nabisco crackers, Helena Rubenstein cosmetics, Singer sewing machines, and Monsanto insecticides were opening one after another. "The common market is starting," he said. "The Army will guarantee the essential liberties. I give to the Guatemalan workers this ONE motto: Work."[2]

Industrial development from the late 1950s into the 1970s involved the limited growth of modern capital-intensive, light industry that produced for a regional middle- and upper-class market framed by the Central American Common Market.[3] Post-1954 governments stimulated this growth by offering exemptions on income taxes and import duties to Guatemalan and foreign businessmen. Supported by U.S. loans, and in line with the postwar expansion of U.S. investment in manufacturing enterprises in Latin America, many U.S. companies opened in Guatemala. Though its industrial development was distinguished from that of many other countries for its restricted scope, Guatemala was not an isolated or exotic relic; it was an area of the world capitalist system where major multinational companies established homes.

In 1959 foreign investment represented 0.8 percent of the total value of investment in industry; by 1975 it represented 48 percent. By then, foreign-owned industry produced 30 percent of the total value of industrial production.[4] Elite Guatemalan families that had accumulated wealth from agriculture, commerce, and finance invested in manufacturing without leaving behind their other holdings and within the context of a modernization shaped by foreigners. They sought ties with U.S. businessmen, and they, like U.S. capitalists operating in Guatemala, often hired reactionary managers who hailed from Spain, Chile, or Argentina. One worker recalled that TACASA, the Philip Morris cigarette factory, contracted in the 1970s with a Chilean manager who threatened workers with "the tortures given in Santiago's notorious stadium after September 1973."[5] Urban workers coined the term *The Second Conquest* to describe post-1954 industrial development, equating the predominance and behavior of foreign capitalists and managers in industry with their vision of Guatemala's invasion and colonization in the sixteenth century. Industrial development appeared as another violent territorial humiliation—not the progressive, national project proposed by reformists and Communists in the 1944–54 era.

However appealing various ideals of modernization were to the new industrial working class, factories were not. In 1967, when Sonia Oliva was fourteen, she went to the city to study; there was no high school in the rural area of Zacapa where she grew up, and she believed that an education would change her life. In the city she eventually attended night school and found a job in the Japanese-owned ACRICASA textile plant soon after it opened in the early 1970s. The factory shocked her: "The very first thing that amazed me about ACRICASA was the kind of treatment the machines got. The machines, which are *machines*, got medical attention 24 hours a day. Who were their doctors? The mechanics. What were their medicines? New parts, grease, repairs. They got everything they needed to function 24 hours a day without hitches or failures, but we did not. A machine breaks and a mechanic comes running in seconds. Do you realize the difference? The machines had all, the people nothing."[6]

In their leaflets and conversations workers often used the image of a concentration camp or a prison to describe factories, which were usually surrounded by barbed wire, guarded by armed men and police dogs, and patrolled inside by armed supervisors. Conditions and treatment were terrible in new factories as well as old ones. At ACRICASA Japanese supervisors slapped women workers, and when workers attempted to talk to a manager about conditions in Goodyear's recently opened GINSA rubber tire factory, the man simply drew out his pistol to end the conversation.[7]

The high labor turnover rates at factories reflected worker dissatisfaction as well as low skill requirements and flawed company policies. Few factories offered inducements to experienced workers to stay, as machinery was simple and training took place on the job. On the contrary, to avoid pay increases and cumulative social security benefits, companies were motivated to lay off workers.[8] And workers left anyway. One worker told of quitting four factory jobs in the city in three years: a candy factory because he was forced to work nights without compensation, a canning plant because the machinery made him dizzy, a second candy factory because "the pay wasn't worth the grief," and an ice cream factory because he was obliged to put in a fourteen-hour day.[9]

Working staggering numbers of hours, factory workers earned less than a subsistence wage. Throughout the 1960s, the government-established minimum wages in industry averaged Q1.86 a day (Q1 = $1), when, according to the government, urban workers needed Q1.81 simply to feed a family of four, although most working-class families were larger. In 1974, in response to a teachers' general strike, President Colonel Carlos Arana Osorio raised the average daily minimum from Q1.86 to a mere Q1.97 (see Table 2).

Until 1973, Guatemala had the best record on inflation in a region that was itself an oasis of price stability in Latin America in the 1960s. Between 1970 and 1972 prices went up 0.1 percent. In 1973, which saw the beginning of an inflationary crisis, prices rose 18 percent. They climbed by 26 percent in 1974 and 16 percent in 1975, while wages remained at the 1974 level set by Arana. Wages did not increase until a general strike of plantation workers in 1980

Table 2 Government-Established Minimum Daily Wages in Quetzales for Selected
Industries, 1974–1980

Food	1.98
Beverages	2.05
Textile	1.99
Leather products	1.85
Printing	2.12
Paper	1.84
Metal	1.98

Source: Guatemala, Ministerio de Trabajo.

obliged the government to establish an average minimum industrial wage of
Q3.95. By 1977 the government estimated that it cost Q3.62 a day to feed an
urban family of four and Q7.96 to cover "all costs" (food, rent, transportation,
and medicine, though not clothes or school expenses), but in no sector did
workers earn even Q3.62 a day. A Coca-Cola worker described his situation
in 1979, after his union won a wage increase that made Coca-Cola a slightly
better-paying factory:

> I earn Q110 a month because I work six days a week as well as over-
> time. My wife takes in sewing and makes Q30 a month. So that's Q140 a
> month for a family of six. Our rent is Q25 a month for one small room, a
> kitchen and a toilet. Water is Q3 and electricity Q4.20. My wife spends
> Q22 a week on food which is Q88 a month and that means rice, beans,
> and tortillas. My bus fare is Q6 a month so that leaves Q14 for clothes,
> shoes, medicines and so forth. I can't even afford a bottle of Coca-Cola.[10]

The family wage was key to urban survival, which the Coca-Cola worker characterized as not including a soft drink. Industrial workers were desperately
poor. Intense short-term coping formed much of their universe, and wage
struggles tended to stem from the absolute need of minimum food and shelter,
even if workers spent money on baptisms, birthdays, weddings, and wakes.

The factory system, however, did not come to dominate the urban economy.
In the 1960s and 1970s industry enjoyed modest overall growth before it de-

Table 3 Economically Active Population by Sector (in rounded percentages)

	1950	1964	1973	1981
Primary (agriculture, mining)	69	66	59	58
Secondary (manufacturing, including handicrafts, construction, electricity, gas, water)	14	14	18	16
Tertiary (commerce, transportation, communications, services)	17	20	23	26

Source: Guatemala, Dirección de Estadísticas, Censo Poblacional, 1950, 1964, 1973, 1981.

clined as the Central American Common Market was undermined by war and revolution in other Central American republics.[11] In the city, transportation, commerce, communications, and services accounted for more workers than did manufacturing, which never reached beyond 18 percent of the nation's economically active population (see Table 3). Although industrial development created a sizable industrial proletariat for the first time in national history, it generated comparatively few jobs and the new proletariat was relatively small. In the important ten-year period between 1965 and 1974, only about 30,000 men and women joined it (see Table 4).[12]

This is not to say that qualitative change did not take place. Modern, large, foreign-owned industries came to dominate many important branches of manufacturing. Those factories employing more than fifty workers accounted for 70 percent of the value of industrial production by the mid-1970s.[13] Whereas in the 1940s the textile and apparel industry, then the main employer in manufacturing, was composed of small workshops, by the 1970s much textile and apparel production occurred in large plants with a high degree of mechanization and a detailed division of labor and took second place in importance to the food industry. Food, beverages, and tobacco, all minor industries in the 1940s, were major modern ones geared to export by the 1960s and 1970s. These, along with textiles and apparel, absorbed 51 percent

Table 4 National Growth of the Industrial Proletariat

Year	Number of Workers	Number of Factories
1946	23,000	800 (employing over 3)
1965	37,800	1,140 (employing over 5)
1974	65,730	1,860 (employing over 5)
1981	78,080	1,940 (employing over 5)

Source: Guatemala, Dirección de Estadísticas, Censo Industrial, 1946; Encuestras Industriales, 1965, 1974, 1981.

of the industrial work force. But industrial development did not involve a total reorganization of labor in the city. As elsewhere in Central America, industrial development affected craft production without replacing it, and much production remained inside the household.[14] Tailors and seamstresses, for example, continued to custom make clothes in their homes or in small shops while Cluett, Peabody manufactured Arrow shirts for the regional market, and the city's population depended on the household labor of thousands of Maya Indian and ladina women who made and marketed tortillas three times daily and were not counted as part of the formal economy.

In addition, the union movement unfolded in a city in which a significant proportion of factory workers were employed in small and medium-sized firms. By the mid-1970s, when the urban labor movement was at its height, 45 percent of the manufacturing work force was employed in factories of fifty or more workers, 34 percent in factories with between forty-nine and twenty workers, and 20 percent in those employing less then twenty.[15] Only thirty or so factories employed over three hundred workers, and it was among these that unions flourished in the late 1960s and 1970s; the workers who joined them were young, new to factories, and unskilled.

If factories had not been geographically centralized, workers would probably have been unable to build more than scattered pockets of unionism and not a movement. Because of the availability of labor and the presence of at least minimal infrastructure such as electricity and access to ports and an airport, 80 percent of all industry, including 70 percent of all large indus-

Table 5 Estimated Occupational Profile of Guatemala City, 1973 (in rounded percentages)

Manufacturing employees (factory workers, artisans)	28
Service employees	25
Office employees, related workers	12
Traders, vendors	14
Professionals, technicians, managers	9
Transportation employees	6
Agricultural employees	6

Source: Guatemala, Dirección de Estadísticas, *Censo Poblacional,* 1973.

try, was located in Guatemala City. Although they formed a tiny part of the national labor force, industrial workers in the city had more weight. Moreover, the growth of the state administrative apparatus, commerce, finance, and urban population was concentrated in this single city, the only important city in Guatemala. (See Table 5.) Trade unions had the potential to unite with a broader urban movement concerned with issues such as transportation and housing, and with a national movement in which they could act as a broker between the rural poor and the state. Location made it possible for industrial unions to assume an importance in politics far greater than the weight of industrial workers in the national or urban economies.

Guatemala City had not become a truly industrial city, but it had become a large and complex one. The majority of its residents were underpaid wage earners making or moving goods or providing services whether they worked in banks, shops, offices, hospitals, factories, and schools or in the street hawking newspapers and gum. Or they were unemployed. By the mid-1970s unemployment and underemployment were estimated at 20 percent. The greatest "zone of attraction" for rural migrants, Guatemala City absorbed 40 percent of the total number of those leaving the countryside in response to the rapid expansion of large-scale export agriculture.[16] Between 1950 and 1973 the city's population more than doubled, growing from 320,000 to 700,000 residents; by 1980 over 1.5 million people lived there, while the number of jobs available increased by only an average of 1.6 percent each year from 1973 to 1978. Out of the swollen labor market an industrial work force formed that reflected the city's heterogeneity.

Although ladino men predominated, Maya Indian and ladina women were part of the new proletariat. Despite an overall decline of women in the industrial work force from 22 percent in the 1940s to 18 percent in the 1960s, by then they comprised and continued to comprise an important and concentrated minority, representing 45 percent of workers in clothing, 53 percent in tobacco, 30 percent in textiles, and 16 percent in food.[17] Several of the city's few large plants, which were of strategic importance to trade unionism, such as the INCATECU shoe and ACRICASA textile factories, employed a majority of women by the 1970s. Women found jobs in factories and joined unions, even though they lived in an urban society that frowned upon female participation in politics and in the workplace outside of the home, and despite the fact that they became part of a labor movement in which male leaders and imagery prevailed. Sonia Oliva, who began working in the ACRICASA textile plant in the early 1970s and who by 1978 was a labor leader citywide, was an exception for being a woman and a leader, not for being a woman and a trade unionist.

Maya Indians, male and female, were also a minority in the new urban proletariat. Only in a few factories, such as a canning plant that hired only Indian women, and Foremost Milk, which recruited its work force from a nearby Indian town, did they constitute a majority.[18] Modernization in the countryside had affected the position and number of Indians in the urban economy. Before the 1950s Indians went to the city to sell or to work in ladino households. The expansion of large-scale export agriculture in the 1950s and 1960s displaced a number of Indians in the countryside, some of whom then went to the city not only as servants or vendors but also to settle in their own lodgings and to find work; they often got jobs and housing alongside of ladinos.[19]

The relationship between Indians and ladinos was complex in the city. Centuries of discrimination against Indians had made racism part of the implicit social knowledge of all Guatemalans, and the line between Indian and ladino among the urban laboring population was marked. Yet even though Indians lived within a cultural milieu that was specifically theirs, the distance separating lower-class Indians and lower-class ladinos was not always so great in the city in the 1960s and 1970s. Ladinos often had close Indian relatives; no study of Guatemala prepared me for the frequency with which I encountered Indian relatives in ladino workers' homes. However much Indians were held in contempt by the larger society, there existed no sharp or total segregation of spheres among urban wage earners; there were no Indian or ladino streets, neighborhoods, bars, or restaurants. Urban ladino popular culture could not be known independently of the influence of Maya Indian culture. Lower-class urban ladinos loved the marimba music of Indian villages, and many relied on herbal medicine, sought out *brujos* for advice on special matters (as did a group of ladino and Indian trade unionists during the yearlong 1984–85 occupation of the Coca-Cola Bottling Plant), and grew up believing in night visitors such as El Sombrerón, Tzitzimitle of pre-Conquest Maya origin, a little man in a wide-brimmed hat who handles horses and provokes women's undying love.

Despite deep prejudices, and because of the real and perceived shared interests of class between urban lower-class ladinos and Indians, Indian men and women had a large part in a labor movement that did not identify itself as Indian or ladino or speak at length about problems of discrimination against the Maya population. Numerous examples exist of leaders of Maya descent: Gonzalo Ac Bín, a textile worker killed in October 1978; Florencia Xocop, a textile worker kidnapped on June 21, 1980; Felipe Antonio García, a steel worker incinerated in the Spanish Embassy Massacre in 1981; and Coca-Cola workers Manuel López Balam, assassinated on April 5, 1979, Ismael Vásquez and Florentine Gómez, kidnapped together on June 21, 1980, and Mercedes Gómez. In fact, when the violence at the Coca-Cola Bottling Plant was at its worst in 1980, the number of workers of Maya descent who kept the primarily ladino union alive was disproportionately high.

In the 1960s and 1970s, when Indians joined the urban labor movement, racism existed but relations between lower-class urban ladinos and urban Indians were not one-dimensionally hostile or remote. The distinctiveness attributed to Maya Indians by ladino working-class activists varied from the representation of Indians as a tenacious people, as in the remark "when *los indios* join [the labor movement] they always stick until the very end" (this was often said with approval by ladinos, and on one occasion by a ladino making a point about the many ladino traitors in his union), to the odious "*los indios* are stupid" (this comment was made after a self-identified Indian leader of a union with a ladino majority made a mistake). Because of racism, several trade unionists of Maya descent did not publicly identify themselves as Indian, yet that some did identify themselves as Indian *and* their ambivalence in doing so is important: Coca-Cola leader Mercedes Gómez, who described himself as "a natural" but noted that his father was ladino, sometimes appeared in Maya Indian dress during the 1984–85 occupation of the Coca-Cola plant, when for the first time workers wore their own clothes at the work site instead of the regulation brown pants and beige shirt. The presence of workers of Maya descent in the labor movement and in leadership posts, as well as both the ability and the hesitancy to acknowledge Maya origins, attested to the complexity and nonfixed nature of ethnic relations and sensibilities among all workers.

That the new proletariat was primarily ladino had some relation to its small size, the predominance of ladinos in the city to begin with, and patterns of migration. Over the years increasing numbers of ladino and Indian rural people entered the new industrial work force, but it was not swamped by recruits from the peasantry, Indian or otherwise, as many hypothesize happened during periods of rapid industrial and urban growth in other parts of Latin America.[20] Most industrial workers were born in Guatemala City or in nearby towns, rural and urban areas on the southern coast, and the eastern departments of Jutiapa and Zacapa. In the 1960s and 1970s, 40 percent of all union leaders registered with the Ministry of Labor were city born, 30 percent hailed from the southern coast, and the majority of the remaining 30 percent came from Jutiapa and Zacapa. The heavy rural-to-urban migration of the 1960s and 1970s did not mean that either Indians or an ex-peasantry came to comprise the new industrial proletariat, for two reasons: industry did not generate enough jobs to exhaust the existing labor supply, and the zones of greatest out-migration to the capital were areas where wage labor and ladinos predominated, such as the plantation-rich southern coast.[21]

The rural area of the greatest out-migration to the capital was the southern Pacific Coast department of Escuintla. Escuintla had been transformed not only by an expansion of capitalist export agriculture more intense than in other areas of Guatemala in the post–World War II period, but also by the dramatic political events of those years. The agrarian reform of 1952 had its greatest impact there, and so did the counterrevolution of 1954. More than a few of the migrants who entered factories had lived through nothing but this history. Efraín Alonso, who organized a union in Riviana Foods's Kern's canning company in the 1960s, had grown up picking bananas at a United Fruit Company plantation in Tiquisate, Escuintla, which was one of twenty United Fruit plantations in Guatemala. He recalled his childhood: meetings of peasants and rural wage workers in the late 1940s and early 1950s, the fervor that the 1952 land reform created, the 1954 coup and the bodies of many of the adults he knew, riddled with bullets, floating in the river that ran through the plantation. By the time he migrated to Guatemala City in 1955 at age sixteen, he was "disillusioned and knowledgeable about power in my sad country," and he sought out activism and schooling.[22]

His childhood was not exceptional but his luck in securing work in a factory in Guatemala City was (in his case, a company manager recruited Alonso for his skills as a soccer player who could enhance Kern's team). Far more workers, migrant or not, ladino or Indian, found jobs as artisans or in service jobs, commerce, transportation, and communications where they were employed either by the state, the largest employer in the city, or by the private sector. In addition, many made their livelihood in the so-called informal economy, one consisting of car washers and watchers, scavengers and sellers of garbage who made their home in the enormous city dump in Zone 3 and competed furiously with one another for the spoils, children employed by tire repair shops to scatter nails, match sellers, magazine renters, letter writers, blender repair men and women, and so forth. This sector mushroomed during the period of industrial growth; whether by origin or evolution, all informal jobs had a relation to the whole of which they were part and about which they were a commentary. They were a response to economic misdevelopment which did not benefit the majority, they represented a strategy for coping with formal unemployment, and they cushioned the instability and low wages of employment in the formal sector.

Formal economy workers spent a good part of their wages and even sold

A Guatemalan resident locates a means of survival in the city dump. (Photograph by Patricia Goudvis)

their own labor in the informal economy, which for many was the more pertinent of the two. According to one study, most working-class housing in the 1960s and 1970s was constructed by the informal economy at a time when single-household shanties—located on land bought on installment or squatted upon—replaced the early to mid-twentieth-century housing for the poor, the *palomares*, one-story buildings containing a series of tiny apartments that opened onto a common alley.[23] Industrial workers purchased goods in the informal economy that were often made by industrial workers with craft skills who supplemented their factory wage by building housing or making clothes, shoes, or food to sell to their friends, neighbors, and coworkers. In this way everyone saved the money to buy school books and uniforms for their children, a blender, a used typewriter, or a lamp.

Urban workers inhabited a difficult social as well as economic milieu. By the late 1960s Guatemala City was an urban disaster. A sense of being permanently stalled characterized even the modern. Projects to pave new avenues ended half finished, and new middle-class housing complete with indoor toilets had running water only intermittently. Outside of the few wealthy areas in Zones 9–10 and 13–15, whose residents lived inside walled compounds, shopped at well-guarded malls, and knew Miami, Florida, geographically, culturally, and socially better than their own city, Guatemala City was an inhospitable metropolitan area unable to accommodate or service a growing population. Such was the administrative chaos that borders were never drawn between the city and the department of Guatemala, and this led to endless problems about which entity was responsible for garbage collection and water supply in dozens of neighborhoods in the twenty-one zones that comprised the city by the 1960s. Even where responsibility was clear, the city administration had difficulty providing the rudimentary services of collective transportation, water supply, and sewage.[24] Guatemala City grew without planning, as waves of migrants from the countryside and urban residents seeking to reduce their expenses built fragile dwellings in the ravines that crisscross the city. This was a polluted and filthy city by the 1970s, virtually without parks, with few sidewalks, and with gutted streets. The population carved space for its social life in little yards and dirt streets.

For a variety of reasons including political repression and instability of housing and employment, there developed little durable grass roots community organization to shelter the laboring poor from the difficulties of urban life except voluntary fire fighter organizations and Alcoholics Anonymous, groups that depended entirely on their local members.[25] In addition, the city was bereft of private or state-authored systems of relief or improvement because no one with power was interested in ameliorating or reforming the urban population's housing, sanitary conditions, health, or morals. These matters were left to those who lived with them. Public health services remained hopelessly underfunded and the majority of residents received no state welfare services. Though public education had grown since 1954, 40.8 percent of children under age fifteen did not attend school as late as 1978.[26]

The national elites did not justify their power to workers; they did not create the institutions or discourse that gave people the sense of a shared endeavor. Urban residents usually were not conscripted into the military, which thus did not function to "discipline" them or inculcate in them scripts for being.

Modernity in Guatemala City: New shacks and new high rises. (Photograph by Patricia Goudvis)

Nationally produced television and cinema were virtually nonexistent, and publishing was limited. Modernization meant literacy and some new skills for a large sector of the urban population; at least a majority of young people attended school, which was not true in 1940. Yet public schools, a potentially key means of socialization, were notoriously disorganized pedagogically. That gave progressive teachers and students some advantage, which in turn led the military repeatedly to intervene directly in the schools' administration. In the post-1954 era city schools became infamous as sites of rebellion, not of social normalization and pacification. In any case, they offered an eclectic education. In the best high school, students read José Martí and nineteenth- and early twentieth-century Guatemalan writers; in others, they learned that "God created man" and read, or more likely did not read, exceptionally dull positivist texts crammed with lists.[27]

Once minimally schooled, the adult majority had little contact with agencies of social control or welfare outside of occasional, traumatic experiences such as military searches and trips to the morgues, police precincts, and hospitals searching for the disappeared. Even priests were scarce in the neighborhoods where industrial and other workers lived, much less social, health care, and sanitary workers, educators, or housing inspectors. Because of the Liberal party's hostility to the Catholic church in the first part of the twentieth century, few priests worked in Guatemala throughout much of the twentieth century, and almost none of them in urban working-class areas. Between the 1940s and the 1960s the number of priests in Guatemala swelled from 114 to 494 as state-church relations underwent a major shift. But in the city, the church continued to work almost exclusively with and for the upper class, for whom it operated a system of schools. The sole exception was one Catholic Action program for young workers that started in the mid-1940s.[28]

Urban workers were surrounded by poor and middle-class persons in worse, similar, or slightly better situations; they were not segregated or distant from the general urban experience, except for that of the rich. Although types of housing varied by income, the residential areas where industrial workers lived (Zones 1–8, 11–12, and 18–21) were shared with "informal" sector workers, artisans, and the middle classes, and with both ladinos and Indians. Industrial

An everyday street scene in downtown Guatemala City. (Photograph by Derrill Bazzy)

workers lacked the structural advantages that Torcuato di Tella points to in his classic discussion of the formation of class consciousness in Latin America: they did not live in a singularly industrial milieu or in tight homogeneous urban working-class communities.[29] They experienced diversity and contact with comparative strangers. The city's lack of social services and high formal unemployment led to self-reliance, improvised everyday life-styles, and often short-term ties with a variety of people as residents connected by a veritable curse of unrelenting uncertainty sought housing, jobs, aid, and counsel.

Everyday life demanded that people be inventive and accept risk. Perhaps it was the trade unionists' best school. Making one's home on the sharp slope of a ravine that could become a landslide with an earthquake tremor or in heavy rain, living with the constant sentence of the death squads, riding on overcrowded, fast-moving, old, ill-kept buses on roads made more of holes than pavement amid cars with malfunctioning brakes and no rearview mirrors, working hard on an empty stomach, giving birth in a public hospital or at home—in short, all the ordinary demands of daily life—required the same trusting of oneself to the moment and to what was at hand that heroism does and that trade unionism did.

Daily life required some measure of confidence in one's own abilities to make do. Part of working-class common sense was the notion that nothing happens unless you make it happen; this was an indisputable truth in their lives, no matter how little power they had. When Joan Manuel Serrat put music to Antonio Machado's "Caminante no hay camino se hace el camino al andar" (Traveler, there is no path; as you walk you make the path), it was an instant hit in the lower-class neighborhoods of Guatemala City.

In this modern city without glitter or simulacrum, no one bothered to argue that modernization was particularly positive for urban workers, no respectable identity as "worker" was ascribed to industrial workers, and there existed no imagery of the majority of the urban (or rural) population as a potential or actual "good citizenry." The elites did not hope to gain support from an urban population that was neither market nor political base, and they expended almost no effort in trying to do so. Instead, during the period of industrial growth the state revived with new language and methods the pre-1944 tradition of dominating society through violence. Before 1944 unions were illegal and legally suppressed; after 1954 they were legal and illegally attacked by the state and by owners and managers, and matters of violence had changed qualitatively. As the industrial working class expanded in the post-1954 period, as modernization unfolded, thousands were tortured or were "disappeared" and the mangled dead body, present or absent, became the singular image of the national body politic.

This state of affairs was not accepted as natural or necessary by the urban popular classes. It was understood as barbaric and even as unbelievable. No belief system explained the death squads and disappearances; a frequent commentary was "es una 'lica" (it's a movie), a fitting observation in a city where cinema was generally perceived as unbelievable. When industry and capitalist agriculture grew in the 1960s and 1970s without redistributing wealth in the city, there deepened a radical ideological and existential schism between rulers and ruled, rich and poor. More than an absence of hegemony existed among the city poor and working people. There was the presence of spontaneous dissent, of something approaching "inverse hegemony," the view that the state was in its essence alien and dangerous; anything it did was wrong.[30] Although stable organization was unusual in the city, the deep fury that smoldered in the lower-class neighborhoods and within families surfaced with tremendous force from time to time. This happened in the insurrection of March–April 1962, after the 1976 earthquake (when neighborhoods quickly formed vibrant self-help committees that challenged the government's feeble relief work), and in 1978 when the city exploded in reaction to an increase in the bus fare. Either as a sign of respect or as a way to win favor, no language of deference toward state officials existed in the labor movement; trade unionists publicly referred to state functionaries as "murderous psychopaths" and "barbarous, heartless, not human beings."[31]

Hatred for the government and for the rich was a part of popular urban culture. It was well expressed in the city's famous black humor, its unending supply of jokes about presidents and generals, about disasters such as disease, hunger, and earthquakes, and even about torture ("Did you know that Chupina [Germán Chupina, the police chief in Guatemala City and a reputed torturer] was a twin?" "No. What happened to his twin?" "He was born dead, with signs of torture.") Two examples illustrate the texture of a humor that divided the world between the good people and the bad state. In the first example, "Two generals are riding on an airplane over the country. The first one says, 'I'll throw down twenty quetzales and make twenty Guatemalans happy.' The second responds, 'Well, I'll throw down one hundred and make one hundred Guatemalans happy.' The airline stewardess, overhearing the conversation, remarks, 'Why don't you both jump out of the plane and make eight million Guatemalans happy?'" In the second example, "President Lucas García [1978–82, notorious as violent and stupid] is having his shoes shined. Wishing to pass the time and entertain his customer, whom he does not recognize, the shoeshine boy inquires, 'Have you heard the latest joke about Lucas García?' 'But I am Lucas García!' replies the president. 'In that case,' says the shoeshine boy, 'I'll tell it very, very slowly.'" Such bold jokes cast light on, and thus challenged the efficacy of, a political system that thrived on secrecy and invisibility. Humor sustained the monotonous daily battle with transportation, jobs, prices, water, and violence and the will to survive it. It was part of a subculture nourished in workplaces, families, and neighborhoods.

The neighborhood arenas of this subculture were the streets and open-air markets where women, men, young people, and children socialized, bars for men (usually a small back room of a corner store), and soccer matches. Played almost exclusively by men and boys, soccer was unsurpassed as a neighborhood social activity. Soccer was vital to male working-class life: through teams jobs could be found, friendships were made and tested as individualism vied with collectivism on the playing field, and union meetings were sometimes convened on the field after a game.

The neighborhoods that industrial workers shared with other wage earners, such as La Parroquia in Zone 6, El Gallito in Zone 3, La Verbena and La Quinta Samayoa in Zone 7, or Primero de Julio in Zone 19, are not well described by the word *community* insofar as this term suggests the existence of long-standing, cohesive structures and a perception of common culture or history. The waterspouts and the streets, the dust or mud, like feelings of anger, joy, grief, fear, solidarity, envy, and above all the feeling of a common destiny, were shared by a shifting population of poor people who did or did not form deep ties. For their residents, these neighborhoods were points of reference at once fragile and profound.

Cristobal Monzón Lemus, a Guatemalan car washer in Los Angeles, captures the solid yet precarious quality of neighborhood life in his *Camino de adolescente: La vida de Ramón en el barrio El Gallito*, perhaps Guatemala's sole proletarian novel; its publication costs were covered by the dollars the author earned abroad. In Ramón's old neighborhood of El Gallito, there were always memorable local initiatives, such as soccer teams, that fell apart and then were rebuilt as fast as the youngsters' homemade cloth soccer balls. Neighbors were vital to Ramón's life, but they quickly came and went in his troubled youth, as did schooling and a series of jobs. Nothing lasted very long, but everything was important anyway.[32] Trade unionist Marco Tulio Loza recalled that on his street in La Quinta Samayoa (Zone 7), neighbors who talked to each other so rarely that they could not remember one anothers' names quickly mobilized en masse to search hospitals, streets, ditches, ravines, and the morgue for a disappeared youth (who, as it turned out, had migrated to Mexico to work—unlike most of the disappeared—and he turned up a year later to be dubbed Lazarus, a nickname no one forgot).[33]

Given their lack of stable organization, neighborhoods sometimes united in surprisingly forceful ways. Rodolfo Robles remembered no long-standing community group in La Parroquia (Zone 6), but "when some students were shot in La Parroquia [in 1962], the neighborhood exploded. When the issue was protest everyone went, because everyone had received so many blows."[34] On a larger scale were the effective block-by-block initiatives that followed the 1976 earthquake, when thousands organized to tend to the wounded, bury the dead, locate water and food, protect what remained of their homes or rebuild, and channel international relief aid. Marco Tulio Loza recounted how

> we, the youngsters, organized the area. We had a vigilance committee against thieves. We mobilized the fathers to participate but they proved unreliable. We took over a bakery [white rolls were, along with tortillas, a staple] on the block, and baked and distributed bread until the flour ran out. When the relief-aid trucks started showing up, we refused to let them in the street because we wanted to avoid chaos and fights. We told the drivers exactly how much we wanted and we distributed it. We rationed water, we took care of everything and everybody.[35]

Workers had resources. Because more than the phantasmic presence of death squads constituted their milieu, workers experienced more images of existence than torn bodies and more culture than one of terror. The 1954 coup had not destroyed, for example, the liberal discourse that, starting in the late nineteenth century, had shaped Guatemala's modern state, its intellectuals, press, school system, and national symbolism. Notwithstanding state terrorism, in the post-1954 period the language of individual achievement, rights, responsibility, and of the self-determining individual was ubiquitous among politicians, public intellectuals of all sorts, journalists, and educators, no matter what their politics were.

Liberal ideology was also communicated by the foreign culture abundant in Guatemala City in the 1950s and 1960s. For instance, Mexican comics were

Organizing in a city neighborhood: a woman calls for signatures or fingerprints on a petition for titles to urban lots. (Photograph by Derrill Bazzy)

very popular in the fifties and sixties, when young people rented them to read at corner stores. Approved by the Mexican Ministry of Education as "children's magazines," these comics, like other cultural commodities, celebrated the role of individual initiative, power, and imagination in history as they depicted the lives of Marco Polo, Lord Nelson, Alexander von Humbolt, Alexander Graham Bell, Sarah Bernhardt, Beethoven, and even Toussaint L'Ouverture (titled "El Napoleón Negro"). In the 1970s the influence of foreign cultures grew: the number of movie houses increased; the Beatles, the Rolling Stones, and Pink Floyd were popular; *nueva canción* from Venezuela, Nicaragua, Chile, and Cuba could be heard; and television was available to the general population for the first time, broadcasting Mexican soap operas and news and U.S. dramas and comedies. All of these media relayed their own messages of individualism, modern family life, consumer society, and, in the case of nueva canción, lyricism about revolution and the power of heroic individuals.

The 1954 coup and the culture of terror also did not annihilate local urban culture. Everyone in the city knew of John Wayne, Pedro Infante, Donald

Duck, and Mickey Mouse, but these figures had not displaced others that were only preserved in memory and only reproduced orally. The city's popular classes kept alive, possessed, and reelaborated complex characters: el Cadejo, the barking black animal, part dog, part goat, perhaps from medieval Iberia, who protects drunks; Tzitzimitle, of Maya origin, sometimes called El Sombrerón; Tatuana, the colonial witch condemned by the Inquisition who stops husbands from wandering; La Siguanaba, a Nahuatl name for the strange woman who appears by water to entrap men; and La Llorona, well known throughout the region as she wanders weeping for the child whom she killed. These and dozens of stories about the devil, money, love, kindly interventions by the dead on behalf of the living, and so forth were not only part of the popular imagination, they depended on it.[36]

Because the culture of terror tore apart many other social solidarities it reinforced the impact of the most intimate cultural milieu that workers possessed, their families. Survival depended on individual fancy footwork and on family as well; the ethos of individualism and self-reliance did not supplant or displace the importance of family and of familial ideology. In the life stories I recorded to write this study, the individual shared centrality in workers' narrative strategies only with the family, no matter what state the family was in. In response to my query, "Tell me how you became involved in your union," the men and women I interviewed often replied, "Well . . . My father was born in . . . and my mother in . . . ," and then went on to describe what seemed to weigh heavily in their own understanding of their union activism: the broad sweep of their parents', siblings', and other relatives' troubled lives. In the labor movement higher wages were sought in the name of family and risks taken to provide a future and positive paternal images for children; one trade unionist commented, "What kind of man would my children think I was if I did not join the union?"[37] References to the "fight for our families" were as common in conversation and in trade union literature as those to "the fight for the working class" or "the fight for the people." Even male trade unionists who had deserted their children years before fought in their names.

Absent or present, peaceful or not, family was significant. Families were often authoritarian, and they were marked by rigid conventions about what men, women, and children were supposed to think, do, and say, and by the distance between those expectations and reality. The implicit code that women tend to children and serve men, who in turn win the daily bread in the world of work outside the home and protect their obedient, dependent, silent wives and children, was subverted in many ways, whether by inclination or by poverty. Throughout the early and middle part of this century a high percentage of women were single mothers, and women worked outside the home.[38] Poverty meant that everyone was a breadwinner, though fathers often did not provide support because they had deserted their families.

Family members pooled resources, and children worked from an early age to contribute to the family wage. In 1969 eight-year-old Marco Tulio Loza started helping his father make bricks in their yard in Zone 7 (see Appendix). After his father abandoned the family for a woman, Loza became an apprentice to a shoemaker uncle to give money to Loza's mother, who washed clothes to supplement what he earned. After Loza left his uncle following a dispute over pay, he made little wooden marimbas to sell to tourists at the bus terminal. This yielded so little that he tried to immigrate to the United States to better contribute to the family wage, but he was caught and jailed in Oaxaca. After he returned, another uncle found him a job at Coca-Cola, which provided him a steady income for his mother and six siblings.[39] Rodolfo Robles and his brothers and sisters helped their mother, who made and sold tortillas, by finding scrap cloth and pulling out the thread to sell it. At age nine he ran away because his father, who lived with another woman and their children, would not allow him to attend school. After living for a time in an Indian village he returned home, and at fourteen he started working in a print shop and giving his earnings to his mother.[40]

Economic pressures together with the changing and continuing social and cultural configurations of urban life simultaneously and forcefully pulled the family together and pushed it apart. Robles ran away from it because he wanted to study. Rafael Méndez left the southern coast and migrated to the capital when he was sixteen to find work. In Guatemala City, the CAVISA glass factory hired him, and he lived "alone for the first time, did everything by myself and sent money to them [his parents and siblings]."[41] Mercedes Gómez, from the village of San Andrés Iztapa, went to the city to get a job and send money back; he "worked and lived alone, sleeping alone on a straw mat on a dirt floor in a tiny rented room, until my brother joined me there."[42] For one reason or another that had to do with family, being "alone for the first time" was not unusual for workers in the city. Sonia Oliva chose to be by herself because the aunt with whom she lived in the city slapped her and would not allow her to attend high school; she rented a room in a boardinghouse, worked in a factory, and attended high school at night.[43]

Oliva told me the story of her escape from her aunt's domination "to explain how I could get involved in the union. There was no one at home to stop me . . . no husband, mother, father, mother-in-law, father-in-law. I was alone."[44] The power of, and the respect due, familial expectations about suitable female behavior prompted Oliva to conclude that a personal journey away from family was a necessary prelude to her activism. Her story suggests that women trade unionists took a unique path away from their assigned gender roles. That she related this story implies her awareness of how aspects of gender ideology negatively affected her life as an activist in a factory.

What Oliva understood as the significance of being alone, without family, was gender specific. However, in answer to my inquiries about how they became trade unionists, all the people I interviewed both spoke at length about their family life and recounted experiences of separation and aloneness in the city as part of their odyssey leading to social awareness and class consciousness. Their life stories hinted that the ability, and the recognition of the need, to unite with others was preconditioned on the opposite, an acknowledgment of being alone, of one's individual powers, and of the development of independence and self-confidence. Whether reflecting liberal ideology or highlighting in their pasts what resonated with their lonely present as trade unionists, the trade unionists emphasized their solitary battles. One man struggled with alcoholism on his own, another alone challenged teachers who humiliated him, Marco Tulio Loza was proud that as a young teenager he stood up "by myself" to another prisoner in a Mexican jail, another finished high school because of "my own efforts, no one helped me," and so forth. Luis Colocho, a trade unionist at the Ray-o-Vac battery factory, told of learning to hold his own as a young man whom others teased before he could socialize with his peers, of having a "strong interior life," and of "seeking solitude" in the woods to "dream." His decision to stay in the labor movement after three other workers at Ray-o-Vac were tortured to death in 1980 was made not in the midst of a demonstration or in the face of others, but when he lay alone in a hospital bed after losing his leg as a consequence of a gun wound inflicted by a plainclothes detective.[45]

Class consciousness is by definition about a sense of unity and commonality; yet trade unionists stressed their individualization, as well as their recognition of their abilities outside of an accustomed set of people as part of the life that led to activism. Many studies have suggested that preexisting communities, including kin, fuel class mobilization and political consciousness. That was the case in Guatemala City, where city neighborhood life and family gave future trade unionists some values of and experiences in solidarity. However—and suggestive of the view that there is no one truth about the relationship between kin, community, and consciousness—an almost lonely self-validation and the simultaneous discovery of individual power and its limits were part of workers' conception of their path to activism. And for many women, some distance from family was at times imperative.[46]

Expectations within the family and elsewhere about what constituted appropriate male and female behavior affected men and women trade unionists differently. The men often faced families that, torn by anxiety, opposed their membership. But women trade unionists inevitably encountered fierce disapproval from family and not only because of the risk to life. Even though varied representations of women existed in the city, most men—above all, husbands—and many women ardently opposed women's participation in the workplace (outside the home) and in activist organizations. For this reason most women trade unionists were divorced or single, and often they were single mothers; thus many had already parted ways with conventionality even if, as in trade unionism, they had company. Sonia Oliva lived alone when she became a trade unionist, and later she lived as a single mother with her little son. As a trade unionist, a woman, and a mother, she became a nonconformist. To the dismay of many men and other women workers who did not think that her life-style provided good mothering, Oliva brought her son into her world of trade unionism: to demonstrations, to a worker occupation of the ACRI-CASA factory in 1977, and to work one day, near dangerous chemicals, as a protest against the lack of day-care.

To be a woman trade unionist was to struggle against an employer, a violent state, and the conventions on which much love, identity, and security depended. To be a male trade unionist was hard enough, but one important difference was that, for the most part, the personal lives of male trade unionists continued to be rote and conservative because in many respects trade unionism coincided with male gender identity. To be a "real man," a macho, was to protect one's family, to be brave and bold, and to not allow oneself to be abused, humiliated, or dominated. Trade unionism demanded breathtaking public heroism, and this was a male-associated character trait no matter how many publicly heroic women there were. Trade unionism was perceived by men and many women as a macho domain populated by the truly courageous and manly. Machismo was one of several qualities mentioned by male trade unionists as important to trade unionism.

Gender ideology had a powerful effect on men and women in the labor movement. Two important industrial unions, one at the Kern's canning plant and another at the Ray-o-Vac battery factory, were initiated by male workers specifically to protest managers' sexual harassment of female workers. The fact that women were in these factories in the first place signified a breakdown in men's breadwinning capacity, and if managers could sexually harass women workers with impunity, the macho identity of male workers was null.[47] But it was not gender ideology alone that compelled male workers to protect their female counterparts in these factories. Their actions were an expression of their class consciousness and their gender identity informing and changing one another. What counted for both men and women activists was the way senses of self and values influenced each other. Sonia Oliva would not have demanded day-care unless she was a woman and a mother (male trade unionists in other factories who were fathers actually opposed this demand for themselves because it freed their wives from the household), but she would not have fought management in the way she did—bringing her baby to work—unless she had strong convictions about herself as a worker in relationship to owners;

she was one of only two of the many single women who needed day-care at ACRICASA to take this militant step. If they were simply machos, the male workers at Kern's and Ray-o-Vac might just as well have sexually harassed the female workers. If they were acting purely on their class sense, these workers would have done something they did not do: encourage women workers to be in the new unions that the men formed. Male trade unionists' machismo was well colored by their class consciousness, and vice versa, as well as by other convictions. Their culture hero was not John Wayne, Che Guevara, or Fidel Castro but Jesus Christ.

Without doubt, the most important cultural idiom of families and neighborhoods was a religious one. Although the city's residents certainly did not create Christianity, one cannot escape the sense that it was the local population that breathed life into it. Despite the growth of the church's political and social prestige nationally after the 1954 coup, which Archbishop Mariano Rossell y Arellano actively supported, the church stood aloof from the expanding urban population. The work of a conservative Spanish priest who developed a Catholic Action program in working-class neighborhoods in the 1940s–60s was exceptional. Though the state used a religious language, neither the government nor the church encouraged the incorporation of the majority of the urban population into organized religion. Even the slow introduction of religious teaching in the public schools after 1954 was unplanned; many of the young men and women who became teachers did not have to be told to teach the story of Genesis as truth. Throughout the first half of the twentieth century, when the Liberal regimes curtailed the church's power, Christianity had been kept alive in a popular imagery and language, in festivals, in rituals, and in the annual pilgrimages to the Black Christ of Esquipulas and to Antigua. Christianity remained the most important conceptual framework for birth and death, and for all the judgments, diseases, accidents, disasters, triumphs, jobs, and decisions in between.

Despite the paucity of priests, no images in the neighborhoods of wage earners and other poor people were as common as Christ's body on the cross and Mary's figure in some posture of affliction or supplication. Workers adorned factory locker rooms with statues of Mary surrounded by fresh

Fresh flowers and candles are provided for the statue of Mary in the women's locker room at the unionized ACRICASA thread factory. (Photograph by Patricia Goudvis)

flowers and candles, and most unions had their own patron virgin saint. Sacrifice had enormous status. Whatever was worthwhile required "sacrifice"—be it an education, a child, or a trade union.

Religious festivals became national holidays after 1954. However, unlike the drab, state-sponsored Independence Day, these were elaborate and heady popular productions, not commercial or state or even church affairs. The religious calendar included eating and drinking on relatives' tombs and flying kites over the dead on November 1, the burning of garbage on December 7 to rid homes of the devil, and the Christmas posadas and the display of hand-made intricate miniature nativity scenes on Holy Night. Holy Week was known for neighborhood-crafted carpets from colored sawdust, pine, and flower petals and the Burning of Judas, when young people made effigies of Judas and attached to them lists of his "gifts" to local neighbors ("To Don Meme, the crazy, I leave my balls, so he will have something healthy to eat; to Don Pedro, my pants so that he will have something to defecate in") before parading

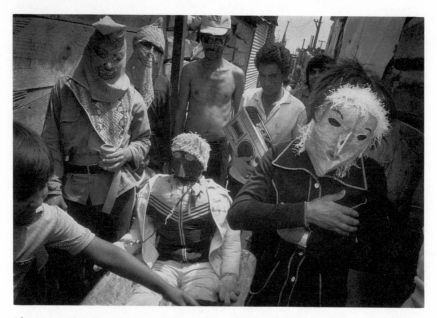

The customary annual Burning of Judas is accompanied by merengue music from a
new cassette player. (Photograph by Derrill Bazzy)

the effigies about and then torching them. On all religious holidays and especially during Holy Week, which was by far the most important holiday, no line
existed between suffering and joy, camaraderie and mockery, life and death,
celebration and mourning. During Holy Week city Guatemalans went to the
beach, drank excessively, and paid money to carry the huge floats of scenes of
Jesus in his life, his death throes, or his death as double penitence for a sinful,
merry life. The denouement of Holy Week was the spicy soup for hangovers
served everywhere the Monday after the Sunday of the Resurrection.

Such popular religious culture was its own school of life, one that encouraged participation and depended on improvisation and imagination. In addition, humor energized it at the same time that death was acknowledged and
given a lively presence. For better or worse, local religious culture protected its
practitioners from emotional demoralization and the ethical vacuum of state
discourse. It was the character armor of many working people, a way to keep
their balance while the earth shook, a way of understanding power. Lorena
Ibarra, a secretary without ties to unions or political groups, recalled her good

fortune when she was kidnapped off the street almost in front of her house in El Gallito (Zone 3) by three men who pushed her into their new car and blindfolded her. After driving around for hours they left her in the middle of the night on a deserted street in a part of the city she did not know. She stood there trembling, when suddenly, as if out of nowhere, there appeared a small and obviously poor man with a kindly face who almost wordlessly showed her the long way to her own doorstep. When she turned to thank him he was already far down the street, disappearing into the dawning light as if ascending into it; he was, she explained, a real saint.[48] Given the religious terms of life and empowerment for many, it is not surprising that people who spoke a class-based religious language started unions in factories in the 1960s.

No trade unionist, however, told me a story like Lorena Ibarra's. However inspired by the values of saints, the trade unionists did not claim that saints guided them. In describing their lives, these workers made central *their* individual strength and *their* own capacity to overcome great difficulties, whether alcoholism, an inferiority complex, the loss of a leg, the challenge to fight in a Mexican jail, fathers who failed to provide, obtaining an education against all odds, army sweeps, an earthquake, poverty, or fear. They built their life stories around lonely moments of rebellion, personal decision, triumph, and self-realization that gave deep validation to their lives. In their narratives, trade union activism was one of a series of events in lives in which self-identity and worth were forged in the course of defending themselves against contrary forces. None of them doubted that God, capitalism, accident, and the like played a part in their life's unfolding, but at the same time they thought that they could have power over themselves and thus control their own destinies. Such voluntarism, a belief simultaneously false (they had so little power over their lives) and true (if they did not stand up for themselves they would fall), made making history possible. It was the wisdom of working-class activism, a shrewdness that had to be about real power, with saints only looking on in approval as workers found their own way.

3

See, Judge, Act: The Young Catholic Worker and Trade Unionism, 1960–Early 1970s

The Guatemalan Catholic church never intended to provoke militant working-class organization. Yet in 1920, according to tailor Silverio Ortíz, the writings of Bishop José Piñol y Batres against the anticlerical President Manuel Estrada Cabrera and the bishop's subsequent arrest were "points of departure" for the urban artisans who took up arms against the dictator.[1] The artisans' politics soon surpassed the bishop's: in the 1920s a few of them founded the first Guatemalan Communist party, and after years of suppression in the 1930s and early 1940s, they and other Communists went on to lead the labor movement in the 1944–54 reform era. Dependent on state tolerance, their ability to build unions following the 1954 coup was limited. When young activists from the Young Catholic Worker (JOC) had more success than Communists organizing unions in the 1960s, this was a second occasion of labor activism inadvertently inspired by the Catholic church. During a decade when state terrorism intensified, and new factories spread through the rapidly growing and changing city, the Young Catholic Worker's emphasis on personal change, identity, and self-empowerment resonated among workers.

Evolution of the Young Catholic Worker

The roots of the Young Catholic Worker lay in the Roman Catholic church's efforts to gain male working-class adherents in Europe. The Belgian priest

Joseph Cardijn created JOC in the early 1920s to "conquer" male workers and "return them to Christ." JOC, as it developed under Cardijn's ideological leadership, opposed "Communism and Capitalism because they are materialist, class-based and authoritarian." The movement condemned capitalism for placing "money before social obligation," industrialization and urbanization because they were "decadent," machinery because it "enslaves," and "immoral" liberalism for fostering the "false science of industrial progress and the free economy." JOC recognized that the worker was not an "instrument of labor and production, but an intelligent human being, created in the image of God; this personal character cannot be violated." JOC conflated class and familial loyalties; Cardijn's own "conversion" to the working-class mission took place by the deathbed of his father, a worker who died from "overwork and sacrifice to assure his son's betterment." Cardijn swore over his father's cadaver that "my life would be dedicated to changing the working-class condition." Cardijn proclaimed that JOC aimed to change the world. He told young workers that "the world is in your hands" and encouraged them "to set in motion a complete transformation of the moral and material condition of the worker . . . who is not a machine to exploit." From the outset Cardijn defined JOC in relation to his competitors among Belgian workers, the Communists. As he saw it, it was "either Moscow or Rome."[2]

In the late 1920s JOC received authority from Rome to be a specialized branch of Catholic Action, a form of the "lay apostolate" encouraged by popes from the beginning of the century and given formal status by Pope Pius XI in the 1920s. Responding to the challenge posed by Communist, Socialist, Protestant, and Masonic groups, Catholic Action aimed to turn nominal Catholics into practicing ones by bringing religion into their daily lives through secular activities within the context of religious study, and by drawing them into the structure of the church as lay apostles. That the laity could be apostles was novel as an official idea, and Catholic Action gave the masses, previously envisioned as sheep, a new role as shepherds. The motto adopted by Catholic Action and JOC was "See, Judge, and Act"—to see reality in all its aspects, to judge it morally, and to act to change it.

By declaring the masses capable of perceiving reality, by proclaiming them capable of being judges and actors, and by bringing them and their concrete problems into the church, JOC created a dynamic that often led to political activism long before the advent of Liberation Theology in the 1960s. In Europe, JOC groups were gathering places for morally serious people and breeding grounds for anticommunist rebels who studied, and self-consciously adapted, notions from the left. Priests brought JOC to Latin America in the 1930s to combat the loss of youth from the church's ranks, and JOC played an important part in working-class life in many cities, where its political effect varied. From the Buenos Aires branch, for example, grew the centrist Christian Democratic continental trade union confederation, the Latin American Confederation of Workers (CLAT), and in Brazil the military abolished JOC in 1964 because its members were trade union militants.[3]

In Central America, Catholic Action by the late 1940s was the church's main response to what it defined as its three major problems: Protestantism, communism, and the scarcity of clergy.[4] The Guatemalan Catholic church in particular, because it thought it was living under a Communist regime in the 1944–54 era, encouraged Catholic Action. A Guatemalan branch of JOC was launched in 1947 under the guidance of a Spanish priest named Gilberto Solórzano, who worked closely with Archbishop Mariano Rossell y Arellano and envisioned JOC as similar to the right-wing Opus Dei.[5] The church, Rossell y Arellano, Solórzano, and Catholic Action opposed the 1944–54 reformist governments of Juan José Arévalo and Jacobo Arbenz. But aside from routine anticommunist articles in its newspaper, *Avance Juvenil*, JOC remained aloof from formal politics. It only aimed to raise the moral and cultural standards of young workers. JOC did not perceive working-class culture as positive or as a source of truth; workers needed to cultivate an ability to rise above their horrendous material and spiritual situation.

Intertwined with this orientation toward self-help and self-improvement was the "lesson"—effortlessly grasped in Guatemala City as the years passed—that modern troubles were caused by modern times. Few wage earners in Guatemala City would have taken exception to what JOC denounced as modernization's sins: consumerism, the new and ignoble "proletarian condition," and the entrance of women into factories. A few anticommunist intellectuals in Guatemala who supported JOC's work, such as lawyer José García Bauer, advocated a return to a romanticized precapitalist corporate world as an answer to the problems of the post–World War II era.

Father Solórzano started young men's clubs in working-class neighborhoods such as La Parroquia (Zone 6) and El Gallito (Zone 3) in the 1940s, and these slowly became a part of neighborhood life. After the 1954 coup destroyed virtually all other youth organizations, and as the city grew chaotically and industry developed in a hodgepodge manner, JOC—small as it was, never involving more than a few hundred young workers—became the best-organized and largest grass roots youth group in a city with little community organization. The clubs of roughly fifty male members each met at least once a week by the late 1950s, when Solórzano started separate young women's groups that oriented its participants toward a life spent in the household attending to husbands, offspring, and parents.

The sole intra- and interneighborhood organization, JOC had an impact on daily life. Sometimes recruited by religious parents and more often by zealous JOC members who were assigned to "conquer" others, the young men and women in JOC battled adult and youth alcoholism, taught literacy, and cleaned up neighborhoods; the young men helped one another find jobs and fought injustice on the job with intensity and enthusiasm. Solórzano, however, opposed forms of struggle that were as systematic and as potentially contentious as trade unionism.[6] In the mid-1960s a more open-minded priest named Abel López, who did not disapprove of unions, took over the work of guiding JOC. López was influenced by the floodgate of energy and creativity opened in Latin America by Vatican II, and by the new practice of "going to the poor" to encourage critical thought and social action. The Guatemalan Catholic church hierarchy did not support the growing number of priests drawn to what would soon be known as Liberation Theology.[7] The church gave JOC less backing as it became more progressive, and without church patronage JOC declined in size to fade by the end of the 1960s. But for over two decades JOC had recruited to its clubs a particular sort of urban working-class youth: socially aware and nascently class conscious, serious, restless, and religious. Through its ranks passed important future labor activists such as Julio Celso de León, Teresa de Oliva, José Mundo Alvarez, César Galicia, Salomón Prado, José Pinzón, and Adolfo Hernández, all of whom belonged to the first generation of JOCistas, and Miguel Angel Albizures and Alberto Colorado, part of a second one. Over the years, the politics of these and other ex-JOCistas varied, yet all of these men became worker-intellectuals who provocatively engaged with the world around them.

The Young Catholic Worker was seminal. At JOC clubs young people talked, played sports, produced little plays, read, sang, went on excursions, pilgrimages, and processions, held conferences and retreats, and performed Christian rituals. Together they read Pope Leo XIII's *Rerum Novarum* (priests discouraged Bible reading), the church's late nineteenth-century declaration of Christian social justice and exposition of the moral obligation of the proletarian crusade against its own exploitation. From a text that also encouraged nostalgia for a mythic golden age of harmonious social formations, JOC members learned that the working class was a vanguard, that the mission to save the working class was a divine one, that the workers' apostles could only be the workers themselves, and that workers should be dignified men who "challenge history . . . and fight to liberate themselves from the Slavery of the Machine, Capital and the State."[8]

They also read novels in JOC. Two novels, *When the Sirens Become Silent* and *The Companion*, deeply impressed the young Miguel Angel Albizures, who in the 1960s read them by candlelight in his parents' home in La Parroquia (Zone 6), where he was born in 1944 and where he grew up amid complex political events that fiction helped him locate in a world wider than La Parroquia, as full as that one was. He recalled that

the author, a Frenchman, or Belgian . . . had an anticommunist outlook, but all of a sudden I was looking at strikes in Europe. In hindsight the novels were a little backward, but they posed real situations. To this day, I remember facts about the city called Lille. I even remember the names of the trade union leaders and the differences between them. They were very moral people, very committed, who sacrificed with great force and power. These novels opened my vision to the world. They were very important to me. I saw that the Guatemalan working class was not alone.[9]

The novel that stayed in Julio Celso de León's mind for four decades was *The Courage to Live*, which told the story of a young man who faced up to the difficulties posed by tuberculosis.[10]

JOC emphasized that people had the power to transform life. In its clubs there was pragmatic talk about reformation within many contexts, including that of self, family, community, and labor-capital relations. JOC members, for example, discussed various approaches to wage payments and concluded that Taylorism and piecework made machines out of workers, and that only a just minimum for all was morally appropriate.[11] "Seeing" a problem was the first step, "judging" the second, and "acting" the third. As Albizures explained it,

We talked about everything—work, justice, education, prostitution, about the sexual abuse of women in general and how women could say "No." And after we discussed something, say a person's behavior, he had to make a commitment to change it, and then there would be a review, a check, the next week. It was very strict.

In our neighborhoods we formed groups which talked about family problems, alcoholism, jobs, unemployment, and the community. Each case was discussed and an action attempted. Take the alcoholism of a father—we would suggest that the son could talk to the father and point out how it was affecting the whole family, or they could talk to the mother. Or when there was a serious problem of unemployment we would all try to find a job for the young person in question and sometimes we did. Or neighborhood issues—sometimes we painted a house, swept streets, or if there was an area near a bar where people were always assaulted, we tried to help with a patrol. Or work—a *compañero* had a problem about safety conditions in his factory. We met, discussed why the factory was unsafe, and then we would decide on concrete forms of action like having the group leaflet the factory from outside while the *compa* stuck up a big poster inside saying something like, "We have dangerous working conditions and we need to improve them."[12]

Another former member said that what attracted him to JOC was "this procedure 'See, Judge, Act.' This was a revelation, a method of living which I use to this day—to analyze reality in all its many causes, and to change it with all the consequences that brought. The issue was always what *action* to take in the face of x problem; like an injustice in a factory. Most of us were workers so that came up often." He said that he and others felt committed to overcoming the daily obstacles to individual and social betterment, and to being "integral and authentic persons who took responsibility for our destinies."[13]

JOC underscored the sense of individual responsibility that was already part of urban popular culture. It taught moral self-empowerment, and it constructed an identity for workers as historical protagonists. As Albizures and others testified, JOC primarily concerned itself with personal, work, and community problems rather than political parties or positions. Unlike the Communist emphasis on state power because that was where "real" power resided, JOC concentrated on persuading working-class people to cultivate their own powers and to take action; for JOC petitioning the state was explicitly not a concern. Through its "method of living," "See, Judge, Act," it offered youth a means of doing something about life as a way of life. It promoted an ethos of intellectual and practical antipassivity and of voluntarism, one that resonated with the local wisdom that "you can do something if you really try to do it." At the same time it developed personal confidence and a concern for others, and it presumed an ethical approach to social problems. In a worldview where nothing was morally neutral, judgment was implicit in knowledge. The judgments were obvious: exploitation, torture, alcoholism, wife beating, prostitution, and unclean neighborhoods were evil.

The significance of "See, Judge, Act"—what was seen, what judgments were applied, and what actions were taken—was specific to society, class, and time, as were the lessons that Albizures drew from anticommunist novels that French workers might have disdained in the 1960s. In another place and time

Young men converse at a JOC meeting at the end of the 1950s, including future labor union leader Julio Celso de Léon (*second from right*) and JOC leader José Angel Berreondo (*at Celso de Léon's left*), who was assassinated in 1962. (Photograph courtesy of Miguel Angel Albizures)

JOC's "collective self-help" ideology might have functioned to shield the state or employers from class struggle. In Guatemala in the 1960s it provoked trade unionism, a struggle against employers and inevitably against the state as well. It is not difficult to find explanations for this outcome in many aspects of Guatemalan life: state terrorism, increasing working-class poverty, feeble methods of socializing youth into dominant norms, and the young age at which people entered the work force, a phenomenon that transformed working-class youth groups into workers' circles. But this outcome had to be formulated. In the dryness and poverty of post-1954 intellectual life, young people were not exposed to an array of ideas but they did the best they could, selecting from what was available, adding and reshaping ideas to step toward a new sense of personal value and of alternative ways of living; this was original, deliberate, and creative, not rote.

It would be misleading to label as only "religious" social phenomena that absorb and adapt religious forms of expression and leave it at that. Although there exists no polarity between the religious and the nonreligious, there is a difference between the two. Religion influenced the young Guatemalans who started trade unions root and branch, but they were not promoting it. To varying degrees they were impelled by the egalitarianism that they had culled from Christianity's rich and ambiguous repertoire of politics, ethics, and utopias, but in contrast to the later Liberation Theology, neither JOC nor the labor organizations that its members started were trying to change the church or religious doctrine. Liberation Theology simultaneously justifies class struggle on doctrinal grounds and argues that Christianity is "really" a worldview that supports the struggle of the oppressed. JOC made no such claims; it predated the heyday of Liberation Theology. In many countries, including Guatemala, its members moved away from the church as a framework instead of trying to bridge their distance from it or, as with Liberation Theology, launch a countermovement within it.

JOC taught a relative degree of independence of thought and action without drawing people into the isolation of individualized nonconformism. It was well suited to Guatemalan conditions: though anticommunist (at least until the mid-1960s), it inclined members to radicalism in a society where trade unionism was an aberrant social activity. JOC was simultaneously nonconformist, in its emphasis on working-class self-defense in all arenas of life, and conformist, in its establishment of Christian and priest-supervised groups to which parents could send their errant children. JOC was "safe" yet riddled with ideas that led the young to move on in "dangerous" directions.

After the 1954 coup, which Solórzano and international JOC leader Joseph Cardijn, who visited Guatemala in the 1950s, supported, many JOC activists were increasingly troubled by the loss of workers' rights. By the late 1950s some became preoccupied with the sad details of workers' struggles in which they were not involved, as well as with international questions.[14] For example, in 1959 the secretary general of JOC in Guatemala, José Angel Berreondo, at the invitation of Cuban JOC members who supported Fidel Castro's July 26th Movement, went to Cuba to attend the Revolution's first May First celebra-

JOC youths welcome Belgian priest and international JOC leader Joseph Cardijn to Guatemala after the 1954 coup. (Photograph courtesy of Miguel Angel Albizures)

tion. By 1962, the year Berreondo was shot dead in Guatemala City, Solórzano and the church were barriers to the historical protagonism taught by the Young Catholic Worker. They discouraged any sort of political activism, including JOC participation in trade unionism, in part because the Autonomous Federation of Guatemalan Unions, whose formation had been endorsed by Archbishop Rossell y Arellano and JOC in 1954, had been taken over by the Communist Guatemalan Labor party. As a result of the church's intransigence, several young workers left JOC, as Julio Celso de León put it, "to do what JOC had told us to do: ACT against injustice."[15]

It was after the March–April 1962 urban uprising, when thousands of workers struck and students took to the streets to demand the resignation of President General Miguel Ydígoras, that Julio Celso de León, Teresa de Oliva, José Mundo Alvarez, and César Galicia (from the first generation of JOCistas who came of age under the conservative leadership of Gilberto Solórzano) left JOC to form the Christian Workers' Front (FTC). Members of FTC went on to create the National Federation of Transport Workers (FENOT) in 1965, the Central Federation of Guatemalan Workers (FECETRAG)—which replaced the FTC—in 1966, the Guatemalan Federation of Peasants (FCG) in 1967, the National Central of Workers (CNT) in 1968, and the Bank Workers' Federation (FESEB) in 1969. Of these organizations, CNT, as a national central, was the most important. It united into one group the several peasant leagues in the FCG and the unions of bank, construction, transportation, and factory workers in Guatemala City. By the mid-1970s CNT would be the most important urban labor organization since the 1954 coup, one that projected an imprecise yet fiery "revolutionary" line.

After Celso de León and others quit JOC in 1962 to successfully launch Christian unions, which procoup ideologues had tried and failed to establish after 1954, JOC drifted leftward. In the early 1960s Gilberto Solórzano left the Young Catholic Worker and responsibility for it fell to the priest Abel López, who was attuned to the thinking that eventually crystallized in Liberation Theology. López encouraged a new generation of JOC members to collaborate with unions. Thus in 1967 JOC assisted strikers at the new CAVISA glass factory at a time when the Communists hesitated to support militant class action. One year later, both former and current members of JOC organized the National Central of Workers. The idea for CNT had come from an Argentine ex-JOCista, Emilio Maspero, a leader of the Christian Democratic continentwide Latin American Confederation of Workers. At the suggestion of Abel López, with whom the Argentine spoke in 1968 during a visit to Guatemala sponsored by the Guatemalan Christian Democratic party, Maspero contacted former JOCistas in the peasants' union and in the existing Christian federation, including Celso de León and de Oliva.[16] They met and soon launched CNT, the new central, with the participation of younger workers still associated with JOC, such as Miguel Angel Albizures.

By the time CNT was founded, the Young Catholic Worker was a small organization. When its support for trade unionism alienated the Catholic church, JOC floundered completely and was supplanted by the labor movement. At that point Albizures got a job at the new Shulton Old Spice cologne factory and organized a union using the method of "conquering" workers: organizing them into small personal discussion groups and converting them to a vision of themselves as powerful protagonists. The union was launched on the day that

Albizures had coffee in the Shulton cafeteria, the one reserved for management. The point was that "one's own small action could change the world."[17]

Albizures explained how he went from JOC to CNT:

> We [in JOC] began to see trade unionism as a further step. You were a worker, exploited, you were working and had a relationship to others who worked. Trade unionism presented a possibility for change, for talking about the exploitation you experienced in flesh and blood and for becoming what we called "the integral man," the historical subject, through the transformation of oneself—not drinking, not accepting injustice. It presented a way of talking about the very value of being able to demand, and demonstrating to people that their situation was not singular. They were not alone, isolated from others.[18]

JOC gave the sense, indispensable to sustaining class and personal struggle, that workers had the power to think and act, and that they were not alone. United with others, they could stop drinking, or end crime in a neighborhood, or say no to sexual abuse. Within JOC, young people perceived themselves anew as "subjects" instead of "objects." They took that perspective into factories, where they remained "subjects" as trade union organizers, and where the struggle against alienation and for personhood was, along with demands for improved wages and working conditions, a part of workers' protests against the kind of society and industry in which they lived and worked. The young workers who left JOC and started unions had rebelled against the fixed meanings of JOC's discourse, which in their interpretation led to a certain kind of trade unionism. The ideology of the union movement that these workers created belongs to their hard-wrought intellectual history.

The Emergent Trade Unionism

Containing multiple trajectories, the Christian Workers' Front, the first labor group organized by ex-JOCistas, described itself as militant, antigovernment, anticommunist, and, in a qualified way, Christian. The founding statement of May 1, 1962, read:

We aim to organize all workers and peasants in a defined union because we are convinced that neutral unions, such as those which collaborate with the government, are far from fulfilling the aspirations of workers and far from presenting a solution to the imminent danger of Communism. . . . The Christian name only means we are inspired by Christian doctrine and we choose Christian morals and method, but this does not mean submission to religious or extra-temporal norms. We are concerned that the present structure of society be radically altered and the union movement is part of the base of that new society. . . . We want a more just economic system, an economy which serves workers, and not an economy workers serve.[19]

Six years later, CNT, the front's heir, was founded at the height of death squad activity under President Julio César Méndez Montenegro (1966–70). By then CNT did not designate itself as Christian or anticommunist, and it spoke openly of social revolution. It was explicitly anticapitalist and emphasized, as JOC had, the need for personal transformation. Unlike JOC, however, it connected personal change with social revolution. In a typical statement from the early 1970s, the central wrote:

CNT, whose task is the integral personal and collective advancement of the workers, which will only be possible through a radical change of the economic, political and social structures, proclaims its task as Social Revolution, of which the workers are the vanguard. . . . CNT declares itself independent of Governments, Political Parties, Bosses and the Church. The CNT derives its inspiration from the values and the fundamental needs of the Human Being. . . . The exploitation of the worker is not only economic, it is fundamentally *human*. As a worker, he is impeded from making his own decisions, from taking responsibility for his own acts, and made dependent and subordinate. . . . The Human Being should be the principal subject and aim of all social institutions. Liberty acquires vigor when the responsibilities of the human life are assumed and a commitment to the community is made. Man can know, dominate, and transform the nature of all things. Because of that he spiritually transcends the material world.[20]

"Spiritually" transcending the material world meant understanding and controlling that world, not being subjugated by it. The reclamation of humanity's spirit, which lay in its ability to "know, dominate, and transform the nature of all things," was paramount. CNT advanced a humanistic, rationalistic definition of workers who in Guatemala were assigned no positive definition; it did not exalt or deprecate the rank of "worker," as do both socialist and capitalist ideologies in many-layered and often contradictory ways. Instead, it advocated the abolition of that status of worker in favor of what it argued was an inherently positive and powerful status, that of human being, much as Karl Marx once wrote of the need to affirm the "species-being," and as twentieth-century Christian existentialists, who shared intellectual roots with Guatemalan trade unionists, spoke of forming the "integral" person. What was wrong with society was not only that workers were poor but also that some people had to be workers. CNT stated:

> This system denies the right to BE, to CREATE; it converts man into an object. Instead of forming the individual, it deforms him, and places him in a dependent position. In view of this negation of man as *being*, we ask what kind of education do we need? One which permits the reflection that accompanies the action which makes a free man who participates in his personal destiny and in collective destiny. An education with these goals: (1) To understand oneself clearly and deeply; (2) To understand others clearly and deeply; (3) To understand objects clearly and deeply; (4) To understand situations clearly and deeply.[21]

These concerns and this language seem strange if one assumes that unions are only about jobs, or jobs and politics. But CNT had the capacity to empower by virtue of the culture it created. Its concern with being, independence, and clarity is not surprising in a society where existence was constantly put into question by a terrorist state that thrived on secrecy and negated human personality, talent, and right by reducing people to raw material and flesh, which it then stole away and cut up. According to CNT's declaration of principles, "A unified labor movement is the indispensable condition for the full realization of the personal and collective destiny of the integral individual." The National Central of Workers urged the creation of culture, which it defined as "the result of human experience, the work of man. The necessities of the realization of his integral person give existence, form and content to culture."[22] In the critical conjuncture of the late 1960s in which CNT developed, when bodies were literally being torn apart, CNT offered the inverse image—wholeness.

This concern with being and personhood was visible in struggles at the shop level. For example, in late 1974 a few workers at the La Elegante factory asked for the minimum wage and were told by the owner, Antonio Malouf, to "go to hell." Paying less than the minimum daily Q1.19 established for the textile industry, Malouf prodded workers with sticks and used a megaphone to shout insults such as "Move it you old whores" to the largely female work force. The small group interested in unionizing asked around their neighborhoods until someone directed the workers to ex-JOCista Miguel Angel Albizures, by then fired from Shulton Old Spice and a full-time CNT organizer. On his advice, they formed an ad hoc committee and wrote their first leaflet. Although they were unaccustomed to writing, Albizures had urged them to do so, based on his philosophy that people needed to do these things on their own. In the leaflet, they explained their position:

> We are announcing to all workers that in view of the problems that we have suffered in the factory, we have decided to organize to defend our rights which are upheld by the Constitution and the Labor Code, which grants the right to unionize. We have taken this decision because of the threats, humiliations, shouting, insults, low salaries, unjustified dismissals and job instability and because we think that workers have the right to better treatment, better pay and the right that our dignity as human beings be respected. The most important thing in the factory is not the machines or the money as the owners always had us believe; the most important thing is us, the men and women who with our intelli-

gence and strength move the machines. Compañero workers: Don't be afraid, we have submitted a petition of demands to the courts and therefore you can't be fired [this automatically placed the factory under a temporary injunction forbidding it to dismiss workers]. Compañeros: We appeal to your conscience, your human and social sensibility, to your feelings of comradeship and human solidarity to unite with us in our aspirations and ideals. We urge all those who have not joined up to do so now without fear.[23]

Malouf responded with a letter that read in part: "Dear friends. . . . What abuses do you complain of? Elements here say those things because they do not want the factory to move forward. Here there is affection, sympathy, mutual esteem. . . . We are all human, we can confer peacefully. . . . I want to thank those who are conscious of their duty and say: God pays them and God blesses them."[24] "*Of course*, we are all human," replied the workers in their second leaflet:

We think, reason and feel and because of this we have chosen to stand up to so much injustice and so much humiliation. . . . He speaks of peaceful dialogue, here we listen to shouts and dirty words. He asks, "What abuses?" Doesn't he remember that his wife hit Señorita Elizabeth when she was pregnant? . . . He speaks of humanism. Doesn't he recall we went to him and asked for a minimum wage and he told us to go to h——. He speaks of evil elements. *To the contrary we are people conscious of our dignity and rights and it matters to us if we lose our jobs* but if with our sacrifice we teach that in Guatemala workers are people and not animals, we are prepared. He speaks of respect. To *earn respect one must learn to respect others as human beings.* The problem with Malouf is that he treats us as he wishes because he believes us to be slaves instead of thoughtful male and female human beings. This is *injustice and exploitation.* We will not step backwards, we will show *even if it costs us* our jobs that workers are people, not animals. The señor mentions God in his note; this is ironic. One does not respect God if one doesn't respect people. *God for us is all justice and all kindness,* but in the factory we live in injustice.[25]

Labor militants at the La Elegante shirt factory talk to a reporter in 1974. (Photograph courtesy of Miguel Angel Albizures)

The organizers did end up sacrificing their jobs. The company lawyer, also an employee at the Labor Ministry, found enough workers to start a second petition. Because the Labor Code specified that only one petition could represent workers in a particular shop, the ministry had to decide between the two. It chose the second, thereby nullifying the injunction of the first. The lawyers who worked with CNT in the early 1970s challenged the ruling and lost, military police were stationed inside the plant, and the organizers were legally dismissed.[26]

The La Elegante workers had grievances about wages, treatment, and job insecurity. They invoked the constitution and the Labor Code in their own defense and to calm nerves, apparently with faith in the law but without claiming that it inspired them. They felt entitled to make demands because they understood that they were producers, "the most important thing" to generating Malouf's profits as they moved the machines, and because they were "the most important thing" in an absolute sense within the framework of their own sensibilities about life. Their rationale for unionizing surpassed economics and religion, and they repeatedly raised the question of identity; their rights as "workers" and as "human beings." Although they argued that God and religion were on their side, and not on Malouf's, they did not claim religion or God as a justification for, or a source of, trade unionism. Malouf brought up God first, not the workers. To their essential humanity—that they thought, felt, and therefore acted—they attributed their trade unionism and called to others in the name of human sensibility. If to be people they must lose their jobs and their status as workers, they were willing to make that sacrifice—a sacrifice because then they would be penniless—but one they would make because money was less important than proving, or teaching, humaneness. Over and over the leaflet writers insist that workers are people. This constant defining of worker as person could be interpreted as a way of talking about class or as a rejection of class—not of the abstract category that serves as an analytic tool in unmasking relations, but as the refusal to identify oneself only as a worker in a society where that meant "slave," "animal," "daughter of a whore."

Ties with the Christian Democratic Party

The Guatemalan Christian Democratic party (PDC) collaborated with the National Central of Workers and with the federations initiated by the cadres from JOC. PDC provided funds, and many of its middle-class professionals became part of the labor movement's general staff. Moreover, CNT affiliated with CLAT, the Latin America–wide labor confederation that Christian Democrats supported and whose Argentine leader, Emilio Maspero, had had a part in founding CNT.

The Guatemalan PDC had formed immediately after the 1954 coup as a procoup party of the anticommunist right. However, in the 1960s it moved toward the political center in the same manner that PDCs did elsewhere in Latin America in response to the rise of mass upheavals and revolutionary movements during that decade. Like PDCs everywhere, the Guatemalan party initiated popular urban and rural organizations and advocated social change in general terms. Because of its new organizational work with the poor and its rhetoric of social justice and a new humane order through a "third-path" neither capitalist nor socialist, the Guatemalan PDC attracted to its ranks young men and women from the middle classes who, often as devout Catholics, were distressed by Guatemala's poverty and violence and sought to reform their country through legal means.[27] Among the PDC intellectuals who advised the slowly emerging labor movement were lawyers René de León Schlotter, Gabriel Aguilera Peralta, and Enrique Torres, who helped establish a center for organizers called the Institute for the Economic and Social Development of Central America (IDESAC). University-educated and of middle- and upper-class families, these professionals had access to powerful social circles from which workers were excluded and they understood the state's mechanisms of legal control. Given the complex procedures of union recognition and contract negotiation, as well as the fear shared by many workers of speaking directly to managers and state functionaries, they seemed indispensable to trade unionism. Their presence sometimes conflicted with labor's emphasis on worker self-empowerment, although they often spoke in similar terms.

The prestige of lawyers within the labor movement grew when they found a legal maneuver to prevent employers from stopping unions by firing workers who signed organizing petitions. To unionize any company, twenty-one workers were required to sign a petition and present it to the Labor Ministry, which had to recognize the union within sixty days. However, because the twenty-one petitioners had to be employed by the company in question, if the company fired any of them before the ministry acted, the petition was invalid; many companies simply fired activists to end drives. Lawyers discovered that if the workers presented to the court a "petition of demands," which was considered a "collective conflict of an economic character" (in effect, a civil suit), by law the company was thereby *emplazado*. An *emplazamiento* (an injunction) was a temporary restraining order under which company relations with labor were frozen until the civil suit was settled. Hence, when workers took a petition for a union to the ministry, they could also deliver a petition of demands; if the company then fired any worker, it could be challenged in court.[28] The lawyers thus found a loophole in the Labor Code, and their subsequent courtroom battles were designed to make the fantasy of constitutional right a fact;

in some instances they could not, such as in the case of La Elegante, and in others they could.

A few workers who belonged to CNT, such as Julio Celso de León, were recruited by the Christian Democratic party. Many, however, opposed PDC on the grounds that it was manipulative and politically self-serving.[29] When Celso de León temporarily left CNT to run for office on the Christian Democratic ticket, the intention of many PDC members to use mass organizations to mobilize votes became a clear point of disagreement, one that reflected trade unionists' deep mistrust of electoral politics. By the early 1970s internal divisions were apparent within CNT. Miguel Angel Albizures, Adolfo Hernández, and others opposed the influence of Celso de León and other Christian Democrats. Although CNT did not formally leave CLAT until 1978, by 1974 the Christian Democrats were a declining power within CNT. In addition, as a result of the party's failure to become mass-based by the early 1970s, some of its members became interested in the guerrilla organization, the Rebel Armed Forces (FAR), as an alternative. In response to the growing inflexibility of the political system, these Christian Democrats lost their enthusiasm for legal reform and looked with approval toward the growth of a revolutionary movement.

By the 1970s the Rebel Armed Forces was turning its attention to the city. FAR's leaders attributed its defeat in the late 1960s to the inherent weaknesses of its *foquismo*, the view that the exemplary military action of a small group of combatants in the countryside would bring about the downfall of the state by creating a political crisis. This had not happened, and FAR now sought the traditional Marxist vanguard, the industrial proletariat, to be the backbone for a new mass-based armed struggle against the state. A few PDC members joined FAR and subsequently introduced Marxism into the Christian-inspired urban trade unionism. This is how it happened that workers who formed unions in the 1960s, such as Miguel Angel Albizures and Efraín Alonso, read Marx. They did not become Marxists, but Marxism influenced them.

Efraín Alonso's history illustrates the course of an activist's life and consciousness in the 1960s (see Appendix). Alonso was born on the southern coast, where he worked as a child picking bananas at the United Fruit Company's Tiquisate plantation in the 1950s. After witnessing the dismantling of the laborers' union and the persecution of rural activists following the 1954 coup, he migrated to the city to study and to escape from Tiquisate. By 1962 he was working in road construction and attending night school at a time when "all the students were in the streets. No one studied and everyone talked about Cuba, including me." Because of his school experiences and because he had witnessed the organization of rural workers, the beginnings of land reform in his childhood, and the counterrevolution, Alonso was already interested in trade unionism when he started working at the Riviana Foods' Kern's canning company in 1963; in fact, he was looking for it. A deeply religious man, he came into contact with FECETRAG, a Christian trade union federation of the early 1960s, through a fellow worker. Ideas about gender, which were a part of urban popular culture and which JOC had articulated, were pivotal to the efforts of Alonso and his friends. They started the union at Kern's because "there were these managers, these middle-class young guys with their cute little cars. And when the harvest came they needed a lot of extra women to work so they always picked the prettiest ones. And what they [the managers] did afterwards, they took them to drink on Fridays, on the weekend, I don't know what they did, and these poor women had to give in to what they wanted because they needed the job."[30] With the help of Julio Celso de León and others, the union secured legal status and remained active for many years.

The Christian Democrats cultivated Alonso, who was a bright, eager young worker, and hired him as an organizer. They even sent him to a course sponsored by a pro–Christian Democratic labor federation in Venezuela. But disillusioned by the PDC's attempts to use the labor movement to build an electoral constituency and by the habit of many PDC leaders of red-baiting anyone with whom they disagreed—something Alonso remembered from his childhood with horror—he left the party at a time when many people were deserting it in search of other methods of achieving social justice. One of the lawyers in the labor movement who quit the Christian Democrats and entered the revolutionary movement lent Alonso a book by Marx.

Alonso was active in a neighborhood betterment association, and when an underground member of Rebel Armed Forces contacted him through a neighbor, Alonso agreed to distribute FAR leaflets; not only were some of the ex-PDC members joining FAR, but also several of its leaders were Alonso's former high school companions. According to Alonso, unemployment and his young wife's anxieties finally resulted in his decision to immigrate to the United States. When he left Guatemala City in the late 1960s he felt "disappointed with myself." He settled in New York City, where he eventually began to study theology with priests who endorsed Liberation Theology, and to participate in a community group of Spanish-speaking residents who met regularly to discuss and find solutions to their problems.[31]

A Balance Sheet of the National Central of Workers by 1974

The late 1960s and early 1970s were hard times for trade unionists and for most other Guatemalans. When Colonel Carlos Arana Osorio (1970–74) became president in 1970, after directing a scorched-earth campaign against FAR and the general population in the east, he announced that if it was necessary to turn the entire country into a "cemetery in order to pacify it," he would not hesitate to do so.[32] Constant states of siege, military intervention at the University of San Carlos and city high schools, and hundreds of disappearances and murders characterized his years in office. Arana Osorio forged unity between the army's political wing, the Party for Institutionalized Democracy, and the right-wing Movement for National Liberation, the favored party of most members of a national bourgeoisie that was intolerant of any dissent or reformism. The ruling coalition of the PID-MLN oversaw the construction of state institutions in which the line between civilian and military power blurred, and the military's relationship to economic power altered as officers used their position within the state to buy property. Arana Osorio expressed this change clearly enough the day he inaugurated the Bank of the Army in 1971: "The army is not a servant of private initiative, we are associates."[33]

CNT and its member federations organized the majority of the new unions of the 1960s and early 1970s. The bus workers' federation, FENOT, formed six unions, the bank workers' federation started five, and CNT organized unions in twelve factories, including Kern's, Philip Morris's TACASA cigarette plant,

Goodyear's Ginsa tire factory, the INCASA powdered-coffee company, Shulton Old Spice, and a textile plant, the Atlantic Industrial Company (CIDASA). Because of both illegal and legal repression, union victories barely kept pace with losses, and each victory required a major effort. The workers at Shulton Old Spice won union recognition in 1969 and lost it within a year when the company changed its name and the new enterprise was able to legally fire activists. Before they lost their union, the Old Spice workers had promoted one at the neighboring CIDASA textile plant. About the time that the Shulton union was dissolved, the CIDASA union was recognized, largely because lawyers successfully used the emplazamiento. In 1972 the CIDASA union, unable to obtain a contract, won a strike vote and 280 workers walked off the job in the first legal strike since 1954. CNT mobilized massive publicity, bus workers held stoppages, and several priests issued declarations of support. After sixty-seven days, the court declared the strike "unjust," arguing that the company already paid the Q1.60 daily minimum in textiles and that the market was contracting. Over 100 workers quit in protest, the union faded, and three months later its leader, César Augusto Morataya, was murdered.[34]

Through either the courts or violence, a third of the unions organized between 1968 and 1972 were destroyed by 1973. Many leaders were killed, among them ex-JOCista Teresa de Oliva, assassinated leaving a church in 1971, and bus driver Vicente Mérida Méndoza, kidnapped in 1972. It was an enormous achievement that anything existed at all: in 1973 CNT at least had several factories still organized, a two-story building, a newspaper called *Acción Popular*, and a small staff of volunteers. Despite the constant states of siege imposed by President Arana Osorio in the early 1970s, the labor central sought ways to protest and to have a public existence. For instance, to demand the reappearance of bus driver Mérida Méndoza, CNT members held work stoppages and leafleted and hung banners throughout the city. And simply to ensure that the central's name was in the public's eye, they ran in the annual Max Trott city marathon wearing T-shirts labeled "CNT."

No matter that times were hard for workers not only politically but economically as well, CNT activists were quick to proclaim the morality of the labor movement they were building, and to separate themselves from anyone who, from the central's point of view, fought only for money. In early 1973, 15,000 teachers struck illegally for four months in the longest, largest, and most militant strike since 1954. Responding to the sudden inflation of that year, the teachers eventually won a salary increase of 25 percent, one-half of what they had demanded, twice what the state had offered, and far more than any group of workers had won since 1954.[35] Yet in spite of the strike's militancy, the encouragement it gave other workers to fight inflation, and the strategic importance of a strike by state workers, who numbered over 150,000 nationally and had the power to cripple the state, the National Central of Workers was suspicious of the teachers and their walkout. Concerned with educating the "new man," CNT had criticized teachers before the strike as "agents of the system," and once the strike began, CNT hesitated to support it.[36] In early 1974, when the teachers' organization was unable to turn a small defensive walkout against massive layoffs of its 1973 activists into a general strike of teachers, an editorial in CNT's newspaper pointed out that the weaknesses of the 1973 strike, what it called "economism," doomed that of 1974 to failure. Because they were part of the capitalist system of values, argued the editorial, teachers only knew how to fight hard for money; because they had not transcended those values, they were incapable of a solidarity strike.[37]

CNT did represent unions as a means to material ends, but its *primary* representation of unions was as transformative personally, socially, and politically in their daily functioning and in their aims. Its literature addressed "All workers and peasants who are *protagonists* and not merely *spectators*," and it defined unions as "Voluntary groupings of workers to *study* problems, interests, rights; to *struggle* to resolve these problems; to *defend* the rights which as producers of capitalism's wealth belong to us; to *change* the present society and end all abuses and injustices which today exist among all popular sectors."[38] Keywords had metamorphosed since the days of JOC: "subjects" were also "protagonists," and "See, Judge, Act" became "Study, Struggle, Defend, and Change." A language of class action evolved from one of existential positioning.

In the early 1970s Miguel Angel Albizures, now a man in his late twenties, immigrated to California, where he worked for five months to earn enough money to pay his mother's hospital bills in Guatemala City after she became seriously ill. In California he joined a unionization drive in the large factory where he had found employment. Eager to decipher this foreign trade union-ism, he was soon repelled by it. Albizures recalled that "the boss would give a big dinner for the workers at a good hotel with beer and all and then the union organizers would do the same thing and this was what seemed to decide the issues. I couldn't understand the moral basis of the unions in that country."[39]

4

Possibilities and Repression, 1974–1978

Between 1974 and 1978 intense conflict characterized Guatemala City's neighborhoods and factories, where workers formed more unions than at any time since 1954. The inflationary cycle that started in 1973 pressured already impoverished industrial, craft, service, transportation, and other workers. The 1976 earthquake deepened general discontent, and the social landscape shifted in every sense after thousands mobilized to rebuild their neighborhoods, schools, markets, and workplaces. The popular response to inflation and to the 1976 earthquake occurred during the presidency of General Kjell Laugerud, who entered office in 1974 promising that he would uphold constitutional rule and address social grievances.

Laugerud's mildly reformist rhetoric was a measure of the provisional success of state violence. The same ultraright coalition of the Party for Institutionalized Democracy and the Movement for National Liberation (PID-MLN) that Colonel Carlos Arana Osorio had forged during his presidency (1970–74) brought Laugerud into office. Arana Osorio's temporary defeat of the guerrilla movement, his repeated imposition of states of sieges, curfews, military searches, assassinations, and disappearances had left the country subdued. By 1974 PID-MLN felt secure. Laugerud, its presidential candidate, could afford to replace his friend Arana Osorio's terrorist language with a reformist one to answer the challenge posed by the Christian Democratic candidate, General Efraín Rios Montt, who urged reforms in an appeal to the vast constituency for social change. Never mind that PID-MLN committed blatant electoral fraud to defeat Rios Montt; when Laugerud took office he allowed a small political opening. What distinguished the Laugerud years was not that the state guaranteed rights, but that compared to the extraordinary levels of violence of the 1966–73 period, death squad, army, and police actions killed fewer people. This definition of a "political opening" may have been peculiar to Guatemala, but as the atmosphere changed perceptibly, workers attempted to unionize in virtually all the city's important factories, and by 1978 the National Central of Workers embraced seventy-five member unions in the city and endeavored to construct a national mass movement for social change.

In 1974 CNT was the most dynamic labor organization in the city, far more so than the older Autonomous Federation of Guatemalan Unions, which was influenced by the Communists in the Guatemalan Labor party. A victorious Reorganizing Commission took control of CNT in 1974 to lead it away from a future linked to the Christian Democratic party and toward a strategy based on the power of mass organization. The Reorganizing Commission included Miguel Angel Albizures and Adolfo Hernández, the 1950s–60s' generation of activists who had once been in the Young Catholic Worker, and a member of the next generation, Miguel Cifuentes, born in the city in 1951 and now a worker at Philip Morris's TACASA cigarette factory. These men shared a profound suspicion of formal politics and politicians and never hoped to make the state a neutral or prolabor arbitrator. Miguel Cifuentes remembered the bloody battles against the militarization of his high school in 1963 as "definitive" to his understanding of the need to struggle against the state.[1] But CNT leaders expressed a practical ambivalence: their rejection of the state as a mediator on behalf of workers did not mean that they also opposed militant legal action that would force the state to obey Guatemalan law. They believed in worker self-empowerment, yet they also needed the law and lawyers because trade unionism was about working within the system, even if trade unionists did not think that the system worked. Even the lawyers did not believe that the system worked. By 1974 CNT had a small staff of legal counselors, many of whom were former members of the Christian Democratic party, who were inspired by Christian notions of social justice and a Marxist analysis of capitalism.[2]

After Laugerud took office, workers in many factories initiated organizing drives, though they were haunted by the fear of what could happen even as they tested the new president's pledge to uphold constitutional rule. In 1974, for example, a few workers in the Japanese-owned ACRICASA textile factory, which opened in 1973 and employed primarily women, decided to "*do something, whatever*" about the miserable working conditions; supervisors even slapped workers in the face. Ex-ACRICASA worker Sonia Oliva recalled:

> We didn't have a very clear idea about what we were doing. From what I knew about unions, it sounded very daring to me. I had heard my father talk about railroad workers getting killed in the 1950s. Anyway we proceeded.
>
> One of the workers had a father who was a rail worker so we arranged through her father to meet someone in FASGUA, but the person did not show up the day he was supposed to, and there we were just standing out in the street, and one of the girls says, "Hey! I saw a sign for a workers' group downtown." So we went over there, and it was CNT.
>
> We walked in very humble, eyes down, and said in these small voices, "We are workers and we have all these problems." Miguel Angel Albizures [an organizer for CNT] was sitting there, all smiles—"Oh, sit down." We started to explain how things were, and Miguel Angel talked about a union, and he said, "You have to think about it and decide, but we will give you all the information you need to have one." And that's how it started.[3]

Sonia Oliva and workers like her at ACRICASA and elsewhere took two major risks: they often did not know the people with whom they collaborated well, and they did not have a "clear idea of what we were doing" except that they knew they could get killed for it. "Anyway," as Oliva put it, in the mid-1970s, textile and clothing, food and beverage, transportation, and other workers, in groups or alone, went to the two-story, early twentieth-century building that CNT rented on Ninth Avenue in the busy downtown near the National Palace. Sometimes a friend or relative directed them there, or they heard about the central on the radio. Workers from the INCATECU shoe factory knew nothing of CNT. In 1974 they simply walked into the courtyard of the University of San Carlos Law School and asked everyone they encountered how to organize a union until someone referred them to a student legal aid service, which introduced them to CNT. Because of this sort of initiative, in 1974 alone thirty-five unions formed in the city, as compared to nine in 1972.[4]

The following year a court decision in favor of the new union at the IN-CATECU shoe factory encouraged many workers to think that a new era in state-labor relations really could begin under President Laugerud. Founded in the 1930s by a Belizian-born, naturalized Guatemalan family, INCATECU had unionized in the 1944–54 period, when it produced only rubber shoes. After the 1954 coup, the union was destroyed; the factory expanded production to leather and employed a new, primarily female work crew of 375 workers, some of whom had walked over to the university in 1974 seeking advice about how to unionize. Law professor Mario López Larrave and several of his students guided the INCATECU workers through the procedure for obtaining union recognition and through months of negotiations for a contract.[5] When the talks failed in mid-1975, workers voted to strike. In June they began a legal walkout while the court deliberated whether their action was "just"; according to the 1956 Labor Code, a legal strike was just only if the union proved that the company could meet the strikers' demands. The striking workers camped out in tents in front of the factory, which was located on a major highway, turned the strike into a public event, and drew spontaneous support from workers across the city. After the INCATECU workers had been out for forty-nine days, a judge, to the city's amazement, ruled in favor of the union. This was the first time since 1954 that a legal strike had been declared "just."[6]

The workers obtained this ruling because one of the defense lawyers, Julio Alonso Figueroa, had managed to acquire the company's books. Also an economist, Figueroa, who was murdered three years later, easily proved INCATECU's ability to meet the union's demands. This placed the judge, who happened to be new to the bench, in a difficult position; influenced by Laugerud's electoral promises, she ruled in favor of the workers.

Although the INCATECU ruling turned out to be an anomaly—not only the first but to date also the last time a judge ruled a strike to be just—in 1975

The strike and encampment at the INCATECU shoe factory in 1975. The workers note the uniqueness of the walkout in their banner: it is a legal one. (Photograph courtesy of Miguel Angel Albizures)

many workers considered it to be an excellent omen and an upsurge of union activity even greater than that of 1974 followed. That the ruling did not indicate a significant change in state-labor relations quickly became apparent; within a year workers involved in a union drive at the Coca-Cola Bottling Company had to strategize in the face of a hostile court. Nevertheless, it was the prolabor INCATECU ruling that encouraged workers in plants such as Coca-Cola.

Beginnings of the Coca-Cola Workers' Union

The Coca-Cola Bottling Company (EGSA) in Guatemala City is a national enterprise operating under a franchise from the U.S. Coca-Cola Company. EGSA was established in 1941 by a U.S. airline pilot in downtown Zone 1. In 1956 a Texan Christian fundamentalist and MLN sympathizer named John Trotter took over and expanded production. Encouraged by a Central American Common Market tax exemption as a "new industry," Trotter in 1967 opened a new plant in Zone 11 on eight acres fronting the Boulevard Aguilar Batres at the southern edge of the city. He put up a large building that housed the latest bottling machinery and conveyor belts, cavernous storage areas, and administrative offices. Outdoors, he paved over only a small part of the large lot, while the rest remained overgrown with weeds; broken glass manufactured at the nearby CAVISA glass factory was dumped in one corner, and at night red and white delivery trucks were parked there randomly. A gardener was hired to plant a small rose garden in front of the compound, facing the highway. Coca-Cola grew to be a "3 star" Common Market firm and one of the largest; by the mid-1970s it produced over 200,000 bottles of soda pop daily. By that time it had a history of unionizing attempts: a union started in the 1944–54 period ended with the coup that destroyed reformist government in 1954, and a 1968 organizing drive abruptly stopped when its leader, César Barillas, was kidnapped and killed.

Two weeks after the successful 1975 strike at the INCATECU shoe factory, twenty-two-year-old Ricardo de Jesús Boche Morales, impressed by that victory, initiated a union drive at Coca-Cola with the encouragement of his brother, a member of a CNT union organized in the late 1960s at the INCASA powdered-coffee factory. Jesús Boche had been at Coca-Cola for two months the day he walked into the CNT office for the first time. He barely knew a soul at Coca-Cola, but after CNT legal adviser Marta Gloria Torres informed him that he had to affiliate twenty-one workers, he enlisted the support of co-workers Santos Martínez Campos and Mercedes Chácon Pirir, and the three spoke to others.[7] Warehouse worker Joaquín Rosales, who was twenty at the time, remembered the extemporaneous manner in which the three men went about organizing:

> One day I was loading up a truck, and these guys came over and asked me if I wanted to join a union. I said I didn't know. I thought it was strange that young guys who had just started wanted to unionize. They said it was a secret and I shouldn't tell anyone. I should join or not but I shouldn't talk, blow it and burn people. They said that it was very dangerous given the national situation, so that if one was going to get involved, one had to take into account that it would not be easy. I wanted to join. I didn't like their improvised way of going about things, but I agreed and they gave me a date to go down to the CNT.

Twenty-one workers attended an initial organizing meeting in CNT's building on August 9, 1975. Rosales said:

> We went over to that office like we were thieves or something, one at one corner, one at another, creeping up on the building secretly. I felt very nervous, my hands were sweating. "This is dangerous," I said to myself. I had spoken to friends who said don't get involved in that stuff, it's dangerous. But I had decided I had to do it because the situation in the plant was terrible and the treatment so shameful.
>
> We got into the building and they were waiting for us, Miguel Angel Albizures and a legal person. Albizures said, "Compañeros, you all have come here to form a union. Do you have some idea of what a union is? If you have questions about what a union is please say so." So I raised my hand and said I did not entirely understand unions. He said he would speak thoroughly and quickly so that we could see it was possible and not lose enthusiasm. He grabbed a piece of chalk, stood up by the blackboard and started to explain various issues and pose possible scenarios. We made a petition [of economic demands] and they put an injunction on the factory on August 11, 1975. There were a little over 20 of us at first and within a short time 120.[8]

Looking at the organization of the labor force one would not have predicted that many workers would have joined so quickly. In 1975, 350 workers were employed in eight departments, the largest of which were sales and production. Sales consisted of over 100 "salesmen" and "helpers" (company terms that workers also used) who supplied retailers in Guatemala City and two neighboring departments. The salesmen and their helpers came into the compound briefly in the morning and evening to pick up and return their trucks; otherwise, they were in the streets all day working in teams of three, one salesman and two helpers. The salesmen drove the delivery trucks and handled the sales route; in conjunction with the sales supervisor, they kept accounts and cultivated customers, and they earned on commission. The helpers loaded crates of empty bottles and unloaded full ones at the stores and received one-third of a cent for each crate. What these teams earned depended on the affluence of the neighborhoods; therefore routes were fought over. Getting a good one depended on ties with management, which is why in 1974 one production worker considered salesmen "finks, spies, always befriending the bosses."[9]

The over one hundred men employed in the production division worked inside the plant, tending the machines that washed and filled bottles as they moved down a conveyor belt. Production workers also took the bottles off the belt, packed them into crates, and put the crates back onto the belt, which carried them into the warehouse. The sixty men in the warehouse division stacked the crates and helped the forklift operators, who loaded the crates onto trucks. The remaining departments—long-distance delivery to wholesalers, the laboratory where formulas were mixed, mechanics, maintenance, and internal security—had fewer than fifteen workers each. The great divide in the work force lay between salesmen and all others. The sales department worked without direct supervision, and salesmen working from six in the morning to nine at night could earn up to Q400 (Q1 = $1) a month in 1975, whereas other workers received roughly Q1.10 a day and no more than Q60 a month and were supervised by managers the whole time.

Ties among workers were weak. Worker turnover was rapid, and hostility existed between production workers and salesmen, who in any case were out of touch with the plant all day. There was neither a soccer team nor a cafeteria; the only social amenity was a small bar across the street. Though production people spent the day together, production worker Mercedes Gómez, who had been there for two years in 1975, recalled a bleak situation: "I didn't even know people's names before the union started."[10] Nevertheless, there were *relaciones de paisanos* or that sense of comradeship among people who do not know one another as individuals but feel they do because they come from similar backgrounds or regions. There were also some kinship ties because salesmen often pulled in relatives as helpers. Family had a part in the union's formation, as evidenced by Jesús Boche, who entered trade unionism through kin (albeit a relative outside the plant), and by two brothers, Pedro and Luis Quevedo, who became union members together. But no preexisting group of friends, relatives, or paisanos played a definitive role in forming the union. Joaquín Rosales described the three initiators: "Boche met Santos Martínez in the warehouse. Boche was new, so was Martínez, so they hung out, and one of them met Chácon who was in production, and he was new too"—companions, but hardly close.[11]

When the workers organized, many were strangers to one another or at most acquaintances and only a few were friends or kin. As Rosales indicated, workers took a leap into the dark; he personally did not trust the organizers but he went ahead. Unless one appreciates the general quality of urban life for working people, it is hard to comprehend workers' capacity to unionize in conditions of such perilous uncertainty, at the same time that they lacked the comfort of old solidarities to ease the insecurities prompted by new risks. Vulnerability, unpredictability, and the gamble of relying on acquaintances, rather than the confidence that comes from a close and long-standing community, were familiar aspects of everyday survival.

The union spread from the warehouse. By the end of September 1975, 150 workers had joined. The majority came from production and the warehouse, a minority came from sales (mainly salesmen and not helpers), and a few other workers came from the small divisions such as mechanics and maintenance. Production and warehouse workers, the lowest-paid and worst-treated employees, were the union's backbone. A disproportionate number of salesmen, however, were elected to the first provisional union executive committee, formed in August 1975. Three out of nine members were salesmen (Rolando Maldonado, Pedro Quevedo, and Efraín Zamora), one was a well-paid technician (Israel Márquez), two came from the warehouse (Martínez Campos and Jesús Boche), one worked in mechanics (Víctor Burgos) and two in production (Francisco Abraham Montenegro and Ernesto González). Although production workers mistrusted salesmen, the few salesmen who joined the union were considered "unique," and the elections were not particularly competitive. Furthermore, salesmen often had the air of leaders: they were professionally outgoing men who spent virtually their entire workday talking, and they were accustomed to formalized personal relations. Partially as a consequence of their higher rank, which reinforced salesmen's sense of entitlement, they felt closer to management and capable of dealing with it. Production workers, who would lead and save the union during the worst of the state violence in

1980, generally lacked self-confidence in 1975, accepted that salesmen had more status, and wanted to utilize that hierarchy.[12]

Of the executive committee members, two soon predominated as leaders. One was salesman Pedro Quevedo, a former military man revered for his temper—"Pedro was very macho, no one could push him around." The other leader, Israel Márquez, was a soft-spoken, articulate, and educated technician. Both men were deeply religious and together were said to possess what workers considered magnetic qualities: conviction, clarity, and courage. These words had historically specific meanings: in the mid-1970s courage was synonymous with machismo, clarity referred to the capacity to decode the law, and conviction meant sticking with the union. By 1984, when union members were more interested in the union's internal life, some recalled Quevedo critically as "macho with coworkers" (not "courageous" with coworkers but dominating, although still courageous toward Coca-Cola and the state) and the relationship with Márquez as "good but maybe a little unhealthy. We depended on him too much.") But what stood out in 1975 was that Márquez was kindly and smart, Quevedo was tough, and both were determined.[13]

Workers particularly respected Márquez because of the contradictory configuration of his social standing and his own attitude toward it. He was almost a manager, he received a salary that allowed him a lower middle-class lifestyle, he had an education, and he belonged to the Mormons, a religious group of which most workers did not approve and one that opposed political activism. Once he joined the union, these qualities made him more admirable: an educated Mormon technician was the way he was; it broke all the rules in their favor and he stood to lose all he had. Márquez's presence made the union more "respectable" for many workers who at the same time valued him precisely for his originality and daring in the face of that respectability. According to Mercedes Gómez, "When Israel came in, it had a big effect. He was practically a boss, a technician, and no one wanted to talk to him about the union. When he walked by everyone shut up. But someone asked him and he said, 'With pleasure.' Because of him a lot of people joined and the union flourished."[14] Pablo Telón, a self-taught mechanic from Mazatenango, explained that "nobody thought Márquez would become a trade unionist, that he would become the working class's *best* defender! The company loved him. It impressed people when he joined. He had no reason to."[15] Workers did not join the union out of idealism, but in their eyes Márquez's renunciation of individual advancement and safety for the sake of justice and workers' welfare had real grandeur.

Workers unionized for many reasons: they wanted higher wages, formal work schedules, overtime pay, and an end to favoritism in route distribution and to management's arbitrary powers. Managers ripped up workers' social security cards so that Coca-Cola would not have to contribute to their funds and otherwise insulted workers continually. Warehouse worker Joaquín Rosales recalled a manager kicking him as he worked beneath a truck. Pablo Telón evoked his feelings of humiliation when he explained why he joined:

> I was deemed garbage. Once some equipment was misplaced and they said I had to pay for it out of my pocket. I spent days hunting for the equipment after work and finally found it and gave it to them and they did not even apologize.
>
> Once I had to go out for days after a truck that had broken down in the countryside. It was the rainy season and I came back driving the truck wearing an old dirty hat, and the manager, Uriguen [Julián Uriguen was EGSA's general manager], threatened to fire me because he said dirty people should not be in the truck. *Real tears* rolled down my cheeks.
>
> Uriguen was a beast. He fired people for drinking a soda. That's what it was like. It went on and on like that, so I was overjoyed to see that injunction notice in 1975.[16]

Mercedes Gómez's experience is also instructive. He had found his job in the Coca-Cola production department in 1973 through his brother, with whom he had migrated to the city in order to support their family in a small Indian village and to whom he felt very close. Gómez had many complaints, including that Uriguen, a native of Spain, swore repeatedly at Gómez, a man of Maya descent. The trigger for his joining the union was the company's sudden dismissal of his brother in 1975.[17] One salesman became a union member because he had a poor route and could not earn enough to provide for his family.[18] And as Pablo Telón put it, Israel Márquez had "no reason" to join. All of these motivations would develop new dimensions along the way, as the dynamics of organizing generated many twists.

While workers waited for months after their initial August meeting for the court to act on their petition of economic demands, and for the Labor Ministry to act on their request for legal status, John Trotter sought to defeat the union drive. He repeatedly stated that he would rather close the plant than turn it over to "the Communists." Considering it his legal right to dismiss a new worker on probation, he fired Jesús Boche. But CNT lawyers were able to win Jesús Boche's reinstatement on the grounds that the plant was under an injunction and by law management could not dismiss anyone. In addition, Trotter hired workers from Chiquimula, a region known as an MLN stronghold, at Q3 a day; the higher wage, he claimed, was part of an increase planned for all nonunionized workers. The newcomers were given guns licensed by the police and warned against the "Communist" agitators. These new recruits, however, were generally poor, former rural wage workers whom union members either won over or neutralized.

Then, immediately after the February 1976 earthquake, Trotter had some success. He gave thirty workers loans for rebuilding their homes on the promise that they submit a separate petition of economic demands to the labor court. Thus by late February the court had two petitions from the Coca-Cola workers. Because by law only one petition could represent the workers of a given workplace, the court had to rule which was valid. At that point the union's petition, with 152 signatures, had been before the court for eight months despite the Labor Code's requirement that petitions be processed within sixty days. If the court determined that the second list of demands was valid, the injunction that went with the first would no longer be in effect and the company could fire workers with impunity, as had happened at the La Elegante garment factory in 1974. In early March the union decided to "make a lot of publicity" in order to pressure the court to approve the first petition. Union workers wore T-shirts lettered "Coca-Cola doesn't like unions," decorated Coca-Cola delivery trucks with huge pro-union banners, and on one occasion drove them around the Central Plaza in front of the National Palace, where Pedro Quevedo was arrested for "capricious behavior."

On March 24, at 2:30 P.M., Marta Gloria Torres, the union's legal adviser, discovered that the court had approved the second petition. Because the court closed at 3:00 P.M., which meant that the official notice on the court ruling would not be served until the following morning, the union had one evening to prevent its members from being legally fired. As Joaquín Rosales explained: "We had to act legally and illegally at the same time. We would have been smashed if we broke the law, but we did not have a solid legal tool at that moment, so we stood on fairly odd ground."[19]

Pablo Telón described what union and nonunion workers did next:

We gave the word that nobody should leave the plant because if we left we might not be able to get in the next day. At five o'clock the manager told us that a list was up of dismissed workers and we could go to the Ministry and get our severance pay in the morning [Coca-Cola posted a list before the court notice was served]. We read the list—absolutely 152, every union guy fired. So we started to move. We put trucks across all the entrances, we put trucks in front of doors, we put forklifts in front of trucks, we punctured tires, we took all the keys.

At about seven o'clock the first riot squad bus comes by and then a Red Cross ambulance shows up with all this noise . . . WEEEEEEEER went the sirens. The CNT people were standing around outside, Albizures and Marta and Enrique Torres, yelling, "If they take someone, yell his name." And we're yelling, "We're not going to back down." And them yelling back, "We are with you. Go forward and yell the names of anyone taken." It was a tremendous scene.

Then the police chief goes and talks to Uriguen about who knows what. They came to some agreement and then they called through a mega-phone, "*Attention Workers!* If you don't abandon, we'll have to use . . ." How did they put it? "Force." So they gave us ten minutes, then nine, eight, seven . . . We were fairly frightened and we started to gather water fast, handkerchiefs and water for the tear gas bombs since they say with wet handkerchiefs the gas doesn't affect you. We sat down, wrapped blankets around ourselves and then wrapped ourselves around ourselves, wrapping arms, and then arms around waists and legs around legs—a regular straw mat.

And they're out there counting, and *Bam!* son of a . . . they attacked! One older guy started to leave and we said, "NO, grab on to us!" We met their onslaught with water which sort of startled them.

It took them until ten at night to get us out of there because of the way we'd tied ourselves to each other. Some of the people were really badly beaten up, like [Pedro] Quevedo—[managers] Uriguen and Fong were telling the police who to beat up—and we got some of them into the ambulances sitting there. The thing was not to lose sight of anyone and to count, so that no one disappeared. And we just stayed out there in front. There was no wall in front of the plant then, just the garden, so we all stayed in the garden.[20]

Telón was in a new situation, in the midst of a class action, sitting in a garden and faced with the possibility of losing his job.

The question was what to do. The workers had a potential legal argument for being outside the plant: a company lockout was in progress, not an illegal strike, because the workers had been at their workplaces and the police had thrown them out of the plant. But the problem was the petition on which the court had already ruled, as well as the firings. Clarity had to be both about law and more than law. In the meantime, before a course of action was planned, several of the workers started a hunger strike. Mercedes Gómez said that everyone was very nervous about kidnappings, "but there was press, publicity, a lot of people outside—CNT, all that. People went and got sheets of tin. We established ourselves out there in front like market day—stalls, blankets, pots, food, guitars, children."[21]

What they decided was to camp outside the plant without actually blocking the entrance or declaring themselves on strike. They were inspired by the INCATECU shoe workers' encampment in 1975, except that the Coca-Cola workers thought that they were in a more difficult position because they had a court ruling hanging over their heads. Mercedes Gómez called it a "tight situation":

Either you left to find a job elsewhere, or you stayed. And you knew, even then, if you stayed, you'd have to go on with this until God took you. I decided to stay. My mother wanted me to leave. She said I had many skills—baker, carpenter—and I could find work elsewhere. But something urged me to stay—maybe the attitude of the leaders. I could not abandon them because they never slept or ate, they kept at everything. I wasn't a leader, just a base member, but still I stayed.

I told my mother to go off and get food because I was staying. My brothers came and told me to leave. I said, "Help us, go get money. Other people from unions are bringing money and food. Why don't you, since I am your brother?"

A small armed group was going into the factory to work, and one of the leaders used to get up and talk to them in a very friendly manner. "Get with it!," he'd say. Some of them would pull out guns, and he'd say, "Don't be kindling wood, help us, don't work," or "Go into work but don't do anything."[22]

Propelled by his brother's firing to enter the union in 1975, when the time came to decide whether or not to desert the union in 1976, Mercedes Gómez faced a family that wanted him to leave, and he did not. He drew his family to him on the basis of kinship loyalty, but his decision to stay belonged to him, not family. Gómez now trusted certain people because they did not fail in a situation that was his and not familial; that represented a new and different type of bond, one of class. What at one point might have appeared to be a family code of solidarity was now a class code. What it meant to Gómez to be a union member took on more definition: not to be "kindling wood"—burned up sustaining the company; the "something," of leaders "keeping at everything"; dedication to justice for workers. Camping outside Coca-Cola without knowing what kind of pressure could be applied, without knowing what would happen and sensing that something terrible could, involved a greater commitment than simply joining the union. About eighty-five workers stayed in the garden, fewer than the number fired, and some of their wives joined them. If families or wives supported the encampment, it was because their kin

Coca-Cola workers smile at a press photographer during their 1976 encampment. (Photograph courtesy of the Coca-Cola Bottling Company Workers' Union)

urged them as kin. Few families understood or agreed with what the workers were doing. The wives of Pedro Quevedo and fellow union member Manuel López Balam cooked for the workers, but their husbands never discussed the union with them.[23]

CNT immediately formed a Committee to Support the Coca-Cola Workers comprised of trade unionists; thus it structured what had happened spontaneously in response to the INCATECU workers' encampment in 1975. The legal advisers went to other unions and pointed out that if the Coca-Cola union failed, if the court decision in favor of the second petition was allowed to stand, the legal system could doom all, as the La Elegante case had demonstrated in 1974. The support committee grew to include the CNT unions such as those at INCATECU shoe, Kern's canning company, and Philip Morris's TACASA cigarette plant, as well as the unions in FASGUA, the Bank Workers' Federation, a large paper workers' union on the southern coast, and workers from the IODESA cottonseed oil plant in Escuintla. Among its other members were two organizations that had originally been launched by organizers financed by the AFL-CIO in the 1960s and whose members were now searching for more militant allies, the Sugar Workers' Federation (FETULIA) and the Federation of Guatemalan Workers (FTG). Groups of workers from nearby factories came by the encampment and joined the committee as individuals. By this time, prompted by the decrease in state violence and the favorable 1975 court ruling on the INCATECU strike, reporters from the city's four daily newspapers were organizing a media workers' union. As a result of a new spirit of boldness among journalists, Coca-Cola workers were first- or second-page news every day and the heroes of several feature articles.

The union dramatized its significance. The projection of Coca-Cola workers to the rest of the city as powerful and prominent nurtured that feeling among the workers in front of the plant and elsewhere. Coca-Cola workers distributed thousands of leaflets, leaving the encampment in shifts to rally support at union meetings and in schools, which many of them were entering for the first time. The union's almost daily press releases emphasized the foreign nationality of Trotter and his managers; the simple justice of their demands for higher wages, benefits, and a union; the legality of their cause; and the intensity of their commitment: "We prefer to die with dignity than live at the hands of foreign exploiters."[24] They created an uproar in the city.

The encampment continued, effectively stopping production because so few workers entered the plant. Apparently Trotter did not know what to do, and he simply waited. The established channels offered the workers no further means: the court had ruled. The union had to take the initiative. On March 30, six days after the encampment began, a newspaper announced, "The workers of Coca-Cola say that for the first time since 1954 all labor organizations, regardless of ideology, will hold a historic meeting tomorrow at seven in the evening to discuss measures."[25]

The Formation of the National Committee on Trade Union Unity

On March 31, 1976, twenty Coca-Cola workers met with forty-four delegates from other unions, including affiliates of CNT, FESEB, FTG, FASGUA, and FETULIA. They represented groups of wage earners located mainly in the capital and a few in the nearby towns of Amatitlán and Escuintla and in other parts of the southern coast. The meeting resulted in the formation of the National Committee on Trade Union Unity (CNUS), a title suggested by labor lawyer Mario López Larrave and taken from a labor unity group of the 1944–54 period. The purpose of CNUS was to unite unions and union federations and confederations into a broad coalition that could confront the state. This step reflected the recognition of the extraordinary nature of state and society: if the law was meaningless, if the state fundamentally resolved all labor conflicts in favor of employers with or without the law, then all unions would have to take up each struggle with the state, with or without the law. CNUS stated, "The non-application of the minimum guarantees the law contains leaves us with either the immediate action of the president or the united action of the workers."[26]

On April 3 CNUS announced that forty-eight unions would strike unless the dispute at Coca-Cola was resolved in favor of the union and demanded a meeting with President Laugerud. As a result, representatives of the union, CNUS, Coca-Cola management, and the Labor Ministry came to an agreement and with that proved CNUS's point: real social power would pit the effective power of workers against the authoritarian power of the state. With forty-eight unions threatening to strike, Laugerud spoke to the ministry, which pressured Coca-Cola to rehire the workers with back wages as well as to agree to negotiate a contract and sign a statement recognizing the union. In this extralegal manner—extralegal because according to law union recognition was granted through an administrative process, not a presidential intervention—the Coca-Cola workers' union legally became the Coca-Cola Bottling Company Workers' Union (STEGAC). The workers celebrated outside of the plant with fireworks and mariachis in the cool evening air.

To put this story another way: the Coca-Cola workers attempted to organize through legal means. The legal means were slow, and taking advantage of time, Trotter tried various methods to foil the union, finally rounding up some workers to submit a second petition. The state then had to rule on the two petitions, and in its ruling the court broke the rules of the legal game in favor of the employer, as it had dozens of times before, because by law the court should have acted upon the first petition months before.

The moves made by the Coca-Cola workers from that point on were characterized by tenacity and commitment; as Mercedes Gómez had said, "you knew . . . you'd have to go on with this until God took you." They were also thoughtful measures, whether that clarity emerged out of long discussions or happened on the spot. Workers were angry and astute enough to see that they were completely cornered by the rules of the game and so decided to stop playing the game. Even before the recognition of STEGAC, the union and its legal advisers had not, for example, proposed challenging the ruling on the second petition in court. Instead, the workers stayed in the factory. By remaining in the plant and then occupying the area in front of it when they were kicked out, the union had changed the game, not the rules, by taking the struggle into an arena neither legal nor illegal, as Joaquín Rosales noted. They were not on strike or obstructing production or officially fired, yet Coca-Cola was not producing soft drinks. In this way the union created a crisis, which like all crises carried a high risk. Once the workers took the issue into terrain where the courts could not act, the state either had to use official violence again (but this time against workers sitting in front of a factory), or wait out the workers, or bring in the death squads. The Coca-Cola workers made a move before the state did and escalated the conflict by bringing in more players when the state had none yet on the field, neither the courts nor assassins. Within days, they organized a national labor organization that then threatened solidarity strikes. The workers won by creating a situation in which the state had to resolve social problems the way it classically did—"informally," outside of the law—except that this time the state resolved it in the workers' favor. The key word *clarity* now meant a deep understanding of the state and society, not only of the law.

Trade Unionism and a Mass Movement

The National Committee on Trade Union Unity functioned ideally at the time of the Coca-Cola conflict, and its image as a combative, unified front of national popular organizations had élan and contributed to its prestige. Within months and without an office, a telephone, or legal status, delegates from the growing number of urban unions and from student and community groups met as CNUS whenever the need arose in whatever location was convenient.

CNUS's formation followed the February 1976 earthquake by weeks. The very establishment of CNUS and the great expectations it raised for labor militants, as well as the victory at Coca-Cola in early April, were in part based on the mass activity and protest that surged in the wake of a disaster that left tens of thousands dead and 300,000 homeless in Guatemala City alone. Secondary and primary students organized to demand the rebuilding of their schools, factory workers fought for relief aid from their employers, and neighborhood committees, which were often started by students or trade unionists, flourished everywhere in the city as residents mobilized to find and bury the dead, provide emergency medical care, prevent robberies, dig latrines, recuperate or improvise cooking facilities, locate and distribute water, food, and building materials, and even entertain one another. In one form or another, these groups lasted for several years. Into 1977, 1978, and 1979 students were still taking militant actions to force the rebuilding of schools destroyed in 1976, and neighborhood committees fought for paving, water, sewage, electricity, transportation, schools, and lower food prices until repression stopped them by the end of the decade.

The aftermath of the earthquake was an experience in local power in the face of state corruption. Residents often had to expropriate virtually by force relief aid hoarded by government agencies. Members of unions and of student and neighborhood groups such as the National Movement of Pobladores (MONAP) sometimes turned up at CNUS meetings together. They easily assumed antigovernment stances.[27]

CNUS attempted to place itself in the center of events, and it leafleted extensively in a city where leaflets were read, discussed, and passed on. A typical

CNUS leaflet, responding to the government's postearthquake slogan, "Reconstruct Without Ceasing to Produce," read: "What is there to reconstruct? The workers have no property. What they [government and business] want to reconstruct is their world of capital. We workers and peasants have a responsibility to pull humanity out of exploitation and injustice and fight for full liberation."[28] At the enormous CNUS-organized May First demonstration in 1976, four weeks after the victory at Coca-Cola and three months after the earthquake, the tenor of nostalgia for the 1944–54 years prevalent in May First marches during the 1960s had vanished. Projecting strength, energy, and urgency, CNUS demanded such sweeping changes as a general wage increase, fixed prices, an end to death squads, withdrawal of the military from the workplace, and land reform as if plans for gaining popular power were under way. In the spirit of underestimating state power and overestimating trade unionism, one trade unionist said after the earthquake, "The movement overflowed, the government was no longer free, it could not do as it wanted."[29] Yet CNUS was only loosely woven into the spontaneous mass activity and politicization that followed the earthquake. And in many important labor arenas it was powerless.

CNUS could not stop several employers from utilizing the earthquake to destroy unions. For example, immediately after the disaster the recently unionized Aurotex textile plant was shut down by its owners on the ground that the building had been damaged. The company then dismissed the 120 unionized workers both with a court order and at gunpoint. When the plant reopened, the union no longer existed. In mid-May 1976, weeks after the May First march, two thousand full-time ladino and part-time Indian workers went on strike during harvest time at the largest sugar plantation in the country, Pantaleón, located near Guatemala City. The General Association of Farm Owners (AGA), in the midst of an international market boom for their goods, brought enormous pressure to bear on the strikers. CNUS was unable to mobilize far-reaching support or to prevent, through counsel, the strike's defeat and the strategic weakening of the union through state and company manipulation.[30] At the end of May CNUS attempted to help 230 union workers who were locked out of the IODESA cottonseed oil factory in Escuintla when its owner, the Kong family, claiming lack of materials, shut down operations. After one of the unionized workers was killed, fifteen more were arrested and obliged to do military service, and seven were kidnapped and beaten, the case was brought to court and the union lost.[31]

The state and owners faced a more dynamic adversary in the labor movement after the earthquake and the formation of CNUS, but they were not restrained by it. Despite his concession to the Coca-Cola workers, President Laugerud had no intention of legitimizing mass movements by negotiating with them; therefore violence increased in response to the challenges presented by growing popular mobilization as well as by CNUS. Moreover, in the aftermath of the earthquake the army's power increased. It assumed responsibility for earthquake reconstruction nationally and established military commissions to reorder civilian life through the Committee on National Reconstruction (CRN), which quickly became and remained a stable, aggressive institution with an unlimited scope of activities.[32]

This is not to say that the trade unionists' vision of their movement as "overflowing" was without truth. The urban labor movement had more members and more of a public that read its leaflets and heeded its calls than at any time since the 1954 coup. Few in Guatemala City did not know of CNT or CNUS or the Coca-Cola workers. By the end of 1976 CNT's two-story building was an important and well-known working-class social center. Though sensing danger, as the Coca-Cola workers had in 1975 when they attended their first union meeting there, workers assembled anyway. Sometimes they arrived just to talk on more than a mundane or veiled level; almost every week for months a group of women and their children from a nonunionized textile plant met to discuss jobs, health, men, unions, national and regional history, politics, and the nature of capitalism.[33] The larger unions each had a small office in the building; the one mimeograph machine cranked constantly, the one telephone line rang continually, and workers covered the walls with murals of victory. Union meetings and study groups convened, birthdays were celebrated, couples were married, and the dead were waked. By early 1977 the CNT building was becoming a national center. Peasants and rural workers heard of CNT on national news transmitted by radio, which in this decade spread into the countryside.

That a place existed where they could receive counsel drew rural Guatemalans who wanted to present their grievances to the state. At the same time CNT reached out to the countryside by opening a regional office in the provincial capital of Huehuetenango in the western highlands.

As new workers joined CNT, its leadership expanded to include many of the new recruits at the same time that the lawyers and activists of the early 1970s, such as Marta Gloria and Enrique Torres, Danielo Rodríguez, Miguel Angel Albizures, and Miguel Cifuentes, remained. Pragmatic, CNT's staff advocated the approach that had evolved since the end of the 1960s: organize twenty-one workers into a union, place an injunction on the company, petition for a union, negotiate for a contract, and, as necessary at any point along the way, foment direct mass action.

After the earthquake urban workers were increasingly inclined to engage in illegal direct action. In 1977 more workers struck than at any other time in the country's history, and many workers new to conflict at the workplace took unaccustomedly bold actions. Against the advice of CNT's legal staff, women and men workers at the ACRICASA textile factory seized the plant and, keeping the riot police out by threatening to blow up the boiler if they entered, camped inside the factory compound for two weeks until they won a contract.[34] Municipal workers occupied the municipality building to win a small wage increase. Bank employees worked in nonregulation clothing (women in mourning, men in soccer clothes), held illegal stoppages, and staged rallies inside the banks for an industrywide increase. The Association of Telegraph and Radio-telegraph Operators (ATRG), the association of employees at the Guatemalan Institute of Social Security (IGSS), and the Association of Nurses' Aides (AGAE) formed the Emergency Committee of State Workers (CETE), the first alliance of state workers' associations. Despite the fact that CETE did not join CNUS because of the continuing tensions between state and private sector workers, the Emergency Committee was of strategic importance for the entire labor movement. CETE threatened to strike immediately after it was founded even though state employees were forbidden to organize, much less strike (in early 1978, 150,000 state employees would participate in a sit-in in government buildings).

On almost any day in 1977 photographs of smiling, illegally striking workers filled the newspapers. Working-class combativeness dazzled union leaders. CNT, CNUS, and local union literature voiced invincibility: "Repression will not stop us, the people will win," was the oft-repeated slogan. And why not? Even though increasingly "parades followed coffins," no one went into hiding when labor lawyer Mario López Larrave was killed in June 1977; 20,000 marched in his funeral procession with their faces bared and their fists held high. Twice that number demonstrated when high school student leader Robin García disappeared in August, and 50,000 marched at his funeral after friends found his tortured body. By November 1977, when a small group of miners in the western highlands inspired national mobilization, the ascendancy of *the people* seemed uncontestable.

The CNT office in Huehuetenango, organized by a local activist named Mario Mujía, had affiliated a union at the tungsten mine, Minas de Guatemala, in the small, predominantly Mam-speaking town of San Idelfonso Ixtahuacán in the Cuchumatanes Mountains near the Mexican border. At the end of 1976 the union, representing 320 mine workers, started to negotiate for a pact.[35] After a long period of futile talks, the company announced in November 1977 that it was closing the mine immediately, even though workplace closure was a complex legal procedure requiring months to accomplish.

Mujía suggested, and the union agreed, that to dramatize their plight the miners walk the 250 miles from Ixtahuacán to Guatemala City. On November 11, seventy started out. The other workers and all the workers' wives and children remained behind to ensure that scabs would not be brought into the mine in the event that the company suddenly reopened it, and to prevent hoodlums from entering and causing damage for which the union would be blamed. CNT activists also decided to publicize the plight of the many workers fired from the Pantaleón sugar plantation as a consequence of their strike in 1976 by having the Pantaleón union organize a "March of Dignity" from the southern coast to arrive in Guatemala City at the same time as the miners. Many members of CNT thought that the miners' march could unite the various worlds of Guatemala: the Maya Indian highlands, the southern coast, and the capital.

The miners walked down from the Cuchumatanes Mountains along the Pan American Highway. At all of the many towns and villages along the way, as they passed through the poverty-stricken rural departments of Huehuetenango, Quetzaltenango, Totonicapán, Quiché, and Chimaltenango, huge crowds greeted them with marimba and food, provided them lodging, and met them to discuss mutual problems in momentous "general assemblies."[36] In Guatemala City, where progressive journalists and radio announcers had taken the offensive in reporting on social struggles, the mass media gave the march frontline publicity, covering its every move—"The miners are now leaving Quetzaltenango, where the entire city turned out to greet them, heading for Nahualá where they will be by nightfall" and the next day, "The miners received a grand reception in Nahualá where the Indians there formed a security cordon around them as they entered town."[37] Poems heralding their approach appeared in middle-class journals, and the march was baptized "The Glorious March of the Miners" before the miners reached Guatemala City, and even though only a few weeks back most urban Guatemalans had not known that a mine existed in the Cuchumatanes.[38]

Politicians urged a settlement before the miners arrived in the city. Former mayor Manuel Colón Argueta, who was trying to take advantage of Laugerud's opening to launch a reformist party, the United Revolutionary Front (FUR), attempted to intervene on the miners' behalf, but they rejected him in a newspaper advertisement: "Please do not exploit us . . . by using us for your political ends. This march was not *your idea*. What we are living through is not for you to take advantage of."[39] Alarmed by the miners' radical tone, and by what the popular mobilization on their behalf could mean in an already embroiled city, the Laugerud government successfully pressured the company to agree to reopen the mine, pay back wages, and negotiate a contract. The Labor Ministry then sent this news to the marching miners, along with a bus to take them back to Ixtahuacán. The miners agreed to the settlement but decided to go on to the capital anyway: that is what they had voted on when they left Ixtahuacán, the Pantaleón workers had already started out, people were expecting them, and most of them had never been to the capital and wanted to see it.

Urban trade unionists wanted to see these militants from the provinces, and several workers from the ACRICASA textile plant and from Coca-Cola took a bus up the Pan American Highway and walked back down with them. When the miners entered Guatemala City, a Coca-Cola worker recalled how moved he was as he watched them, sunburned and covered with dust, meet the sugar workers from Pantaleón: "I was with a compa from the plant and I told him I felt like crying. He said to me, 'If we think we suffer in the plant, look at them.' I felt awakened, there was this sensation of energy in my body, all those songs about poor people and justice suddenly sounded true. I realized how important it was to identify yourself with what is just."[40] The press estimated that 150,000 people marched with the miners and the sugar workers from the edge of the city to the Central Park, where a miner addressed the crowd in Spanish, his second language. The miners stayed in the CNT building for a few days before returning home. They saw the sights, went to the national zoo, and received medical care, visitors, baskets upon baskets of food, and two thousand *quetzales* donated in pennies.

Trade unionists repeatedly used words such as *euphoric* to describe how they felt seeing the miners arrive in Guatemala City, and it is clear why. The march and the reception it received constituted unrefutable evidence that a defiant national organization of Indian and ladino peasants and urban and rural workers could be built. In the interviews I collected to write this book, the Glorious March of the Miners was always the climax of trade unionists' reconstruction of the labor movement during the Laugerud regime, its best post-1954 years. Yet however much this display of unity made leading a national movement seem within the reach of urban labor, the day-to-day relations between rural and city groups were weak. In fact, the rural support that had fanned the miners' urban welcome was mobilized primarily by base communities of peasants and rural workers that would crystallize one year later into the Committee of Campesino Unity (CUC), with which CNT had no ties. Further, as optimistic and excited as the demonstrators were because the miners had won, many recognized that the march took place as much within a darkening political landscape as within a brightening one. The huge banner leading off the thousands who paraded to the Central Park bore a breathtaking, tragic "demand": "*For The Right To Live.*" Hardly triumphalist, or euphoric, or revolutionary, the significance of the words on that banner was very frightening.

What could one really get from this state and this society without having to turn them upside down? The question for the labor movement was whether it had to threaten, and then mount, national demonstrations to win every dispute; several important worker conflicts occurred in rural areas following the miners' march but none resulted in a massive mobilization.[41] And although the Glorious March of the Miners showed the breadth of mass political consciousness, what did it win? The Pantaleón workers did not get their jobs back, and within four years the miners' union had been decimated by physical violence. The right to live was not "granted," much less a contract—three leaders of the miners were killed in a row, one of them tortured to death while his murderers forced his wife to watch.

Was Trade Unionism Viable?

Members of the Guatemalan bourgeoisie had not changed their minds about unions. In 1976 and 1977 thirty-seven unions in the city won legal recognition and forty-four were destroyed through a mixture of legal and illegal maneuvers. For example, one of the many new unions born after Laugerud took office was organized in late 1976 at the large Helenoplast plastics, owned by the Guatemalan Abularach family. When the company refused to negotiate in early 1977, the union exercised its legal right to call a strike vote. Before the vote the company fired ten activists, despite an injunction, and then had two of the ten arrested on charges of stealing. When a CNT lawyer won a ruling that the firings were illegal, the company blithely stated that it "refused to accept the intervention of the authorities."[42] Shortly afterward, the strike vote was held. It took nineteen hours for a labor inspector to poll the factory's 250 workers. As the labor inspector asked each day-shift worker if he or she wanted to strike, an army officer listened and an army intelligence jeep sat outside, while the night-shift workers were locked in the cafeteria and threatened with dismissal if they voted for the strike. The union lost the vote. The legal framework within which lawyers had fashioned their tactics had become extralegal power: the strike vote was carried out by officials who broke the law, and the army's presence made it officially clear that workers would face extralegal violence if they voted to strike.

The company, however, was not content with defeating the vote and the contract, or with firing ten activists and having two of them arrested. One morning in early March, the plant manager stood outside the gate and prevented the entry of the seventy-nine workers who had voted for the strike. These workers camped out at the entrance. CNT lawyers claimed that Helenoplast had started an illegal lockout and took the issue to court. At this juncture, a new revolutionary group, the Guerrilla Army of the Poor, blew up the plant manager's Mercedes Benz. The government publicly connected the union with the guerrillas, and the court declared that the company had not locked out the seventy-nine workers; thus they were striking illegally and were fired legally. The union became inactive.[43] Guerrilla action did not solve the workers' problems, but neither could the union nor the legal advisers. After losing their jobs and their union, many workers thought that by bombing the car at least EGP had made some retribution.

The Revolutionary Organizations and Trade Unions

Cadres from the guerrilla movement had survived the defeats of the late 1960s and had turned to nonmilitary organizing, which would allow them to return to military activity in the late 1970s and early 1980s on a far broader scale than that of the 1960s. By the mid-1970s four guerrilla groups had evolved: the Rebel Armed Forces (FAR), the Guatemalan Labor party (PGT), the Guerrilla Army of the Poor (EGP), and the Revolutionary Organization of the People in Arms (ORPA). Their members included peasants, rural and urban workers, artisans and students, and middle-class professionals. FAR, EGP, and ORPA were directed primarily by middle-class men who, frustrated by their country's historic inability to implement modern reforms and to develop a mass party, had become guerrilla leaders. Artisans and middle-class professionals still led PGT, as they had for decades.

By the mid-1970s the four guerrilla groups agreed that the *foco* theory of revolutionary war, whereby a small armed vanguard engages the military and creates a crisis that leads to revolution, had led to failure in the 1960s, and each aspired to build a broad movement for social change. Beyond that, they diverged. ORPA never became involved in urban unions (although it had cadres in the city) because it thought that the rural Maya Indian population was the main vehicle for revolution. Others did. The Guerrilla Army of the Poor, whose public existence dated from 1975, believed that Guatemala was on the verge of a mass revolutionary war that would start in the countryside and revolve around Indians but would embrace other groups of poor people, urban and rural, as well. Its central concern in the city was winning adherents to the EGP and creating a preinsurrectionary atmosphere, so that when the countryside rose up, the city would fall quickly. EGP cadres attempted to remake trade union struggles to fit this plan. Of all the guerrilla groups, EGP was the most vocal, militant, and disdainful of state power. It declared that victory would come soon, and it grew rapidly both in the countryside and in the city, where it attracted university and secondary school students, middle-class professionals, and some workers.

PGT, Guatemala's Communist party, had a history and a presence in the labor movement. PGT members used their wide prestige to argue that labor struggles should be confined to legal ones. As when they were in the forefront of the 1944–54 drive to build national capitalism, the Communists continued to seek alliances with elite political parties as a method of wresting reforms from the state. Unlike EGP, ORPA, or FAR, PGT pursued armed struggle erratically as a means of applying pressure when other ways were closed, and not as a strategy for taking state power. The PGT had no mass line and implicitly rejected Indians as agents of social change because of their ethnicity, which the Communists perceived as a "culture of poverty" obstructing the formation of class consciousness. As elsewhere in Latin America in the 1970s, the traditional Communists were the moderates of the left and its watchdogs. They saw the growth both of other clandestine left-wing groups and of CNT and CNUS as a threat to their claims of representing the working class.

The oldest guerrilla group, the Rebel Armed Forces, had begun to implement a new strategy of mass-based revolution after it split from the Communists in the 1960s. Some of its members had operated underground in Guatemala City since the early 1970s, and by the middle of the decade FAR had influence in CNT through at least one of the legal advisers, Danielo Rodrí-guez. Believing that a proletarian-led worker-peasant alliance would be the backbone of revolution, FAR wished the urban labor movement to expand quickly, to seek allies in the countryside, to raise broad social issues, to deepen its understanding of capitalist exploitation, and to expose the state as a class dictatorship. In its publications and study circles, FAR encouraged workers to move from the recognition of the criminality of the state and of capitalists to an analytic view explaining why state and capitalists behaved as criminals and why workers could have power over them. Possessing a more prolonged vision of the development of revolutionary upsurge than did EGP, it proposed exhausting legal forms before abandoning them. FAR was the most classically Leninist group in the sense that it invoked the industrial proletariat as the class upon which revolution would hinge, ideologically if not tactically, yet one lost to economistic spontaneity without its vanguard, FAR.

As the labor and urban movements grew, the men and women who be-longed to FAR, PGT, and EGP participated wherever they could in unions, professional associations, unity groups, and student and neighborhood orga-nizations. For instance, by early 1980 PGT and EGP, as well as FAR, had secret members in CNT. The stakes were extremely high, and they competed with one another for influence over workers. With great anger, Miguel Angel Albi-zures described the intense competition between these groups as "fighting for a piece of the cake."[44]

The revolutionary groups related in varying degrees to trade unionism, but the trade unions did not involve themselves in building a revolution. When workers went to CNT in 1976 or 1977, they sometimes heard about surplus value, as expounded by legal advisers, students, or other workers who were in contact with FAR. Or, here and there, they learned versions of world history as presented by members or sympathizers of the Communist Guatemalan Labor party. Many labor activists of the 1970s could recite the traditional Commu-nist view of history's stages—primitive communism, feudalism, capitalism, socialism, communism—or explain the labor theory of value as truth without knowing the names of these theories or from whence they came. Revolutionary urban cadres did not reveal their political identities to workers, for whom full-fledged revolutionary theories and practices remained opaque.

Trade unionists did not operate under the leadership of a vanguard party, and their work was not coordinated with that of a revolutionary army. More important, no matter how much tactical advice trade unionists took from revolutionary cadres, they did not think that they were making a revolution, even if one could deduce from their literature that they should have and even if they thought someone should. On the other hand, revolutionary groups were heard by trade unionists. The most basic ideas of FAR and EGP—that capitalism was at the root of Guatemala's problems and controlled a state impossible to reform, that revolution was needed sooner and not in a distant PGT future—were effortlessly adopted by some workers and were already held by others. These ideas were not esoteric, illogical, or complex; it was hard to find a procapitalist worker in Guatemala. It was less perilous to express such ideas than it had been, for example, under President Arana Osorio, and revolution seemed easier to contemplate under President Laugerud.

In other words, the appearance of a political opening accompanied by the flagrant refusal of the state and the bourgeoisie to redistribute wealth to a starving population without stable housing or minimal medical care did not win the state or capitalism adherents. Rather, it facilitated workers' ability to support a vague notion of revolution as an ideal goal that had multiple meanings. Revolutionary discourse held great sway over workers who never really thought about seizing the state and taking power. Speaking of trade unionists she knew in the late 1970s, ACRICASA trade union leader Sonia Oliva commented: "Who would not have supported revolution in Guatemala? And who understood what it would take, or what it meant? The answer to all these questions is not many."[45]

The Ethos of the Workers' Movement

What was the character of trade unionism? Though not revolutionary, the labor movement was nevertheless pointedly antireformism and thus broke with the very premises of trade unionism even while activists struggled to manipulate the law. In 1977, for the first time, trade unionists revised their view of

Guatemalan labor history by rejecting the time-honored trade union representation of the 1944–54 period as a "golden age" for the working class because the government was prolabor. In its declaration commemorating the anniversary of the October 1944 Revolution, CNUS asserted: "Although many think that the Revolution was of great significance for the working class, the working class was neither government nor opposition. It was a revolution made by the petty bourgeoisie, and facilitated capitalist development. . . . The lessons of this history are that the working class must have self-confidence, and not trust the state or the parties of the petty bourgeoisie."[46] In early 1978 CNT quit the continental Christian Democratic Latin American Confederation of Workers (CLAT) because it was "reformist," "lacked ideological definition," red-baited, and opposed the organization of CNUS.[47] This was the culmination of many years of strife between CNT and CLAT: CLAT had helped initiate CNT in 1968 but its support of the Christian Democratic party offended Guatemalan trade unionists, who had opposed the attempts of CLAT and the Christian Democrats to control CNT since the early 1970s. When CNT left CLAT in 1978, it lost its sole source of significant funding and became one of the few major confederations in Latin America without ties to an international, a political party, or a state.

CNUS and CNT, the most influential labor organizations in the city, counseled workers to use and exhaust legal methods in their day-to-day organizing, but by early 1978 their spokespersons simultaneously warned them to live beyond the law. A CNUS leaflet urged workers to "organize without depending on official recognition! Take the right to free speech without depending on the capitalist press to give it! Ensure the right to live without asking that of the State which has always repressed us; instead, adopt forms of work and personal measures which prevent our physical elimination! Take the right to protest!"[48] The 1978 Third National Congress of CNT condemned "opportunists, corruption, political parties, ultra-revolutionary radicalism, left opportunists, economism, government trade unionism and the bureaucratization of unions" in favor of the "autonomous and democratic organization of workers, peasants and shantytown dwellers" who would fight alone "for the liberation from oppression and exploitation to which the capitalist system submits us."[49]

Without a revolutionary practice, without being bound to the specific ideology of socialism, and opposing capitalism, reformism, and even the (improbable) emergence of a labor party, the trade union movement proposed no political program as clearly as it advocated that unique political and cultural values be a way of life. Trade unionists' ideas about what winning meant expressed these values. For instance, one of the few unions to obtain a contract in the mid-1970s was the union at the Philip Morris TACASA tobacco factory. It was an excellent contract, one that left the businessmen's association, the Coordinating Committee of Agricultural, Commercial, Industrial, and Financial Associations, worried and drove Philip Morris to ship tobacco to a plant in El Salvador. Covering over four hundred permanent workers and one hundred temporary ones, the union contract provided for job descriptions, security, and wage policy as well as a general wage increase. The union won 75 percent of transportation costs to work and 50 percent of medical expenses, a doctor inside the plant several days a week, layettes for newborns, one month pre- and postnatal leave with pay, literacy classes, and a glass display case, "one-half of it for news about other workers, one-half for poems by TACASA workers and union notices."[50]

Union leader Miguel Cifuentes related his concern that the material victories did not diminish workers' broader sense of what was important in life:

> The 1976 pact was our contribution to the labor movement in the way it was achieved, in the understanding behind it and in its emphasis on social demands and not money per se. We made a point of asking for programs that would benefit workers culturally, like literacy classes. To have the literacy class was a trade-off, we lost money for that. We got people into small discussion groups to discuss the pact and there we talked about other things besides the pact.
>
> Character development was THE issue in every sense. In the midst of discussing the pact we were also discussing personal and social problems, like drinking as a personal problem, or like what was happening to other workers in Guatemala as a social problem. The point was not to forget that it was the job of the union to help people with these human problems

and create the sense among people that they in turn should help others with their problems as well.[51]

Cifuentes and others at TACASA were worried that workers would not "look beyond the factory" as a result of "economism." In a country where the majority had so little, he and others were intensely solicitous both that workers earn more and that they not make money the sole object of their struggle in order to avoid becoming prey to what they identified as a "consumerist mentality," one that they feared would transform workers forever.

At the same time, toward the end of the 1970s, several revolutionary groups cautioned trade unionists against economism in the Leninist sense of an apolitical bread-and-butter trade unionism. What was at issue for Cifuentes and other trade unionists was not so much that people be political in the narrow sense of the word, but that they be socially minded and humanist in the broadest sense of those words. What Lenin meant by economism was apoliticism, what Cifuentes meant was falling spellbound to commodities. He did not oppose economism because of the strategic need for workers to understand the state and hence, according to the Leninist model, be "political"; his was an ethical value, a moral opposition to economism, a Christian message of the sorry fate worldly vanity would bring.

To promote the humanism for which they fought, labor militants at TACASA devised their own imaginative moral and intellectual activism. By early 1978 the union had taken on the heroic role of general propagandist against a rotten world and explicitly attempted to deconstruct messages embedded in consumerism. When the Philip Morris Company began manufacturing a brand of cigarettes called "Commander," the union issued leaflets arguing that this was an attempt to normalize the militarization of society. This little campaign against the giant of consumerism was emblematic of the labor movement's ethical politics: on guard about moral ideas and ideals, it fought cultural manipulation. The TACASA union regularly bought radio time to comment on current events and to urge attendance at demonstrations. As its sign-off slogan, it used a quotation from José Martí, the best writer a few workers had read in high school: "No one has the right to sleep in peace while a single unhappy man exists in the world." It would have been difficult to have found a more demanding statement of purpose.

Inspired, trade unionists deepened their sense of problems. Clearly the state was terrible and capitalism as well, but what prevented people from understanding and acting more comprehensively? The answer was alienation from reality, concluded the TACASA union, and hence came the art of making provocative banners. When 100,000 people demonstrated in the city in June 1978 against the massacre of 125 Kekchí-speaking men, women, and children in the town of Panzós, the delegation of 150 workers from TACASA carried a huge banner, as tall as the tallest buildings in the downtown area, with the words, "Guatemala, '78, Headquarters of the World Tournament of Murders. We repudiate the Massacre at Panzós, Union of Workers at TACASA." Conceived after several long discussions, this banner was made in a few evenings of painting at the CNT building. What was so special about it and other banners the union made? According to Miguel Cifuentes:

> That banner, and all others, was the result of our understanding that it is easier for people to understand things through drawings or symbols. You can put words on a banner and some people will read them, but a drawing attracts their interest more. The banner about Panzós is a complicated example of this, it basically had words, although there was a small map of Guatemala covered with a skull and crossbones in the corner. But you see these words were very special because what drew people was a familiar image and a startling contrast between events.
>
> Let me explain. In Guatemala most people don't have TV, but they stand around watching it through the store windows downtown. Now at that time a world soccer cup match was going on in Argentina, so everybody was watching TV, and we noticed this, there had just been a massacre and half the world was standing around in the street watching the soccer game. I like soccer but I also see alienation in this instance. On the TV every few minutes would flash over the image of the game the words, "Argentina, '78, Headquarters of the World Tournament of Soccer." So we decided to make a visual relationship between an event which

monopolized national attention and what was going on in Guatemala. We used the exact same lettering and spacing, we just changed "Argentina" to "Guatemala" and "Soccer" to "Murders." It drew people.

Cifuentes described two other banners that were made after General Romero Lucas García assumed the presidency in July 1978:

> Lucas García's campaign slogan was "A loaf of bread the size of people's hunger," so we made a banner with a large very malnourished man carrying a huge loaf of bread with a machine gun in it to make the point the government spent on arms not food, and that the arms it bought would have to be the size of the people's hunger. We wrote, "People of Guatemala, this is the loaf of bread the size of your hunger that Lucas García offers you." We painted a vulture with bloody hands and the face of Chupina [director of the National Police].
>
> When Mario Mujía [CNT organizer in Huehuetenango] was killed [in July 1978], we took off on the radio announcement for tourism that you hear constantly: "In Guatemala we have everything—beautiful women, beautiful volcanoes, beautiful mountains." We painted a woman in jail with her fist high, and a tortured man's body, and opposite them the riot squad with tear gas and arms, and underneath the slogan, "In Guatemala we have everything." These banners were very forceful and they did not concern only us, the union, they concerned the popular situation. We were not a capitalist union, we were not interested only in ourselves.

Cifuentes emphasized that workers kept "inventing," as he put it, to explain how trade unionism persisted: "We flowered because the working class is deeply creative, this wasn't the work of so-called intellectuals. It was this creativity which allowed us to survive. If you look at the years 1978–80 and the number of trade unionists murdered, you would conclude everyone must have been driven insane and given up, but you see this is not so. People keep finding a way. This is working-class creativity."[52]

It was to the power of creativity that Cifuentes appealed in the face of horror. He thought that creativity—not simply representing life but rearranging

The banner made by urban workers at Philip Morris's TACASA cigarette plant to protest the killing of over one hundred Kekchí-speaking men, women, and children in the Guatemalan countryside in May 1978. (Photograph courtesy of *Alero*)

images on a banner in order to rearrange life, rephrasing objective and subjective realities to transform them, making culture to make history—made trade unionism possible. By designing their banners these workers made clear that the tragedies they evoked on them had not destroyed what could be thought or accomplished. Rejecting the world as it was, Cifuentes stood with other activists on the edge of a new and original kind of self-affirming and liberating politics, without being able to go much further.

Although they had no revolutionary program, trade unionists disclosed possibilities for exceptional, radical social being and action. They wanted to live beyond the real limits, and they pressed for the creation of a world of resistance that was no one else's project or property, a countersociety always busy with the details of thoughtfully combating the barbarism that threatened it.

5

Martyrs and Triumphalists, 1978–1980

The dead weighed heavily on us, thousands of pounds, tons. But they also weighed the other way, picking us up, if I'm getting across what I mean.
—Miguel Mármol

The labor movement had grown during the Kjell Laugerud years (1974–78), and so had the army's power. Military men assumed more positions in state administration and more of them became capitalists, particularly in the countryside where they both oversaw and profited from the development of isolated areas. Laugerud's minister of defense, General Romero Lucas García, headed a project to construct a highway from the Atlantic Coast through northern Guatemala into Mexico, and he and other army officers acquired large tracts of land in this area earmarked for oil exploitation, cattle ranching, and cardamon plantations. Capitalist development threatened lands farmed by Indian peasants, who, if they protested, were attacked by the army. The worst instance of this took place in May 1978, when soldiers massacred 125 Kekchí-speaking men, women, and children who had gathered in the town of Panzós, Alta Verapaz, to affirm their ancient right to lands claimed by entrepreneurs.[1]

In July 1978 General Lucas García, land and factory owner, in fact, co-owner of a meat-packing plant where a union was then being destroyed, became president of Guatemala after "winning" the rigged elections that concluded a campaign in which no party, including the Christian Democrats, talked of reform. Two new left-center political parties, the Social Democratic party (PSD) and the United Revolutionary Front (FUR), which like the labor movement had developed in the context of Laugerud's opening, abstained, as did the majority of Guatemalans, with only 15 percent of those eligible voting. Within a few months of Lucas García's inauguration the army began bombing the highlands, signaling that rural social conflict had become the civil war that would last into the next decade, as thousands of Indians and ladinos in the countryside united in various ways with the guerrilla organizations.

The city started to live in the shadow of the countryside. At the end of the 1970s the city "smelled of revolution."[2] A Coca-Cola worker thus described a milieu in which the laboring poor felt that revolutionaries would sweep down from the mountains, as they seemed about to do in Guatemala and then did in Nicaragua, a country whose own intense struggle city Guatemalans followed carefully and passionately. Furthermore, revolutionaries had a real presence in Guatemala City not just as clandestine cadres within popular organizations. Armed masked women and men suddenly appeared on buses or street corners or even inside schools leafleting and expounding on the "seizure of power" before vanishing. The city's poor people were not revolutionaries, but they were *aficionados* and none more than many labor activists who felt that revolution was their last chance. One union newspaper editorial admonished: "Don't you think we need a revolution to transform and overcome the critical situation in which the Guatemalan people live? Dare to think, dare to have an opinion, dare to struggle . . . while there is still time."[3]

In October 1978, a few months after Lucas García took office, the urban poor rebelled. Unparalleled in national history, this uprising had its roots in stagnation of the economic growth of the 1960s and early 1970s, the appearance of revolution as a possibility, and the simultaneous exhaustion of means available to or invented by urban activists. The uprising burst the boundaries of trade unionism and then led nowhere. The state responded by increasing violence against a trade unionism that in the end was unable to organize a social movement to represent a constituency that included shantytown dwellers, state workers, unemployed youth, secondary and university students, informal sector workers, housewives, and other workers in addition to organized labor.

By 1978 many popular organizations existed in the city, where the panorama was dramatically different than it had been in 1974. Virtually every high school had a student association dedicated to helping students, workers, and peasants, and these had united into a central, citywide high school group that regularly sponsored demonstrations and defiant musical concerts presenting nueva canción from Nicaragua and Venezuela. At the University of San Carlos, competing guerrilla groups had student fronts that engaged the constant attention of the student body and faculty. Several neighborhood associations that arose in the wake of the 1976 earthquake continued to be vibrant and, like high school students, had a citywide coordinating committee by 1978. Urban pastoral agents influenced by the Liberation Theology began to coalesce, and they gave public voice to their version of Christianity through a new organization called the Committee on Peace and Justice.[4] In addition, state workers joined together in 1977 when they formed the Emergency Committee of State Workers (CETE), an organization without legal status because the Labor Code forbade state workers from unionizing.

By early 1978 CETE embraced fifteen associations of state employees including those for postal, hospital, and road workers, teachers, printers, telegraph and radio-telegraph operators, nurses' aides, and social security workers. Representing over 150,000 workers nationally, CETE suddenly emerged as the largest labor organization in the country. Its power came from the coherence of several of its member associations, which were started as mutual aid societies in the late 1950s and 1960s after the 1954 coup dismantled and banned the state workers' unions. Because these associations had grown as social clubs and not unions (they did not criticize or try to negotiate with their employer), they benefited from an internal cohesion that had developed over time.[5] CETE, however, transformed these associations into organizations that confronted the state. CETE had spent the year 1977 attempting to negotiate wage increases, and in early 1978 its leaders decided to take advantage of the competition between political parties on the eve of the March 7 presidential elections to press its claims. On February 24, 150,000 state workers went on strike, disrupting the country, preventing the printing of ballots for the elections, and leaving the army, which at that time relied to some extent on state telegraph and telephone services, with limited means of internal communication. For the first and last time behaving as a party that sought political gain by siding with striking workers, the ultraright Movement for National Liberation in early March supported, and the National Congress passed, a small wage increase for state workers, and CETE suspended its strike.[6]

May First 1978 reflected the growing national and citywide turmoil and suggested the direction it could take. For the first time since 1954, the urban May First march attracted hundreds of rural workers and peasants, many in Maya Indian dress. They met up with nuns, priests, and parish members from the Committee on Peace and Justice and joined the large contingents from urban neighborhood associations, high school and university student groups, CETE, the National Central of Workers (CNT), the National Committee on Trade Union Unity (CNUS), and individual unions from Guatemala City and the neighboring towns of Amatitlán and Escuintla. The parade was distinguished from previous ones by the diversity of organizations participating and by the prominence of banners calling for "Revolutionary and Popular Government."

The October 1978 Uprising

Shortly after Lucas García took office in July, a series of bus drivers' strikes paralyzed the capital for months. The strikes began after a group of nonunionized bus drivers from four companies that had repeatedly prevented unionization met in June at the CNT headquarters to devise a method of fighting for a wage increase in the absence of unions. By 1978 few companies had unions, although many bus workers had been organized into unions over the previous two and one-half decades.[7] Two bus workers' federations, which by now were virtually paper organizations with little active membership, were registered with the Labor Ministry. One was the Union of Automobile Pilots (SPAS), initiated in the 1950s by Communists within the Autonomous Federation of Guatemalan Unions (FASGUA). The other was the National Federation of Transport Workers (FENOT), started by Christian labor militants in the 1960s and affiliated with the National Central of Workers, which was more militant than FASGUA or SPAS.

At the June meeting the drivers decided to dust off the name of FENOT to give an air of formality to their call for a citywide wage of Q10 ($10) daily, improved service, and retention of the five-cent fare. The cost and quality of public transportation were already nightmarish for the city's consumers. At five cents transportation was a major expense as well as unsatisfactory: customers waited in long lines to get into overcrowded and dangerous vehicles. Because the buses only ran on main roads, riders were often obliged to pay the inflated fares of special microbuses, which were usually owned by the same bus companies, to go to and from bus routes.

The city's municipal council, which established the wages of drivers employed by the 350 companies that owned the 857 buses in service, did not respond to the drivers' demands. So in early July, the drivers started progressively longer work stoppages. By the tenth of the month, the stoppages lasted all day. Then the drivers simply took all of the buses and drove them to the only place that was beyond the jurisdiction of state authorities, the University of San Carlos, which had autonomy from state control and had been a stronghold of progressive politics since the 1954 coup.

Many students, led by supporters of the militant and vocal Guerrilla Army of the Poor (EGP), welcomed the drivers on the university's spacious lawns with food, drink, entertainment, and words of encouragement. Fearing army or police action on the campus, the Communists in the Guatemalan Labor party (PGT) argued that the drivers should leave and accused the National Central of Workers of provoking a fare increase by endorsing the drivers' actions.[8] The university's rector intervened in the dispute to authorize the drivers' presence at the university over the objections of the Communists, who led the oldest and most influential student association. The drivers, with their buses, camped on the university grounds until the Labor Ministry "agreed to study the issue of the minimum wage, which the Minister conceded should not be less than Q7 a day because that is the minimum necessary for the family to survive in Guatemala."[9] With only this promise "to study the issue," the bus drivers temporarily resumed work. During this first and brief strike, membership in informal committees, not unions, of drivers tripled.[10]

To understand the dispute between the revolutionaries, which foreshadowed others, it is necessary to recognize that the four guerrilla groups operating nationally—EGP, the Rebel Armed Forces (FAR), PGT, and the Revolutionary Organization of the People in Arms (ORPA)—had not yet formed a united front for national liberation. Instead, they competed furiously: in the city EGP, FAR, and PGT battled with one another to win the loyalties of workers; ORPA had urban cadres but the focus of their work in Guatemala City was not unions.

Taking brazen actions in the city and the countryside, EGP predicted that a revolution would happen within a short time; it attracted many adherents to become the largest of the four groups by the end of the decade, when its combatants were active in over two-thirds of Guatemalan territory. It condemned PGT for not supporting aggressive attacks against the state, and it criticized FAR for having a long-term approach toward revolutionary warfare. FAR, on the other hand, warned against "burning stages" in the revolutionary struggle and advanced a strategy summarized in the slogan "struggle, achieve something, pull back, consolidate, wait, repeat this process."[11] FAR and EGP had sharp differences, but they supported the bus drivers' illegal strike and accused PGT, which did not, of placing obstacles in the drivers' way.

In late July 1978 Labor Minister Carlos Alarcón Monsanto finally delivered on his promise to study the problem of the bus drivers' wages by forming a commission of representatives of CNT, FENOT, SPAS, the labor unity group (CNUS), the church, the Congress, the powerful businessmen's association, the Coordinating Committee of Agricultural, Commercial, Industrial, and Financial Organizations (CACIF), and the bus owners' association. Supported by the church, Alarcón Monsanto proposed a Q4.29 wage (despite his own claim that workers needed more), while the bus owners insisted that they would comply only if the fares were increased. In early August FENOT and CNUS left the commission because it was a "farce from the outset"; SPAS remained and supported a fare increase because "it recognized the business isn't profitable."[12]

Because wages were not raised, the drivers, declaring that "from no point of view will we accept an increase [in fares]," called a second strike, which SPAS opposed.[13] This time, to avoid a dispute within the left at the university, the drivers took the buses to a highway circling the city, deflated the tires, and stood guard as detectives drove by spraying rounds from machine guns over their heads.[14] Again the city was without public transportation. At that point President Lucas García signed an agreement granting the drivers Q5.13 a day.

The owners refused to accept the president's decree and impounded the hundreds of buses still in their possession, while drivers inflated the tires of the hundreds of buses that they held and went back to work. However, because the owners hid the other buses and would not pay the wage increase, the drivers struck again, and for a third time the city was paralyzed, this time by both the owners, who hoarded whatever buses they could, and the workers, who would not drive those in their possession. The mayor of the city "confessed" his "impotence" and "begged" Lucas García's intervention. When state officials proposed that the city manage the city buses, the mayor replied that the state should perform that function. CACIF decried these recommendations as "socialistic," and the ultraright MLN suggested that the military take over urban transportation.[15] On September 27, after three months of disrupted urban life and incompetent state mediation, Lucas García met with the bus owners and the mayor. From this meeting came the proposal to raise the fare from five cents to ten in order to "motivate" but not to "oblige" the owners to pay higher wages.[16] The following day, September 28, the municipal council ratified the proposal.

The bus drivers rejected this plan, which "hurts our neighbors, friends and class allies." But on September 30, a Friday, the fare went up even though the bus owners offered no wage increase and while the drivers were still on strike. That day young men and women from working-class areas of the city such as La Parroquia in Zone 6, El Gallito in Zone 3, and others in Zones 7 and 12, which had a history of protest, built barricades across principal streets and fought with riot squads that tried to dismantle them. During the evening and over the weekend, delegates from over 150 unions, neighborhood and state employee associations, and student groups met as an emergency leadership coalition in a secret location.

Two sharp divisions existed within the emergency coalition. The first was between secret cadres representing guerrilla groups, who disagreed about pace and tactics. The second was between the state workers' association

(CETE) and private-sector trade unionists in CNT and CNUS. Trade unionists thought, and had for over a decade, that state "employees," as they called them, were "only interested in themselves"; that they were "state bureaucrats who oppressed the poor" and wheelers and dealers well connected to state officials, who were the trade unionists' enemies.[17] After a heated dispute about whether to call for a national general strike in the private and public sectors, CNT, CNUS, and CETE agreed to take different actions. The emergency coalition declared that on Monday the state workers would strike once and for all against the state, and CNUS and CNT would call progressively longer work stoppages in the private sector. Wishing that trade unionism provide a framework for this urban struggle, the emergency coalition agreed upon its slogan, "For a Trade Unionism Committed to the People." According to one former leader of CETE, state workers were redefining themselves as militant workers dedicated to "serving the people," but, he said, they received no recognition for that change from trade unionists.[18]

Independently of this meeting, over the weekend, thousands of residents secured their neighborhoods with anything within reach in anticipation of attacks from the police or army. A young man recalled: "In my neighborhood over 2,000 of us built barricades with stones. We blocked the two entrances to the neighborhood, one with a bus a driver had donated, and the other with an old car. The riot police came in the morning, but they could not get in so they fired at us from their side of the barricade. Then at 3:00 P.M. the riot squad got thousands of men through a ravine that borders the area. They stayed until midnight, arresting people, and two older men who had nothing to do with anything were killed. A young boy was also killed. Thousands waked the three."[19]

Many young people in these sections of the city identified with revolution and thought it was imminent. After youngsters had barricaded off the neighborhood of Carolingia in Zone 19 over the weekend, they declared it a "liberated territory." By Monday morning, October 3, when the police had occupied most of these neighborhoods, including Carolingia, fighting spread onto the main arteries of the city and into the vicinity of the public schools, which were held by students who stoned police with pieces of cement and rock that had remained inside their unrepaired school buildings since the time of the 1976 earthquake.[20] By Monday afternoon, fighting reached the downtown area, where the young people who composed the crowds of street fighters did not loot the dozens of fancy stores lining the main avenue. They burned buses, tried to block or entrap riot police, and set fire to some commercial establishments and to the outlets of Pollo Campero, a fast-food chain presumed to be owned by Nicaraguan dictator Anastasio Somoza. The slogans they quickly spray painted on the walls expressed their anger about a higher bus fare that would pose economic problems and about the larger issues of power and justice: "Down with the assassin Lucas García," "No to the fare increase," "Somoza is shit," "If Nicaragua wins so will Guatemala," and "Vivas" to revolution and to particular revolutionary groups.

The emergency coalition's efforts to lead coordinated protests were disastrously uneven. On the same Monday, October 3, the CETE strike began with great force as thousands of state workers simultaneously seized the national post office, printing, and telegraph buildings; the municipality building; the social security administration; and several hospitals. But the next day workers struck for two hours in only six factories—Kern's canning company, INCASA, ACRICASA, TACASA, Industria Harinera, and Foremost Milk—and in several banks, although CNT and CNUS had called for "general" work stoppages. Over the following days it became painfully clear that the trade unions did not have enough factories organized to paralyze the private sector, and that even where they did unions were weak, a fact reflected in declining membership. Thousands of state workers remained throughout the week perilously barricaded in their buildings, and work stoppages in the private sector dwindled. The emergency coalition did not have the strength or the internal consensus needed to direct the urban uprising, had such a thing been possible. In addition, within the emergency coalition increasingly vocal cadres from revolutionary groups disagreed as to whether the insurrection "should" escalate into even greater militancy or retreat in view of a potential massacre.

What ended an uprising that no one was leading except the anonymous street fighters who carried it on every day, was not massacre, but triumph. Suddenly, on Friday, October 7, the municipal council restored the five-cent fare. Moreover, although forty people had been killed (some quite selectively, such as CETE leader and telegraph worker Arnulfo Cifuentes Díaz and trade unionist Gonzalo Ac Bín from the ACRICASA textile factory), hundreds had been arrested, and thousands had been fired from their jobs, the state had used restraint, all considered. The army was not mobilized, as it had been in the Panzós Massacre in May and as it now was almost constantly in the countryside, and the police and paramilitaries did not massively kill.

The restoration of the five-cent fare by the state was unexpected by the emergency coalition, which met over the weekend. CETE proposed a national general strike to demand the rehiring of the three thousand state workers fired during the preceding week and the release of the hundreds jailed. But CNUS and CNT hesitated, arguing that the fight had been to lower the fare. On Monday, however, the emergency coalition declared: "We won't stop striking until the buses are running, people are rehired, prisoners are freed, and security forces are out of the neighborhoods and work centers. We call for a general strike."[21]

CNUS and CNT organized no general strike over the weekend, whereas CETE already had a week-old walkout under way. On Monday, October 10, the country and not just the city was crippled when 90 percent of the state employees struck. On October 11, faced with an uneven opposition—united state employees, demobilized private sector workers, and diminishing street protestors, the state attacked its own workers. In the morning, the police pulled people out of the hospitals, the National Printing Office, the Municipal Building, and the National Post Office, where they had to dynamite their way in. In the afternoon, CETE leaders met in the Telegraph Building, the last one they held. Marcos Antonio Figueroa recalled that the leadership knew "we were actually alone" and wrote a statement ending the national strike: "We realized the movement had only one road, total confrontation, and too many would fall. The document was CETE's farewell, and we cautioned people to go into hiding. We foresaw the repression that would fall."[22] The CETE leadership never had a chance to release its statement. The riot squad entered the Telegraph Building in the early afternoon. Figueroa and a leader of the teachers' association were arrested, then "kidnapped" from prison, held for two days, and threatened with torture in front of mirrors before they were released into the basement entrance of a city jail.

On October 13, the emergency coalition announced that the strike was officially over, even as support for the urban uprising grew in the countryside, where members of the Committee of Campesino Unity blocked the Pan American Highway at major crossroads in the western highlands. The statement ending the strike noted the ambiguity of the strike's termination and forecasted a treacherous future: "We are aware that the solution is inadequate. This struggle has shown us that the government is incapable of solving our problems, and the people have torn this conquest [lowering the fare] from the state. However, the price has been tragic. We must find new forms of struggle which will allow us to defend ourselves against the repression."[23] Victory or defeat? And what did those terms mean now?

The state had fired thousands of workers and now fired more. CETE, illegal to begin with, was officially outlawed and the legal status of CNUS and CNT suddenly was "subject to review."[24] The fight to increase the bus drivers' wages ended in complete failure; although their earnings were raised by presidential decree in August, the drivers never saw a cent of the increase. Instead, they were harassed, hundreds lost their jobs for participating in the illegal work actions of July, August, and September, and the competing bus drivers' federations, FENOT and SPAS, ceased to function.

On the day that the strike ended, October 13, members of the military high command met with important civilian state officials. The government had just experienced the worst urban uprising since 1962 and faced a crisis of domination because the revolutionary organizations were winning followers and engaging in successful armed actions in rural areas. To destroy the guerrillas' ability to take advantage of urban unrest, the government officials decided to reduce urban civil society to a pale shadow of its fragile self.[25] From the first half of 1978 to the second, when Guatemala became an international symbol of repression, documented kidnappings increased 72 percent and torture increased 152 percent.[26] The student body and faculty of the University of San Carlos and the newspaper, radio, medical, and legal professions were decimated by violence, as were the church, the labor movement, all manner of student and popular organizations, and any imagined or real oppositional party, such as the Christian Democratic party, the Social Democratic party, and the United Revolutionary Front. It was already the case that the state kidnapped and killed poor people, but now it turned on the middle class as well, fearing its potential for leadership on the left. Shooting progressive professionals in their cars became so common that every few days the press reported similar events: Professor so and so was shot while driving her son to school, or pediatrician so and so was shot in his car as he waited for the light to change. Artist Roberto Cabrera, who would soon seek exile, immortalized this scenario by exhibiting on the lawn of the University of San Carlos his startling metal sculpture of a man just assassinated, slumped over the wheel of his car.

Members of the governing bloc, as well as the wealthy and not-so-wealthy owners of property (such as bus owners), wished to rule over their social, political, and economic milieus without negotiating with any social class other than their own and without encountering strong disagreement from within their own circles. Even Francisco Villagrán Kramer, Lucas García's vice-president, a moderate who objected to the violence, had to leave Guatemala. In retrospect, one could say that state officials had foresight. In Nicaragua, the Sandinistas won in part because of sharp disputes between sectors of the middle class and Somoza. No such fissure—not to mention the flowering of a popular lower-class urban movement—was allowed to develop in Guatemala.

Hundreds were obliged to go into exile or were assassinated. The president of the university student association, Oliverio Castañeda, was shot to death in front of thousands at a demonstration on October 20, 1978, and his successor, Antonio Ciani, was "disappeared" in November. On December 3 the elderly Communist tailor, former PGT militant, and former FASGUA leader Miguel Valdés was tortured to death. Five days later Coca-Cola union leader Pedro Quevedo was murdered delivering soft drinks. In early 1979 Alberto Fuentes Mohr, a former foreign minister and vice-presidential candidate, and at the time head of the new Social Democratic party, was killed, and shortly afterward Manuel Colón Argueta, former city mayor and leader of the middle-class, reformist United Revolutionary Front, met the same fate. Death threats against the Coca-Cola union's legal advisers, Marta Gloria and Enrique Torres, forced the couple and their children into exile. Three murder attempts were made against Coca-Cola union leader Israel Márquez and another man was assassinated by mistake in his place before Márquez fled to Costa Rica in early 1979. ACRICASA union activist Sonia Oliva was kidnapped with her small son, beaten, and held briefly before being released on the condition that she leave Guatemala (see Appendix). Kidnapping attempts were made against CNT and CNUS leader Miguel Angel Albizures and TACASA activist Miguel Cifuentes before each, after wearing disguises and sleeping in different places, went into exile.

Miguel Cifuentes recalled his horror and resolve:

> I had just attended the funeral of Meme Balam [assassinated Coca-Cola worker Manuel López Balam] and I was living in hiding, but the day came when I had to go to the Municipality to renew my residence card [Guatemalans are required to carry residency cards]. I was walking in front of the Civic Center [a large complex of buildings housing the municipal administration in downtown Guatemala City] when suddenly a white Toyota jeep without plates stopped, and out jumped at least four detectives with machine guns in their hands.
>
> My reaction was to run but I couldn't. I felt my legs very very heavy under me, and a sensation that fogged my vision, a red color that obscured my sight. It was horrible. It was the first time I really felt what terror is. I was paralyzed.
>
> Then I started to get a hold of myself and I talked to myself, I said, "I don't have to let myself be seized." I made a very personal decision that I was going to try by all means possible to prevent them from taking me alive, that I would prefer to die, to oblige them to kill me then and there, than to give my family the grief of thinking that I had been disappeared, that I was a prisoner somewhere, being tortured, and who knew when if ever my cadaver would turn up, and what it would look like.
>
> So I achieved the ability to act. I drew together all my strength and things went so quickly. I ran across the street, where I saw another car on the other side, with armed detectives getting out and coming toward me.

I started to run zigzag, right down the middle of Seventh Avenue. There were a lot of people, because it was midday at the Civic Center; what with all those offices and the Supreme Court, everyone poured out at midday. I ran and got inside a municipal building and then left and then hid for a few days until my compañeros arranged my departure.[27]

The question was, how could trade unionism function under these circumstances of intensified repression? The National Central of Workers adopted security measures forbidding almost all activities in its building; those members of the executive committee who remained alive and in the country decided not to shut the CNT facility in 1979 only because that, in effect, would be declaring the central defunct and, by extension, trade unionism untenable.[28] Regulations for a semiclandestine trade unionism were at first adhered to and then not, as they made the central's work too cumbersome. Member unions were accustomed to swift action from the CNT office in the form of leaflets, press releases, advice, and a convenient place to assemble. The central tried to find a way for trade unionism to persist by participating in a new organization, the United Front Against Repression (FDCR). By mid-1979, however, FDCR functioned primarily as a group in exile and, in any case, workers could not utilize it to win their immediate demands.

By early 1979 and into 1980, CNT and CNUS spoke with ever more urgency and frequency of revolution as a means to resolve simple trade union struggles that remained forever unfinished if not completely lost. The trade unionists who still remained active throughout workplaces in the city became increasingly defiant. A CNUS press release of 1979 declared that "the oppressor starts to tremble because the end is near," and individual unions raising their shop floor grievances openly and repeatedly expressed support for the Sandinistas before and after they took power in Nicaragua on July 19, 1979.[29] Trade unionists did not seek to amplify or reproduce the new forms that had emerged in the mass urban struggle over the past years, such as the bus workers' informal committees and the emergency coalition of October 1978.

In late 1978 and into 1979 bold occupations of embassies and churches typified a new style of urban combativeness that depended more on the sharpness of confrontation with authority than on the mass support that had backed past actions such as the 1976 sit-in in front of Coca-Cola or the 1977 Glorious March of the Miners. In late 1978, for example, seventy workers from the Duralita asbestos plant—with their faces masked by bandanas, sunglasses, and low-drawn wool caps—seized the Swiss embassy to prevent the Swiss-owned plant from closing in response to the industrial slump of the late 1970s. The novel use of heavy disguise suggested, as the press noted, a uniform of urban revolutionary warfare. The workers remained for a few days, holding the ambassador and his staff hostage, until the company agreed to reopen, which it did for a short time. In mid-1979 twenty masked workers from the Mexican-owned Panantex textile plant occupied the Mexican embassy to protest a shut-down, "death squad threats and the presence of plainclothes detectives in urban factories with their guns drawn," as well as to denounce a proposal that the Guatemalan army intervene in Nicaragua against the Sandinistas and to demand the reopening of Panantex, the right to live, and the release of a recently kidnapped bank worker.[30] The negotiations of these demands, which were directed against the state, the army, and a foreign company, did not go well, and the workers left the embassy with only the promise of severance plus nine months' pay.

Shortly afterward sixty Maya Indian rural and industrial workers from the El Izotal plantation and the Tejidos San Antonio textile plant in the nearby town of Chimaltenango occupied a church in Guatemala City, as they explained it, "taking the temple of God as the ultimate action" to protest layoffs.[31] The priest called the police, a worker named Miguel Archila was seized and tortured to death, and even more workers were laid off. "The blood of Miguel Archila flows inside the thousands of sons of the people who fight for a better life. Today, more than ever, we fortify ourselves and our commitment to the struggle. The repression will not stop us," exclaimed a CNT press release.[32]

Life Never Lost: The Cult of Martyrdom
and the Reversal of Murder

Some union members audaciously battled their employers and the state, but many more became cautious. The majority of workers at the Duralita and Panantex factories, for instance, had not joined the embassy occupations, though in both cases the majority supported these minority actions. It was true that wage earners, students, housewives, and other urban residents still participated, now well masked, in citywide demonstrations: over 100,000 people attended the May First march in 1979, and the funeral processions of assassinated activists grew longer and longer that year. Yet all protest groups in Guatemala City, whether of students or in neighborhoods, had fewer and fewer people attending meetings, and workers were withdrawing from unions. By the end of 1979 the Coca-Cola workers' union, for example, had decreased from over two hundred members to sixty, and other unions suffered similar declines.

Trade unionists had a difficult time sustaining themselves, and they drew upon their own lively sense of themselves as a good-humored community of survivors. A CNT labor adviser remembered: "We became very close. That helped us. We used to laugh a lot. You could write this as a kind of comic-tragedy or a tragic-comedy. We used to joke about what photograph each of us wanted up on the wall [after their deaths], and what words we wanted under it." "We were half-suicidal," she added, a comment reflecting the position of activists not wanting to die but not willing to withdraw from the labor movement and thus risking death to defend what they felt was valuable in life.[33] When a trade unionist remarking on the number of deaths in his union said, "Yes, it's true we lost many lives, but . . . we never lost life," he laughed at the irony of what he thought was the truth that saved trade unionism.[34]

Losing members and not winning battles, the labor movement fought with what it had, its losses. In 1978, as violence and defeats increased, the term *martyr* became a key word in the urban unions. Those who were assassinated or disappeared now became martyrs who belonged to a labor movement that represented them as spiritual leaders. This cult of martyrs had its roots in a religious popular culture that glorified sacrifice and honored the images of the bleeding body of Christ nailed on the cross and of the enduring Mary, which Guatemalans placed on walls and furniture in homes and workplaces throughout the city. It was reinforced by pastoral agents who now publicly spoke of the biblical characters whom they identified as martyrs for the cause of social justice when they presided at the burials of murdered trade unionists. Yet, however inspired and comforted by the Christian religion and their deep belief that there could be no achievement without suffering, trade unionists were not pursuing purification and redemption through the sacrifice of their lives. Their cult of martyrdom sustained them in the face of deaths that they did not seek.

Following the assassination of CNT organizer Mario Mujía in 1978, CNT declared 1978 the "Year of the Martyr Mario Mujía," and this appeared on all of its leaflets and press releases. As deaths mounted, the meeting hall in the CNT building was named "Room of the Martyrs," and as activists were murdered or disappeared, their photographs were hung on the wall; people met under them. Posted in the office was this poem:

> If you have not come here to give
> your heart, your life
> don't bother to enter
> because in your entrance is your end.
> If you come to find
> a bed, a soft moment,
> don't bother to stay here
> where the most beautiful flower is a wound.
> This is a place appropriate
> only for your sacrifice.
> Here
> you must be
> the last to have
> the last to sleep
> the first to die.

In each ending was another step forward, because out of each death life continued; barring this, why enter? After Mario Mujía's murder, a union published this analysis: "A person lives through his actions and his deeds. The physical life of a person can disappear from its original form, but it is never completely destroyed. Supporting this thesis, we say: Mario Mujía lives through the thoughts and deeds which he realized in his life. Mario! Your bones will serve to nourish the fire which keeps the working-class struggle alive." [35]

In statements such as these and in their own minds, trade unionists began expropriating and repossessing the deaths of their companions at the hands of the state, which was the state's weapon against them, as their own weapon. They took up their murdered dead, and not arms. When the ex-president of the Association of Telegraph and Radio-telegraph Operators (ATRG), Arnulfo Cifuentes Díaz, was killed during the October 1978 uprising, fellow telegraph worker and leader of the ATRG, Marcos Antonio Figueroa, spoke extemporaneously at his funeral:

> A bitterness has grown within us, filling us with contempt and hate for the leaders of the state who, with coldness of psychopaths, murder those who feed them. . . . Arnulfo, your blood will not run in vain. Today more than ever, because of your blood, we will not be intimidated. Your murder has turned panic to anger. For each leader who falls, ten more will arise. Our blood will continue to run in the streets, but we will continue to fight for our interests. You will pass to be a star in our sky, lighting our path to freedom. [36]

Central to the making of history in Figueroa's thoughts was death by murder, multiplying struggle instead of diminishing it, turning "panic to anger," darkness to light, retreat to advance. In the way trade unionists commemorated their assassinated companions, they guaranteed victory and life. If the state aimed to stop trade unionism by murdering trade unionists, a straightforward enough tactic, the trade union movement would regenerate life through murdered trade unionists—a far more complex maneuver.

As the number of assassinated and disappeared grew, so did the imperative to connect the generation of working-class history to murder and kidnapping, to show that these particular deaths created life. Recalling, repeating, and invoking the names of workers who had been killed or kidnapped became trade union style. These names marked the progression of the history of the oppressed, and their recollection was resistance to government repression. The conscious sustaining thought was, as stated by a worker at the CAVISA glass factory, "These people made our history, they are not forgotten. And if it happens to me, I won't be either, and the struggle will go forward, instead of stop."[37]

Trade unionists recomposed their Christian belief in life after death into a formulation of death through state murder as transformation into life and not expiration of life. In early 1980 one leaflet writer even abolished death as a consequence of state murder, which in turn would only bring closer a final victory wherein revolution on earth and the kingdom of heaven seemed to merge just as life and death did in his leaflet: "We firmly believe that all those who have given their lives for their brothers have not died, and the blood that flows will bring us closer to the Reign of Peace, which is the fruit of justice and brotherly love."[38] Murdered activists were especially alive and could use their state-inflicted bodies against the state. And if they were not really dead, the state's power was a fiction.

There also existed among workers more intimate communications about their experiences with terrorism. Marcos Antonio Figueroa, who was born in the capital to a domestic Indian servant and a ladino telegraph operator, and who became a leader of the radio-telegraph workers and of CETE in 1978, told the following story of his own kidnapping:

[After riot police pulled Figueroa and others out of the Telegraph Building, which the state workers held, on October 11 at the end of the October 1978 uprising, they were taken to the Second Police Precinct.] There were about 800 workers, and they had us in the patio in long circles. They came around with a list, asking everyone's name, and I knew I'd better not lie because they already knew. So I said, "Marcos Antonio Figueroa." The detective went down the list and there was my name circled in red. They pulled me out, myself and Roberto [a leader of the public schoolteachers]—no one else. They sat us down in a basement garage and then a little sports car came along. Some men got out and told us to get in.

The truth is, this was the first step to disappear us, because they threw us on the floor and put a rug over us. One guy said, "Accelerate, and go through the red light because there is a crowd of people out there." They started to sing a song to make fun of us: "Dove, my little white dove, communists, trade unionists." We felt something awful would happen to us.

They took us to a place where there were little houses, and semi-dark offices, and into a structure where iron hung—perhaps it was a stable for horses. Very strange. And people inside, playing cards. In any case, there were cells and they put Roberto and me in one of them. We noted that others had been there—the wall had scratches in it.

There we were, alone. It was silent, so we talked about our lives. Occasionally, a masked man would come and murmur, "Who are you?" We'd reply, "We're from CETE."

At around 1:00 A.M. they took us out and put us in a van, and started to drive away. We felt that they were taking us to a place to kill us. But the van didn't go anywhere. It parked again. At around 5:00 A.M. someone got into the van again, and started it up. We felt horrible again, as if the moment was drawing near. But no, he parked the van where it had been in the first place, and they took us back to the cell in the stable. I don't know what this was—orders, counterorders, who knows? It seems this was a center for paramilitary groups. There were many men with masks on, coming and going, shouting at each other.

At 7:00 A.M. a uniformed policeman came into the cell. That calmed us because we thought at least this isn't the paramilitary. But at the same time, this worried us. Perhaps it was the paramilitary and if they were letting us see this, it's because we weren't going to be around to tell it. Then the policeman came near and said, "I know you are from CETE, and your friends are looking for you two in all the prisons. If you have a message, write it." Roberto had the CETE stamp in his pocket, so we stamped that on a piece of paper with our initials. We never found out who received this. Roberto and I evaluated this incident, and decided it was the result of the affection for us among public employees, and that the policeman did this with good intention.

Soon after, they took us out, blindfolded us, tied our hands and put us in a vehicle. We were terribly worried, chilled, fatigued. Perhaps at 10:00 A.M. we started and drove for what I calculate was four hours up steep inclines and then down again, on a dirt road, perhaps in a coffee plantation, because of the terrain. Finally we stopped, and I heard branches against the top of the vehicle, peasants talking, dogs barking, hens, chickens, an airplane taking off. I had no doubt we were in some finca with its own small airport.

At around 2:00 P.M. they took off the blindfolds, and we saw the inside of the vehicle. It was a U.S.-style Volkswagen bus, with curtains and carpeting. Elegant. And in front of us was a huge mirror in which we saw ourselves seated, exactly as if we were in a beauty salon. Next to the mirror was a shiny chrome metal box. At a certain moment they opened it, and it had what looked like surgical instruments inside. I noticed a pipe as well, possibly connected to the motor. I realized this was a torture chamber: the mirror—so that one watched what was happening to oneself; the pipe—to asphyxiate people, heat them or burn them. At that moment I felt completely powerless.

They covered our eyes again and another person entered. I heard radio equipment. Since I am familiar with that, I recognized those little noises, and some communication was made with another radio. I felt it was a transmission to the National Palace or a military base. The person started to speak to us. He didn't lecture us or interrogate us. He started to chat, simply that. Why had we started the strike? How old were we? Did we have children? He said, very calmly, "And your friends, are they looking for you?" "We don't know, perhaps," we replied. "And you think your friends are worth dying for?" Our eyes were covered, but we were very close, Roberto and I, almost hugging. "You want to overthrow the government?" "No," we said. "But you have some relation with CNT, with EGP?" "No," we said. He asked who the head of CETE was and we replied we had none, we were all in charge. He was a young, educated type, perhaps a lieutenant or captain, I could tell.

When he asked us why we went on strike, and we explained about the firings and the death of a compañero, Arnulfo Cifuentes, I took the opportunity of telling him that we had information that the government, the presidential palace, was involved in the death of Arnulfo Cifuentes and we had left these documents with compañeros, and if anything happened to us, they would release that information. We had to say this, because something very serious was going to happen to us.

With that he cut the discussion. He shut off the radio. Perhaps even the president or the defense minister had been listening, and perhaps they had made a decision about what to do with us. The man left, our blindfolds were removed, and we could see again. We could see tree branches against the windows, and a man sitting in the corner of the bus, with a hood on, and you could see very thick glasses behind the hood. He must have had terrible eyesight.

We decided to ask him if he was going to kill us. A moment comes when one simply wants to know. He didn't reply. We talked to him for a while, although he never said anything. We used the word *compañero* to address him; after all, he was a state employee. Then the men who had driven us out of the police precinct climbed back in and they said, "You're lucky, you're going to be handed back to jail, as official prisoners." I felt a bit calmer and started to talk with them on a more human level.

I said I was glad to hear that, because all we were doing was to help the people of Guatemala. I spoke of the cost of living, and said if they had children they surely did not have enough to clothe them. Roberto and I started to speak of these fundamental human issues. And they talked some and said it was true. There wasn't enough to take proper care of children, but one had to be careful about what one was getting involved in. I felt we reached a real communication.

And there is something which I think will never disappear. No matter how evil people may be, they continue to be people. And there is some human element, something of kindness, because at one point they stopped to eat something, and they asked us if we had eaten yet. We said no, and yes we'd like something. Roberto told them I had an ulcer, and they said, "Don't worry, we'll get milk," which they did. And since we were tied up, they fed us with their own hands, putting the milk to my lips to drink, and we all sat together for a few moments eating. I will never forget this, the detectives, accustomed to kill and maim, consoling someone with an ulcer. Humans have many aspects, and if we take advantage of the good ones, make them coherent, we can advance further than we know.[39]

Not only death by murder but even this journey into hell could be interpreted in a hopeful manner by trade unionists. Here, of all places, was an experience in human kindness, a lesson in the human potential for greatness. According to a friend, Figueroa was badly beaten at some point, perhaps after he was shown the instruments of torture and before the army officer entered the van. If this was the case, then he chose not to mention what would alter the memory he wished to cultivate, treasure, and reproduce of the good done to Roberto and himself, and of their ability to persist as themselves, without charade or deformation, summoning their powers in a situation of powerlessness to attempt to recruit their kidnappers, their fellow state employees, to new understandings and solidarities. As Figueroa told the story, he and Roberto answered silence with communication, sightlessness with imagination. He underscored that, while completely vulnerable, in the possession of unusually dangerous men, he and Roberto had maintained their self-possession: they threatened the army officer with incriminating information held by workers, and Roberto even requested special care for a body that the kidnappers could have carved up once and for all with their instruments of torture. Figueroa believed that he and Roberto were released because the kidnappers feared CETE's ability to expose them. In recounting his experience this way, Figueroa saved the world for himself. The cult of the martyrs inverted murder into life; this memory of survival transformed terror and fear into renewed courage and faith in humanity.

Figueroa soon left Guatemala. The truth was that while living in hiding, as he now had to in Guatemala, he could not be an effective activist. In fact, when faced with capture by the state, most trade unionists sought exile—the policy of individual unions as well as CNUS and CNT. When it became apparent that they were in immediate danger of being seized and killed, most avoided the horrible death they knew awaited them. When labor activists honored their assassinated companions as makers and guardians of working-class history, or reversed the significance of a kidnapping, they were not urging workers to march off to die or to be disappeared. They were protecting a sense of self and a vision of humanity that made struggling to improve human life a sane proposition.

Just as many labor activists went into exile if they had the choice and the chance, workers left unions as a consequence of the repression. As much as bravery, a cult of martyrs, and a reversal of terrorism breathed life into an activist worldview in the worst of all situations, these did not give life to the popular movement for more than the briefest period. Workers and other poor people in the city were truly frightened. Terrorism was as effective as it was meant to be, not because it transformed the urban poor according to the image of the tortured body into torn and extirpated beings, but because the majority of the urban population involved in unions or other protest groups chose to retreat, reasonably enough. The city was not the countryside: the urban poor lived under the state's eye, and the only organizational forms of struggle available to them, such as unions, were too exposed and too predictably doomed. If a revolution had swept down from the mountains into the city, no doubt they would have embraced it.

The Countryside Explodes

Until 1978, three types of organizations existed in the countryside: peasant leagues, which grouped *minifundistas*, sharecroppers, and tenants who marketed goods and fought for land together; cooperatives of peasants and artisans who pooled resources to buy and sell; and a very few unions. The line between peasant leagues and cooperatives was sometimes thin, but generally peasant leagues had broader concerns than cooperatives and were more militant. Loosely tied to FASGUA, and almost completely destroyed by repression by the end of the 1970s, the leagues were rooted in the 1944–54 period when they fought for land with Communist support. The cooperatives became widespread in the 1960s under the auspices of foreign and national development programs. The Committee of Campesino Unity was a fourth type of organization. Making no distinction between rural wage workers and peasants or between seasonal and permanent wage workers, it united all of these to oppose ethnic discrimination against Maya Indians and the oppression common to poor rural Indians and ladinos. CUC employed direct action to acquire land and higher wages, and it organized self-defense committees against the military.

The history of CUC has yet to be written, but it apparently evolved out of the cooperatives and leagues, the 1976 earthquake reconstruction committees, Catholic Action groups, and the new loss of lands in the 1960s and 1970s, when large-scale capitalist agriculture extended into the countryside. Moreover, many of its leaders had been involved in groups that were reviving ethnic consciousness among Indians in the highlands.[40] What had started as a series of grass roots base committees dedicated to the defense of land, lives, culture, and community crystallized into CUC soon after the 1977 Glorious March of the Miners, which brought together the workers on the southern coastal sugar plantation of Pantaleón with the Mam-speaking miners from the distant highlands, and for which the base committees had organized enthusiastic, widespread support. CUC joined CNUS and became nationally known for the first time when hundreds of its members arrived from the countryside and marched, mostly in Indian dress, in the city on May First 1978 under the slogan "Clear Head, Heart of Solidarity, Fist of Combat." Twenty-six days later, the army conducted the massacre at Panzós.

CUC had success in 1978 and 1979 organizing its local committees in the highlands and on the southern coast. On January 31, 1980, the committee directed the most dramatic embassy occupation up to that time, as thirty Maya Indians and their supporters took over the Spanish embassy to protest the army bombings of villages in the department of Quiché. The occupation ended in over thirty-nine deaths when police firebombed the building and almost killed the Spanish ambassador, who then had to be protected from Guatemalan security forces by other ambassadors, an incident that created an international scandal for which the Lucas García government was everywhere condemned. What is less well known is that a month later CUC initiated the most strategic and forceful strike in Guatemalan history when it led tens of thousands of sugar and cotton workers in a work stoppage on the southern coast plantations that crippled the nation's key export sectors.

The strike began on February 18, 1980, at the Tehuantepec sugar plantation in Santa Lucía Cotzumalguapa, where 700 Indians and ladinos stopped work to demand Q5 a day. Armed with machetes, groups of strikers walked to neighboring plantations to extend the strike. Within two days, 75,000 seasonal and permanent Indian and ladino workers had paralyzed sixty plantations, and the two largest mills in the area, Pantaleón and Santa Ana, were seized by armed workers. The strike's organizational core consisted of CUC committees in most places and unions in a very few.

The strike spread to the town of Escuintla, where market women joined in, and to the largest factory in the area, the Papelería paper plant, located inside a plantation where workers were striking. The roads along the southern coast were jammed with men, women, and children. They stopped trucks, pierced tires, dumped sugar and cotton, or burned the trucks and their cargoes in huge fires. Military police, riot police, detectives, and soldiers from the nearby Puerto San José army base tried to clear the roads as workers battled with stones, sticks, and machetes. National Police Chief Germán Chupina flew into the Papelería factory courtyard in a helicopter. The farm workers surrounded the factory, which the industrial workers had occupied: "He [Chupina] said he would evict the workers with bullets. We said he would die too, because the workers had the boilers ready, and he flew off."[41]

After two weeks, the government raised the minimum wage in the countryside from Q1.20 to Q3.20, a 186 percent increase covering 800,000 workers in cattle, cotton, coffee, sugar, rubber, and cardamon. Immediately after this apparent concession, the government began a counterattack. As with the October urban insurrection, the state first yielded and then advanced against the popular movement; it was waging civil war, not negotiating with civil society. The wage increase was not enforced, thousands of plantation workers were laid off, and hundreds were kidnapped. Many of the strikers responded to this aggression by joining the Guerrilla Army of the Poor and in smaller numbers the other guerrilla groups, the Revolutionary Organization of the People in Arms, the Rebel Armed Forces, and the Guatemalan Labor party. As one worker explained, "in view of the situation, unfortunately we have to defend ourselves with the same weapons the army uses. We, the Guatemalan people, the peasants, the 'Indians,' as they call us, we have the right to defend ourselves and the only road we have left is to take up the same arms the army uses against us."[42] In the coming months and years well over 100,000 Maya Indians participated in guerrilla warfare, and the army responded with a campaign of genocide against the Maya population.

When the strike started, CUC was part of CNUS, as was CNT. During the strike, members of CNT and CNUS in Guatemala City provided legal and other types of support and negotiated directly with the government in the capital. At the time the government offered Q3.20, CUC was demanding Q5. But at a meeting held in the capital, attended by one CUC member, leaders of CNT and CNUS agreed to accept Q3.20 in the name of the Committee of Campesino Unity, thinking that the increase was a victory and that to continue the strike would have been hard on the strikers; already many workers were surviving on sugar cane, some seasonal workers from the highlands had left the area, and the army was bringing in tanks. When the CUC delegate reported back to the committee, CUC indignantly rejected the settlement, angered that the urban CNUS had been so feckless as not to defend the Q5 figure, a just wage for rural workers. The committee wanted to continue the strike, but word had already spread of the settlement and the strike was ending. After some complicated negotiations between the two organizations, the infuriated CUC withdrew from CNUS.[43] From the city, CNUS tried to fortify the weak unions on the southern coast, such as the one at Pantaleón, for the fight to enforce the Q3.20 daily wage. But the unions did not have the work crews organized and CUC did. After the February–March strike, rural wage laborers began to abandon the workplace struggle for the revolutionary one.

On the strength of the CUC strike, wages in the city were also raised. CNUS had taken advantage of the February–March CUC strike to demand a daily wage of Q7 in industry, commerce, services, and construction, at a time when the minimum earnings in these sectors were between Q1.70 and Q2.50. CNUS could not call a general strike in any of these sectors; only nine factories held brief work stoppages in support of the Q7 demand. But on the advice of William Bowdler, U.S. undersecretary of Interamerican Affairs, the government in April established a new minimum ranging from Q3.75 to Q4.12. Bowdler argued, "If the conservative Guatemalan government fails to promote some political and social reforms, it will be incapable of stopping the polarization of the country and will find itself in the same tragic situation as Nicaragua and El Salvador."[44] The only substantial wage increase won in the urban private sector in a decade thus appeared as the result of insurrectionary rural struggle in Guatemala and revolution in Central America, and it happened when CNUS and CNT were divided from rural workers and frailer than they had ever been.

Catastrophe

The National Committee on Trade Union Unity and the National Central of Workers continued to present themselves as stronger than ever and on the verge of a victory. Both despite and because of the weakness of unions and the unrelenting repression in 1980, CNT and CNUS sponsored a militant May First march. Trade unionists thought that it would have been surrender to relinquish May First by not calling people into the streets, especially if they were still willing to go. Over 100,000 marched, most of them masked. CNUS and CNT pronounced themselves in favor of "a revolutionary, popular and democratic government," as they had since 1978, and declared that "never before had the working class been so united and capable."[45]

May First 1980 ended in massacre. Gangs of kidnappers seized thirty-six demonstrators as they left the march and tortured them to death. Among the victims were two Coca-Cola workers and three trade unionists from the Ray-o-Vac battery factory whose bloodied, mangled bodies were found wrapped up together in the red-lettered union banner that the three of them—a sister, her brother, and their close friend—had painted the previous evening. This particularly savage attack on the urban popular movement followed others, such as the Spanish Embassy Massacre and the gunning down of several people who attended the funeral for its victims. With no victories in sight, the glorification of death by murder as a means to life started to lose its power, even for activists. "If by dying we would end hunger and poverty, I would die," declared a mourning trade union member at the burial of the Ray-o-Vac workers, "but this blood only enshrouds more homes in lament and causes more suffering."[46]

Throughout May and into June trade unionists were kidnapped or assassinated at the rate of almost one a day. On June 17 alone, three were disappeared. Then on June 21, a young Coca-Cola worker was killed at dawn inside the plant in retaliation for the death of a manager who had been machine-gunned by FAR in response to the murder of Coca-Cola union leader Marlon Mendizábal a few weeks previously. At three that afternoon, over thirty of CNT's most important activists from throughout the city met in the CNT building. Within the hour twenty-seven of them had been kidnapped by plainclothes police. The disappeared included two workers from Coca-Cola, four from the ACRICASA textile plant (including Florencia Xocop and Sara Cabrera, who was seven months' pregnant), and delegates from the unions at the newspaper *Prensa Libre* and the companies Kern's, Induplast, Cemaco, Sistemas Electrónicos, and CIDASA. In response to the kidnappings, there were strikes of varying lengths at Coca-Cola (the longest), ACRICASA, Induplast, Kern's canning plant, Cemaco, Enlozados Nacionales, Esmaltes y Aceros, and Adams's candy demanding the return of the twenty-seven abducted workers "safe and sound." They never reappeared.

The June 21 meeting had taken place at the urging of members of the Guatemalan Labor party who were challenging FAR's influence within CNT.[47] Not all the workers who attended were aware of that, although they knew that the meeting had to be unusually urgent. It should never have taken place. Detectives and death squads were openly seeking trade union leaders, who by now feared for their lives, yet one group of revolutionaries from PGT insisted that important trade unionists meet openly, and a second group from FAR agreed, despite the CNT executive committee's recent decision that no leadership meetings be held in the CNT building. None of the movement's middle-class advisers went to the meeting, although one of them, who was in charge of the building, had been expected.

There can be no doubt that a state agent or agents in one of the revolutionary groups utilized the fight for hegemony to guarantee that the meeting occurred. A proposal to meet in the office on the morning of the twenty-first had already been rejected for security reasons, yet the meeting was held that afternoon. A witness explained: "Two members tied to a Faction [one of the revolutionary groups] insisted on the meeting and accused the others of manipulating fear so that a meeting would not take place. An argument started—to have the meeting, to have the meeting elsewhere, or not to have it. In the midst of this some left and others arrived and decided to have it in the building to avoid a criticism from the Faction. They overestimated the need to have this ideological battle and underestimated the conditions of danger which had led them to cancel the meeting in the morning."

The witness described the kidnapping:

The meeting started, although some left because they felt it should take place elsewhere. At approximately 3:30 P.M. about seventy men heavily armed with machine guns and rifles appeared on Fourth Street and Ninth Avenue. They had on hats or wool caps. They ran toward the door and formed a circle around it, placing themselves by windows. They called by radio and cars came. A Toyota jeep smashed the door down. Others blocked the traffic. We heard the Toyota break the door and two leaders said, "Over the roofs!" but most stayed with their arms up. . . . Four of us went for the roof and made it. One crouched near and heard the detectives yelling, "Goats, let's see if you have balls, so yell the name of a revolutionary group." They were then beaten to get them into the cars. . . .

We watched from a distance. People were carried out like logs. The seven cars were from the narcotics division of the National Police. The head of the narcotics division was among the men.[48]

Immediately after the kidnapping, CNUS pointed out in the last issue of its publication *Unidad* that the rapid appearance of a large, prepared force of kidnappers suggested that the meeting had been set up by an informant. CNUS speculated that the informant had infiltrated a "Faction." This was confirmed to CNUS by the subsequent August 24 kidnapping of seventeen FASGUA leaders and other trade unionists from the Kern's canning company, the CIDASA textile plant, and the INCASA powdered-coffee factory who secretly assembled at the Centro de Retiros Espirituales in Escuintla, a meeting place known only to the members of one "Faction."[49] CNUS tried to mobilize protest, but the popular urban movement was in complete retreat, given the prospect of only more ghastly deaths. With the two mass kidnappings of forty-four men and women, the three most important vehicles of the urban trade union struggle since 1954—FASGUA, CNT, and CNUS—ceased to function publicly.

Miguel Angel Albizures, founder of CNT in 1968 and of CNUS in 1976, a pioneer trade unionist whose career as such ended with the demise of CNUS and CNT, wrote from exile in the early 1980s:

Many of us leading the union movement in 1974–1980 must criticize ourselves. We were carried away by activism, sometimes provoked by the extreme poverty and exploitation, sometimes intentionally by the government, sometimes by the spontaneity of the working class, sometimes by an ideological current. Our forces were insufficiently educated, our vision of the enemy empirical and sometimes ridiculous. We were too open. Underestimating the advances of the state in terms of vigilance and computers, we lost many lives because of our own methods of work and lack of vision. We can't lie to ourselves, the most valiant people have fallen. . . . One grave error was not combatting sectarianism to the death, a sectarianism which made of the workers and peasants objects of the struggle and not subjects, not protagonists of their own destiny. If we are going to recall the words of great theoreticians, let's recall, "The liberation of the working class is its own task."[50]

Citing Marx to criticize the Leninists, who had lent Albizures Marx in the early 1970s, for reifying workers, Albizures happened to choose a quotation that resonated with the concept of working-class protagonism, which he had learned in the 1960s in the Young Catholic Worker. In summing up many problems in his statement, he specifically pointed to the part "revolutionary" factionalism had played in the labor movement's defeat, but he deeply believed in the reality and not just the dream of workers' power. However crushed the trade union movement was by state power, in his view, all of it—misreading the state, not managing the revolutionaries, being provoked, and even being ill-educated—was within the trade unionists' purview, within their capacity to handle or overcome.

In the 1970s Guatemala City had been alive with national protest. By late 1980, it seemed as if all of its subjects or protagonists had been silenced in one terrible way or another. Amid an ugly landscape of state buildings, the downtown area was dominated by memories of dead or absent people. A walk through the crowded streets in the center of the city led past the solid National Palace, the Bank of the Army, the National Police Headquarters, and the ill-kept National Library and past scenes visible only in the memory, past the empty CNT building, past corners and spots where so and so had been chased or shot or taken away.

No revolution arrived to rescue the city. In 1980 no one could have predicted a guerrilla defeat in the countryside. The revolutionaries had as many people intertwined with their organizational work as did their counterparts in Nicaragua and El Salvador. Now one can argue that the revolutionaries failed in part because the bourgeoisie was not divided against itself, as it was in Somoza's Nicaragua. In the late 1970s and early 1980s members of the Guatemalan bourgeoisie put aside discord to place their collective destiny in the hands of the military, which overcame its many internal problems in order to

Exile: CNT and CNUS leader Miguel Angel Albizures addresses U.S. labor activists in California in the early 1980s. (Photograph courtesy of Miguel Angel Albizures)

Absence: the empty CNT building in the mid-1980s. (Photograph by the author)

wage civil war.[51] In any case, there is no evidence that any sector of the bourgeoisie objected to the army's dominance or to its policy of massacring the population to defeat the guerrillas by 1984.

No drawn-out contest occurred in the city. By the end of 1981 army intelligence had cut urban guerrilla units to ribbons.[52] A few trade unionists, however, weathered the storm against the urban movement by retreating temporarily. These survivors protected their history and constructed a version of it to hold out against the state and employers.

6

The Coca-Cola Workers Make and Portray History, 1976–1985

Trade unionism in Guatemala City did not end in 1980 with the demise of the labor centrals and federations as a consequence of the massive kidnappings of leaders and members. War in the countryside overshadowed national life, and the army carried out counterinsurgency sweeps in Guatemala City, rounding up anyone even remotely associated with the guerrillas and entering city neighborhoods in tanks to blow up presumed safe houses. But activists in a few workplaces managed to at least retain their unions' legal status. These unions abruptly withdrew from the political arena and kept silent about the strife surrounding them to avoid being engulfed and consumed in the flames of the destruction of the revolutionary movement's urban organization.

One union that survived was the Coca-Cola Bottling Company Workers' Union (STEGAC). Perhaps due to the hysterical anticommunism of Coca-Cola franchise owner John Trotter, who had close ties with the right-wing Movement for National Liberation and with army intelligence, STEGAC suffered more violent attacks in the 1970s than any other single union. Because of this, by 1978 the union had gained potent support from international labor and human rights groups that allowed it to survive in the late 1970s and to persist under military rule in the early 1980s.

The Internationalization of Labor Conflict
in a Multinational Company, 1976–1978

In 1976 the Coca-Cola Bottling Company of Guatemala (EGSA) employed 350 workers, the majority in sales and production and the rest in the administrative office, the warehouse, the laboratory, the maintenance department, and the mechanics' workshop. Production and warehouse workers were the union's mainstay when it formed back in 1975, and its leadership came primarily from among the few trade unionists in the sales division (even though hostility existed between workers in sales, who were paid on commission and earned more money, and workers in other departments).

As of late 1976, STEGAC had legal status—won during the previous April—but the union had no contract, and John Trotter, a wily lawyer from Texas, divided the company into twelve separate paper entities to avoid negotiating one. STEGAC delayed bargaining until the court ruled in favor of the union's right to represent workers in all twelve new companies. The union's legal advisers, Marta Gloria Torres and her husband Enrique Torres, filed a petition of economic demands under the name of each company, thus placing every paper entity under an injunction. They also submitted to the Labor Ministry statements from employees in each of the twelve divisions requesting affiliation with the union, thereby rendering Trotter's tactic meaningless.

As a result, company intimidation increased. Managers threatened individual workers with death, and Marta Gloria and Enrique Torres brought signed testimonies to that effect to the Labor Ministry. Shortly thereafter two of the workers who had signed affidavits barely escaped being machine-gunned as they left the plant. On the following day, March 2, 1977, Marta Gloria and Enrique Torres were driving home when a jeep driven by an employee of the Ministry of the Interior ran their car off the road, seriously injuring both of them. One week later masked men attacked Ricardo de Jesús Boche, the young warehouse worker who had founded the union, and left him in critical condition.[1] Despite these and other efforts to discourage participation, such as the jailing of three union members on murder charges that were eventually dropped, the union continued to grow and in 1977 comprised almost the entire work crew, including the majority of employees in the sales department. Even antiunion workers recruited by Trotter were won over by persistent union members.

What the repression at Coca-Cola achieved was the internationalization of the labor conflict as a human rights issue after the American Friends Service Committee, which had a staff in Central America, publicized the case in the United States. The Interfaith Center on Corporate Responsibility (ICCR), an organization of Catholic and Protestant groups influenced by Liberation Theology, became interested and, through them, so did a group of U.S. Coca-Cola shareholders, the Sisters of Providence. Throughout mid-1977 ICCR and the Sisters of Providence pressured the parent company in Atlanta to get Trotter to settle with the union and repeatedly questioned him in writing about violence, wages, and working conditions and the illegal attempt to fire workers in 1976. As a result, Coca-Cola called Trotter to Atlanta, where the company advised him to contact a Costa Rican priest named Claudio Solano, who ran the John XXIII Workers' Center in San José, Costa Rica. Father Solano was a professional troubleshooter for companies who later inspired the Central American Solidarismo movement of the 1980s. Supported by Christian Democrats, he had a reputation for smoothing over labor conflicts by developing harmonious worker-management relations based on nonunion agreements. Solano employed Liberation Theology rhetoric, but only as it applied to notions of social peace between adversaries.

Trotter rejected the concept of a mediator, and perhaps at Atlanta Coca-Cola's request, Solano suddenly arrived in Guatemala and offered his services to STEGAC. Because he was a priest and workers were courteous, Catholic, and self-confident enough to not feel threatened by his presence, the union accepted. Thus granted a role in resolving the dispute, Solano convened a meeting of union and company representatives to propose making a direct settlement that did not involve the union as a formal party, an idea rejected by both STEGAC and Trotter. STEGAC members explained that "Solano used the Bible as a banner to co-opt the workers, but this objective was not achieved because revolutionary spiritualists were among our ranks."[2] Nonetheless, Solano stayed in Guatemala.

In December 1977 the Sisters of Providence requested a meeting with Trotter and union members; they also filed a stockholders' resolution that the Atlanta Coca-Cola Company establish labor standards in contracts with franchises. The parent company again called Trotter to Atlanta and threatened to cancel his franchise unless he signed a contract with the workers. Although Atlanta Coca-Cola was notoriously antiunion, it feared adverse publicity and it had its own disputes with Trotter: he billed them for import duties from which he was exempt on Mexican-made syrup, and sales were declining in Guatemala due to administrative mismanagement. Atlanta Coca-Cola disliked Trotter, but it did not want to terminate his franchise before it expired. Frightened by the declining market for their products by late 1977 and worried that multinational companies would desert them, businessmen in Guatemala had won passage of a law obliging multinationals who severed ties with local businesses to pay indemnities equal to three times the profits of the last year of business. On that issue Trotter had the rights of a Guatemalan. Thus, having accomplished nothing with Father Solano and trying to avoid terminating the franchise, Atlanta Coca-Cola bluffed and told Trotter that it would end the franchise unless he settled with the union.[3]

This chain of antagonism together with constant agitation at the shop floor level led to a contract. Trotter agreed to negotiate with STEGAC, and in the presence of Solano and two U.S. religious shareholders a settlement was reached in January 1978. The contract awarded workers respect for union freedom, job security for union officers, improved safety conditions, overtime pay, personal leave, fixed pay scales, promotion and grievance procedures, lockers, the right to use the company telephone, more vacation time, medical benefits, training programs, and a cafeteria. It also established a daily wage increase ranging from twenty to seventy cents and stipulated that the last Saturday of each August, the union's anniversary, be a paid holiday called the "Day of the Worker."[4]

By the time the contract was won, most Coca-Cola workers belonged to

STEGAC and the union had a fairly dynamic internal life even though rank-and-file affiliates tended to rely on the opinions and the initiatives of a few leaders and legal advisers, who in turn were often absorbed by the demands of the national movement. Nevertheless, and in part because of those same leaders, STEGAC regularly held well-attended meetings where all union business was debated at length. Throughout 1976 and 1977 the union had depended for its survival on the richness of the collective, on the constant battle of all of its members against the verbal abuse, beatings, and jailings. Union members had a strong sense of belonging to and ownership of STEGAC. Yet the enormous pressures brought to bear upon them in the form of physical violence, threats, verbal abuse, and bribery attempts had to take a toll.

The first two leaders to desert were Ricardo de Jesús Boche, the union's founder, and Santos Martínez Campos, the first worker whom Jesús Boche had recruited. This happened in September 1977, before the achievement of a pact. As Gregorio González, a young maintenance worker from a poor rural family, related:

Boche was persecuted continually, beaten, sent to the hospital. Then he organized a soccer team, and the company bought him shoes and uniforms for the team. The company won him with this kind of stuff. The managers took him on trips, like to Puerto San José. Then they offered him and Santos 10,000 quetzales [Q1 = $1], and, finally, the two accepted.

The thing is that betrayal doesn't sit well, it doesn't leave one peaceful. Boche talked a lot to me then. He was nervous, desperate, and said, "I'm thinking of going," and "This whole thing is fucked." And that afternoon I knew he had taken the money. He sold himself. The managers sent them to the United States.

I heard later they came back and some people saw Boche around, very sad. If he'd stayed as a leader maybe he would have been killed, but he should have finished his period in the executive committee and then become a base member, which is less dangerous.[5]

González thought that Jesús Boche should have risked his life for the union, but González and others were not unsympathetic to Jesús Boche and Martínez Campos. They were weak, not wicked, men who yielded to the quintessential evil, money, and abandoned STEGAC without trying to damage it.

This was not true of the next two leaders who left the union. Father Solano's continued presence had, in the end, served Coca-Cola's purpose. He had befriended salesmen Rolando Maldonado and Efraín Zamora, STEGAC executive committee members since 1975, who in early 1978 traveled to Costa Rica and studied at Solano's center. In September 1978 they were promoted —Zamora became manager of industrial relations—and they launched the Coca-Cola Employees' Association, a "nonunion employees' group" to rival STEGAC. Mechanic Pablo Telón called them "men without culture or religious principles, only interested in money." Production worker Mercedes Gómez dismissed them with a snap of his fingers: "They passed over to evil, just like that."[6]

Following the October 1978 uprising, threats against trade unionists and kidnappings in the city more than doubled, and the union's legal advisers, Marta Gloria and Enrique Torres, were forced into exile. Although 250 out of 350 Coca-Cola workers still belonged to the union, fewer and fewer attended union meetings or citywide demonstrations.

Committed STEGAC members criticized workers who withdrew from union activities in strong terms. Typically, the union newspaper editorialized:

What's happening, you with hair on your chest? Do you think trade unionists fanatics with their meetings, strikes, demonstrations? They aren't! It isn't fanaticism that we struggle for a better life, nor is it fanaticism that the leaders spend all their time and sacrifice so that others get good treatment in the company. Everyone talks about the Coke union— how daring, valiant, disciplined and so on. This image is deteriorating, we are showing indifference to others—egotism, cowardice and indiscipline. Egotism? Yes, even though the word is ugly.

It fits to ask, *why did Christ come to the world?* He died to revolutionize human consciousness; why can't we follow in his footsteps? He came to tell the world to love thy neighbor as thyself. *Are we doing this?* When a person is killed for defending the dispossessed and one is invited to protest and we don't, is it because this man is not our neighbor? . . . God made us men; we must set aside cowardice and fight so that our children are not exploited.[7]

In a language influenced by pastoral agents of Liberation Theology who called Christ a revolutionary, the editorial urged that Coca-Cola workers walk in the footsteps of a man who loved, sacrificed, opposed egotism, and fought in the name of the future, and it challenged them to be "real men." The STEGAC newspaper also invoked the example of David, who could "take on any mountain of Goliaths," and it published poems by workers that were Brechtian in their insistence on individual responsibility, decision, and action. One, entitled "I'm Against *But*," read in part:

> I'm against the sufferings of the people
> but I'm against the people who suffer and do nothing to prevent that. . . .
> I'm against inflation
> but I'm against the consumer who accepts without protest.[8]

The union's newspaper and its leaflets repeated this theme: No matter what the circumstances or the consequences, the victim must master life and change it.

Yet as tough as this language was, STEGAC activists were too shrewd to think that the world was truly divided between those who stood up to oppression once and forever and those who did not, and they were far too modest to believe that *they* were Christ or David. And as macho as their appeal to other workers was, no evidence suggests that trade unionists were compelled simply by machismo. They thought that the path they had chosen as activists was praiseworthy and righteous, but they followed it out of humility, not arrogance. Their language of persuasion affirmed a trade unionism that required workers to sacrifice their personal safety and ambitions for the good of others.

By late 1978 the trade unionists at Coca-Cola were marked men and women. John Trotter personally told the union's secretary general, Pedro Quevedo, and executive committee member Israel Márquez that he would have them killed. On December 12, as Quevedo sat in his delivery truck in Zone 1 bent over his records, waiting for his helpers, four men fired through the windows into his face from both sides of the truck.[9] Waked in the CNT office, thirty-seven-year-old Quevedo was declared the "First Martyr of STEGAC." His funeral procession was tense and silent, as grim union members took turns bearing his coffin through the streets to the General Cemetery. Production worker Hugo Aparicio, a thirty-year-old native of the western highlands department of Quetzaltenango, vowed "never to take a step backwards."[10] After Quevedo's death, all STEGAC communiqués ended with the sentence, "The proletarian example of Pedro Quevedo pushes forward our struggle against exploitation."

Coca-Cola workers, however, were frightened; and as real as the union's tough language was, it hid the compassion workers felt toward one another. All STEGAC's executive committee members received death threats. Pablo Telón, a mechanic from the town of Mazatenango on the southern coast, resigned from the executive committee, to which he had recently been elected. He explained why:

> I got a letter and I knew immediately what it was since I never got letters and no one but the company had my address. I thought to myself, "This is a death threat."
>
> So I changed my clothes and took the letter and left the house to open it so no one would know. I went out to a field in Zone 12, sat in the middle of it and opened the letter, which told me not to get further involved.
>
> Right after Pedro was killed, I went to the union and said, "Look, I've completed part of my term, but I have to leave the leadership because the same thing will happen to me." They said, "What! Are you leaving the union?" I said no, I would never leave the union, just the leadership. I explained the whole thing to a General Assembly meeting. Everyone took it well, they understood the reality.[11]

Everyone understood that no one wanted to die or see the union crushed, but then what if it was one thing or the other?

Secretary general Israel Márquez neither sought martyrdom nor forsook the union to protect his life: he avoided four murder attempts. In late October 1978, he saved his life by dropping to the floor when his car was machine-gunned. Shortly afterward, attackers tried to kidnap him in a market, but he struggled loose and dashed away. On the morning of January 15, 1979, when police surrounded him as he entered work, he ran through the legs of one of them and escaped onto the back of a coworker's motorcycle. A detective pursued them, firing shots, but when his car stalled Márquez jumped into a Coca-Cola truck whose driver had followed the motorcycle. A week later EGSA published a full-page advertisement stating that Márquez was a thief and an international agitator. The next day, January 23, armed men went to his home, not knowing that Márquez had just sublet it, killed the new tenant, Antonio Moscoso Zaldana, and seriously wounded his new bride. Completely shaken by feelings of responsibility for the destruction of others' lives and worried about his family, Márquez sought asylum in the Venezuelan embassy, where he remained with his wife and small daughter until Costa Rica received them one month later.[12]

Maintenance worker Gregorio González observed that "Israel's leaving gave us great sadness, but his life was worth more because he continued to support us from abroad. He didn't become a life-dead as Quevedo had, where the ideas live but the person does not."[13] Márquez was alive in body and spirit, Quevedo was alive in spirit, saved by the union from "death-death," the extirpation of the spirit that results from the historical amnesia that makes people disappear in a way that kidnappers never can.

STEGAC transformed Márquez's departure into the arrival of a new stage of the union's history. A lengthy ritual of separation, signifying the opposite, ensued. The day before Márquez entered the embassy, he went to the Coca-Cola plant for the last time and spoke individually to his friends, urging them to remain in the struggle. From the embassy he sent an "Open Letter to the Union":

I hope you understand that this [seeking asylum] is not only being done for my personal safety but for others as well. I want to re-emphasize that a union is not composed of a single person or an executive committee. *Rather, the union is all of us and each has a responsibility to it.* The union does not exist because it is legally recognized but because it represents the will of the workers. . . . It is clear to me that the union will never be destroyed. I have taken all the risks and, with a calmness, am awaiting whatever will happen to me, satisfied that our cause is just and our duty, for those who consider themselves Christians, is not just to speak of God and Christ, but to put their words into practice every moment of their lives, demonstrating through deeds the love we feel for those near us. If not, all be hypocrisy and falsehood.[14]

With no way of gauging the severity of the repression in the coming months, Márquez addressed his fellow workers as Christians who must put God's and Christ's "words into practice every moment of their lives" or be guilty of hypocrisy. Eschewing concern for personal safety as his sole criterion for action, he implied that he would not have left Guatemala had it not been for Moscoso Zaldana's murder and explained his own actions before his departure as "awaiting whatever will happen to me, satisfied that our cause is just."

In turn, the union's executive committee wrote an "Open Letter to Israel Márquez" stating: "We won't say good-bye because we know your class consciousness and the pain that our people suffer will not let you be long from us. The experience you have had cannot be forgotten. See you soon, compañero Israel Márquez, your example and our consciousness impel us to continue the struggle that you and compañero *Pedro Quevedo* started. The union is on its feet and so it shall remain."[15] Márquez's replacement as secretary general, Manuel López Balam, a thirty-two-year-old salesman of Maya Indian descent, went to the Venezuelan embassy and gave Márquez the letter and a certificate of honor reading, "Award of Merit for your Union Activity. To Israel, for your honesty and humility." STEGAC's General Assembly also passed a resolution "voting confidence in Israel Márquez. We workers of Coca-Cola have demonstrated our militancy, honor and valor. *Our dignity will not be sold at any price.*"[16]

Prepared for the historical record, these letters and declarations were sent to, and published by, the major dailies. These rituals incorporated the dead Quevedo and the exiled Márquez into the community that now composed the union. Death and exile, which were the price of confrontation with John Trotter and the state, became part of the bonds of solidarity between workers. After Quevedo's assassination and Márquez's exile, the union came to represent and to protect, in addition to workers' immediate interests, the grandeur of Quevedo's and Márquez's lives and sacrifices.

By the time Márquez left Guatemala at the beginning of 1979, the situation within the Coca-Cola plant had worsened, as it had nationally. In late 1978 EGSA had militarized management by hiring four army lieutenants. The new director of personnel, Juan Francisco Rodas, had graduated from the army's officer school, Escuela Politécnica, and then trained as a special forces member in Panama. Rumored to have ties with army intelligence and a death squad named the Secret Anti-Communist Army, he was also a former chief of security for General Romero Lucas García. After his arrival, terror pervaded daily life. Throughout January 1979, armed men in jeeps without license plates intermittently circled the Coca-Cola plant and on many occasions workers slept inside, fearing for their lives if they stepped outside.

In early 1979—indeed, the moment Márquez entered the Venezuelan embassy—the company vigorously promoted the Employees' Association organized by former STEGAC executive committee members Zamora and Maldonado. EGSA obliged almost all new workers to sign membership cards and paid them Q3.50 a day instead of Q2.50, the average daily wage won by STEGAC. The association started a savings and loan plan whereby EGSA matched the Q5 that workers deposited in the fund monthly. It offered scraps of the "good life," sponsoring buffet suppers in first-class hotels, where, according to one former member, "it was like a group of savages assaulting the hotel. Workers weren't used to this. Everyone ate from these long tables loaded with turkey, fish, apple pie and a mixed salad as if they had never eaten."[17] The Employees' Association was not only furthered by the obvious access to funds, but it had the state's blessings as well. Because it had no legal status, Interior Minister Donald Alvarez Ruiz invented a special one, and Labor Minister Carlos Monsanto Alarcón arranged for the formal signing of a "pact of good intentions" between the association and EGSA at a cocktail party.[18] Within a few months the majority of workers belonged to the association, which had come to dominate the sales department.

The Employees' Association was not a union: it had no bargaining power, and workers joined it because they were threatened with losing their jobs if they did not. Within two years the association would appear as a transparent fraud; for example, workers never again saw the money that they had deposited in the savings and loan fund managed by the association's leaders. The Employees' Association was STEGAC's antithesis; it rested on fear and the hope that the company would simply give workers what they needed. The fight for a living wage, initially a reason for joining STEGAC, was now cause to leave it. Although the union had the legal power to negotiate, it could guarantee absolutely nothing but trouble. The contract signed in early 1978 had already been violated on twenty-six counts.

The Small Moral Community

STEGAC remained, a union of dwindling members. In early 1979, 182 workers belonged, compared to 250 in September 1978. Few wanted to be leaders. The executive committee previously consisted of nine members; in late 1978, when Márquez had replaced Quevedo as secretary general, the other members were Efraín Zamora, Rolando Maldonado, and Manuel López Balam from sales; Víctor Burgos and Pablo Telón from mechanics; and two production workers. By early 1979, Telón and Burgos had quit in response to death threats, Zamora and Maldonado had betrayed STEGAC, Quevedo was dead, and Márquez had left. New leaders were elected without competition. With Manuel López Balam reelected as secretary general, they included Pedro Quevedo's brother Luis, who was soon fired by the company; maintenance worker Gregorio González; production workers Hugo Aparicio, Florentine Gómez, and Ismael Vásquez; warehouse worker Marlon Mendizábal; and one other, who resigned the next morning after a family dispute. Production worker Mercedes Gómez replaced him after several other nominees declined to serve.

The union had produced many local leaders, but the word *leader* is too charged in its general usage with a sense of professionalism and differentiation from membership to well express the character of most of the men who had been on STEGAC's executive committee since 1975. No executive committee members were atypical of the rank-and-file members except for Israel Márquez, whose participation in the Mormons was exceptional, and Pedro Quevedo, whose past as a military man was unusual. The men on the 1978 executive committee, like the majority of their predecessors and like Coca-Cola workers generally, were in their twenties and thirties, married, Catholic, and from both ladino and Indian and rural and urban backgrounds. They had grown up working to support families whose lives always verged on disaster, and few had finished primary school. None had experience directing an organization except for one member who had once led a church choir. Eloquent conversationalists and imaginative storytellers, few of them ever read or wrote, even if they were literate. These were self-effacing, religious men: Gregorio González recalled that when he was chosen to be on the executive committee he did not think about his own safety until the next morning, "And then I did, and I thought, 'Why had I given myself such problems?' But I kept thinking and decided with God's blessing I could not go backward. I was so angry about Márquez and Quevedo."[19]

What did distinguish the 1978 leadership were the large proportion of executive committee members of Maya Indian descent and the fact that most of the members were from the production division; this was a reversal of 1975, when salesmen predominated. It was the lower-paid and more-discriminated-against workers who came forward when the situation worsened at the end of the 1970s, more so than did salesmen, who sometimes had illusions about social mobility that could destroy their class loyalties, as demonstrated by the actions of Efraín Zamora and Rolando Maldonado.

In January 1979 the 182 STEGAC affiliates signed a statement, published as a full-page newspaper advertisement, contrasting STEGAC with the Employees' Association: "We were born under strong repression, together we have spent 600 days in jail. . . . Our compañero and Martyr Pedro Quevedo was imprisoned three times. Despite this we continue as an important and unified group. . . . And we do not get the 'prizes' 'good' workers do. They go to orgies at expensive hotels, they are offered houses, land and other things."[20] The union responded repeatedly to the company's strategy of tearing apart some workers' lives at the same time that it thrust commodities into other workers' faces.

When, in March, the Employees' Association started planning a June fair called the "First Great Family Bazaar," it offended every principle for which STEGAC stood. What family was this? EGSA gave points to salesmen for cases of soda sold and the highest scorers were to receive luxurious gifts—electric stoves, refrigerators—at the bazaar. Prizes for what? Secretary General López Balam tried to prevent the bazaar, tearing down its publicity posters and engaging Zamora and Maldonado in loud public quarrels about the ethics of a "family bazaar" at EGSA.

A guilt-ridden Maldonado warned López Balam in late March that he would be killed in a week's time, but the union leader did not go into hiding. On April 5 López Balam was inside a corner store in Zone 6 assisting his helpers as they hauled crates when two strangers entered and greeted him. As he exited they grabbed him, beat him with a lead pipe, and slit his throat. Detectives arrested López Balam's father after his son's murder and held him for days without charge. Twenty-two-year-old Marlon Mendizábal, who hailed from Chiquimula, replaced López Balam as secretary general. Reportedly, plain-clothesmen visited Mendizábal's home and showed him a list of the names and addresses of close relatives. "Don't be foolish," they said, "Remember torture is extremely painful. Are you aware of the methods?"[21] A part of an optimistic generation that had fought in the streets of Guatemala City in the October 1978 uprising, and a believer in the imminence of a new future in his workplace, in his country, and in the region, Mendizábal did not resign.

The Great Family Bazaar was held in June. Its real theme was preservation of self and family: if you were a trade unionist, you would die and your father might be jailed or worse; if you belonged to the Employees' Association, you and your children would receive gifts and life would be intact. Dozens of fathers brought their wives and children to see magicians, acrobats, clowns, and a ventriloquist under a huge banner reading, "Everyone Depends on Everyone." A STEGAC press release attacked this harmony as perverse, asking with whom, not with what, the children of Quevedo and López Balam would play.

The union designated 1979 the "Year of the Cowardly Murder of López Balam." The union condemned everyone in the Employees' Association, and above all leaders Zamora and Maldonado, for López Balam's death. In the mid-1970s commitment to STEGAC had meant "with the workers and against EGSA," the plain "them and us." Now it meant "with one group of workers, against another group of workers, as well as against the company and the state."[22] On May 1, 1979, STEGAC's one-story banner displayed only ugly depictions of salesmen Zamora and Maldonado over the words, "Murderers" and "Assassins."

Growing International Pressure

In the meantime, as the violence continued so did international interest.[23] After Quevedo's death, Coca-Cola's religious shareholders reengaged, and the Interfaith Center on Corporate Responsibility publicized events and made the murders of Quevedo and López Balam important news in progressive international religious circles. In its effort to build a broader campaign against Trotter, ICCR contacted Laurent Enckell, the U.S. representative of the Geneva-based International Union of Food and Allied Workers' Associations (IUF). In addition, Israel Márquez, a passionate and effective STEGAC spokesperson in exile, talked to everyone who would listen, including Enckell, who spoke to other IUF officials. In May 1979, shortly after López Balam's death, the Sisters of Providence brought Márquez to Atlanta, where, at a shareholders' meeting, they presented their resolution that Coca-Cola establish a permanent labor code for all franchises. Márquez and the Sisters won little support among shareholders, but the case received more notoriety.[24] Ohio Congressman Donald Pease wrote to President Jimmy Carter, Jack Anderson mentioned it in a column, the State Department opened an investigation, and, as a result, the embarrassed U.S. ambassador to Guatemala called Trotter to express his dismay and emphasize that U.S. foreign policy included respect for human rights. Trotter responded to the effect that President Carter was a Communist.[25]

As the public debate grew, support for STEGAC operated on two complementary fronts: the international IUF emphasized class solidarity and workers' rights, and Amnesty International and other groups such as ICCR talked of human rights. In July 1979, after STEGAC member Silverio Vásquez barely escaped assassination, the International Union of Food and Allied Workers' Associations joined in a letter-writing campaign with human rights groups, and in August IUF secretary Dan Gallin participated in an Amnesty International–sponsored trip to Guatemala. This was a turning point in STEGAC's history. Gallin met with the union's besieged leaders, whom he felt were extraordinary.

By 1979 Guatemalan unions were among the most isolated unions in the hemisphere because they had rebelled against the strongest continental organizations, the Christian Democratic CLAT and the AFL-CIO's ORIT. Yet suddenly, because an international third camp existed, the Coca-Cola workers' union attracted more attention than any single union in Latin America. IUF, a social democratic international formed in Europe in the 1920s as a centrist alternative to right-wing and Communist groups, had entered Latin America in the 1960s. It competed with CLAT to affiliate unions that were neither radical nor conservative, and its interest in Guatemala was part of a drive to gain status and affiliates where CLAT was losing influence.

In December 1979 IUF joined with human rights groups and the Guatemalan Social Democratic party-in-exile to call for an international boycott of tourism to Guatemala, which by 1979 had become a world symbol of human rights abuses. As the boycott was announced, IUF also arranged a meeting in Atlanta attended by Gallin, Atlanta Coca-Cola officials, Israel Márquez, former STEGAC lawyer Enrique Torres, representatives of the Interfaith Center on Corporate Responsibility, Amnesty International, and several AFL-CIO unions. At this meeting, Gallin demanded that the licensing agreement with Trotter be canceled immediately. Technically Gallin had no jurisdiction because STEGAC was not yet an affiliate of IUF or the AFL-CIO, but he had the power of a trade union international supported by world human rights agencies. When Coca-Cola officials replied that they could do nothing, IUF asked its 160 affiliates in 56 countries to "take actions—consumer boycotts, publicity campaigns, industrial actions."[26] To prevent this, corporate heads in Atlanta had the manager of the Swedish franchise hint to IUF director Sigvard Nystrom that the corporation would end its agreement with Trotter in 1981. They also approached the religious stockholders with the same information, asking them to use their influence to stop IUF's campaign, which the stockholders refused to do. For the first time in its history, Atlanta Coca-Cola faced an international union. The company obviously did not want IUF as a party to a settlement, a precedent with repercussions for Coca-Cola and other multinationals and one that contained the seeds of a new style of international working-class power against multinationals. Meanwhile, IUF affiliates publicized the case. This news reached STEGAC and encouraged it to persist.

The Labyrinth of Death

By early 1980, only sixty-six workers remained in the union and over two hundred belonged to the Employees' Association. Many association members were both sympathetic to STEGAC and frightened. Evert Soto, a young man from the southern coast who had started at Coca-Cola in late 1978, felt compelled to join the association, but he attended the funerals of Quevedo and López Balam. He was nervous that his friendships with union people might hurt him and although he did not end them, he did not enter the union. In any case, STEGAC now operated as a secret society and was inaccessible to most workers; it met in secret and was not even admitting new members. Soto knew about the union only because he had played soccer with López Balam and his successor Marlon Mendizábal.[27] Rodolfo Robles, who had entered Coca-Cola as a salesman in July 1979 and joined the Employees' Association, "could not form an opinion about STEGAC" because it had no presence in the sales department. When Robles approached Gregorio González about joining, Gonzalez said no, that no one could anymore.[28] Marco Tulio Loza was the sole exception. At nineteen he was an excellent soccer player who was courted both by the union's team, its only public expression by this time, and by the company's. EGSA did not fire him when he steadfastly refused to join the Employees' Association, and the union signed him up.[29]

Clandestine—except for its soccer team—and inspired by the promise of revolution in Central America, the union's self-presentation became even more defiant. In early 1980 STEGAC responded to the murder of union member Armando Sánchez, and to Trotter's refusal to renegotiate the 1978 contract,

with this declaration: "We are prepared to fight with our fingernails if necessary to defend the union, cost what it may to whomever. With the militant
example of our Martyrs, Pedro Quevedo and López Balam, we will continue
until we are where we can live. Now with the heroic example of the Nicaraguan
people, nothing can stop us." [30]

The fact was that the union was trapped. STEGAC could not protect workers' lives or defend them at the shop level. It could only report the endless
violations of the national Labor Code and its own contract to the Labor Ministry and then sit by while the ministry did nothing. By now military police
patrolled inside the plant. Mercedes Gómez recalled that the first months of
1980 were "very painful. We were very damaged internally. There was a great
fear everything would stop." In early March the union decided to "make a
campaign for May First, to have a strong presence with statements, leaflets,
banners." [31]

On April 14, within weeks of May First, management suddenly dismissed
twenty-eight of the remaining sixty-six union members. The twenty-eight fired
workers were then followed and their homes were watched; on April 24 one of
them survived a murder attempt after he was shot in the stomach and left for
dead. Mercedes Gómez recalled that by the end of April, the union members
who had not been fired would meet secretly with the others and that "many
would say they could not take it anymore and they left"; by the time of the
May First demonstration, the union was "stunned." At the rally itself, thirty-six
demonstrators were kidnapped. Gómez described May First and its aftermath:

> We thought we had things well controlled. We went as a group divided
> into small subgroups, with members of the executive committee in charge
> of each. When we met after the march to count, someone comes in and
> says Gómez and García [Arnulfo Gómez and Ricardo García, two young
> union members] were missing! We went looking everywhere for them.
> Then someone came and said that he saw the police grab them, so we just
> said, "Let's see what God does."
>
> The next day Arnulfo Gómez was found in Iztapa [a town on the Pacific
> Coast several hours from the capital]. They left him dead where he was

born. They could only have found out where he was born from the company. García turned up in Chiquimulilla [also in the south and several hours from the capital], his hometown. The thing was even García's uncle couldn't recognize him because he was so disfigured from tortures.

I went to Iztapa on behalf of the union to see after Gómez. They had taken out his tongue. In that instant, when I first saw him, I was completely cold. I couldn't think. I wrote everything down. Ismael Vásquez and I went. They had cut his lips with a razor, like a pineapple is sliced. His teeth were broken. His fingernails had been pulled out and they broke his fingers and arms.

I became infuriated in a way I can't put into words. All these people died, and I can't explain why, but that gave me the will to continue.[32]

Death propelled events. On May 14, unknown persons killed Efraín Zamora, head of the Employees' Association and former leader of STEGAC. After Zamora's death, plateless cars were frequently seen in front of the plant, and workers urged Secretary General Marlon Mendizábal either to sleep inside or not go to work. On May 27, three women appeared at the plant gate asking to see Mendizábal. He was sitting in the cafeteria, joking with mechanic Pablo Telón. When he heard that three women were looking for him, he laughed and got up. In any case, he soon had to go downtown for a CNT meeting. He went to the gate. Not seeing anyone waiting, he walked out into the street. Pablo Telón said, "Then we heard plah . . . plah . . . plah . . . I couldn't even get up. I knew."[33] Mercedes Gómez ran through the gate: "A compañero was running down the street, shouting, 'Sons of whores, they just killed Marlon.' I went over and the Fire Department was already there. Everything was strange. I became violent, and threw myself at the firemen. Marlon dead and right next to the plant! That day no one left the plant. We all stayed inside."[34]

Association member Evert Soto described the funeral: "It was the third I'd attended. About 300 of us went by bus to Chiquimula, his hometown, where he was buried. And all the unknown men were there as well, watching us. We demonstrated at the burial site, yelling and demanding the responsible be punished. This is what happens; one leaves one's compañeros in the cemetery and returns back to the plant, not knowing what to do or say, with anger and frustration because one can do nothing about these deaths. One is lost."[35]

Mendizábal's funeral drew other members of the Employees' Association, which started to come apart as a consequence of the May First assassinations and his murder. Mendizábal's death also prompted Atlanta Coca-Cola to send Ted Circuit, a Mexico City–based Coca-Cola representative with the title "Head of Coca-Cola Export for Northern Latin America," to Guatemala, where he publicly offered money for information leading to the apprehension of suspects. STEGAC could do nothing about Mendizábal. It continued to negotiate with the Labor Ministry for the jobs of the twenty-eight workers who had been fired. At this point, five men constituted the union leadership: Florentine Gómez, Ismael Vásquez, Mercedes Gómez, Gregorio González, and Hugo Aparicio.

Then on June 19, the Rebel Armed Forces killed EGSA's personnel manager, Juan Francisco Rodas. An Employees' Association member who attended Rodas's wake on the night of June 20 overheard Rodas's bodyguard, whom the workers had dubbed "Superman," swear vengeance against Mercedes Gómez and vow "to get," if not Gómez, someone. Horrified at the thought of more killings, the association member tried to warn union members, but events moved too quickly. Gómez described what followed:

I was working that night [June 20] on the forklift in the warehouse with René Aldana [a twenty-one-year-old warehouse worker and STEGAC member]. His machine broke, so we were taking turns on mine while one of us would nap. A lot of guys hadn't come in to work because they were frightened something would happen.

Superman and some others entered the grounds after midnight, and someone told us and said that they were drunk, so watch out. I felt nervous because I was the only one on the executive committee there. But Aldana and I kept working and napping, and while I slept he wore my cap because he had none, and it was very cold.

I had gone to sleep in a little side room at around 4:00 A.M. and next thing I knew all these people came rushing in, "Papito!," hugging and kissing me, "You are alright! We heard three shots, and the forklift is still on but you weren't there, we thought you were dead."

I yelled for Olímpico [Aldana's nickname] and went running into the warehouse. He wasn't there. I took a lead pipe and went outside.

I walked around. There is this little shack near the mechanics' workshop, and there I saw fresh blood and I touched it. It was still warm. Then I saw bullet holes in the wall. But there was no body. I went back to the warehouse and said, "They've killed him and taken him somewhere."

We talked to the night watchmen and they said Superman and the others had just driven out, so we figured they killed him and then put him in the trunk of their car and drove him out that way.

This was at about 5:00 A.M. At 6:00 people began coming in to work and we told them, and everyone started looking in the ravines and ditches. And then a group found his body behind a church a few blocks from here.

Gómez continued to relate the events of the same day, the dawn of which had witnessed Aldana's death. This was the Saturday, June 21, when twenty-seven trade unionists, including STEGAC executive members Florentine Gómez and Ismael Vásquez, were kidnapped from the CNT office in downtown Guatemala City by seventy plainclothesmen. Gómez said:

There was a meeting that day at the CNT office and I was supposed to go to it. I couldn't. [Gregorio] González and I went to Aldana's home to tell his family. They blamed me. They said, "They were after you and they got René instead." He was 20 or 21.

I felt sick. Florentine [Gómez] said that if I didn't go to the CNT meeting, he and Ismael [Vásquez] had to go. So I said, yes, they could, but I wasn't going, another day yes, but that day no. Something very strong held me back.

I went home. I got a hold of my wife and told her to take the children away. I went to my cousin's house. He had the radio on, and in the late afternoon, I heard that the CNT office had been surrounded and everyone taken. Twice in one day, I was not killed.

I felt dead. I went to González's house and then Aparicio's. [Gómez, González, and Aparicio were now the surviving members of the executive committee.] What to do? We started mobilizing again to search—morgues, hospitals. And we decided that on Monday nothing would move in that plant.

Coca-Cola was one of eight factories that workers struck on Monday, June 23, to protest the June 21 kidnappings. Gómez described what happened at the plant:

> We went in Monday and we said, *"Nothing moves here."* We said that no one should leave until the compañeros were found. Maybe we were menacing but that's what was necessary.
>
> We said, "We know there are many servile people here but to forget the compañeros is sin. It is blood which is running for the welfare of your families. Here is where you must have your moment of consciousness, *Now!"* Nobody said anything, no one objected.
>
> For nine days we were like this, coming in to work and not working, reading newspapers, telling jokes, but not working. We formed a secret leadership group of substitutes, so that when the three of us were killed there would be more left. There was the idea of taking the managers as hostages for Florentine and Ismael but we opposed this, we were legal. We came in every morning and punched our cards. We weren't subversives, we were legal.[36]

Gregorio González recounted how, after the workers had struck for nine days, "about two hundred detectives came, like an army. They threw us on the ground, faces down, like some of those western movies you have in your country where they massacre people." The heavily armed detectives "stuck bayonets against our brains" and threatened to kill workers unless they stood up to work, which the majority did. González rushed to shut the gate to the plant and stood in front of it, almost in tears, until a group of union members convinced him that unless "the base" was willing to continue, it was suicidal to persist.[37] González happened to be the only union executive committee member at the plant on the last day of the strike because, as chance would have it, on that day the Labor Ministry heard the case of the twenty-eight fired on April 14, and Mercedes Gómez and Hugo Aparicio attended the hearing.

Gómez and Aparicio spent the final day of the strike called to protest the kidnapping of twenty-seven trade unionists in the offices of the Labor Ministry seeking the reinstatement of the twenty-eight workers fired from EGSA back in April, because, as Gómez put it, "we were legal." That day, as the entire Coca-Cola work force lay beneath drawn bayonets, the Labor Ministry agreed to reinstate the fired workers. Neither by definition nor by practice a revolutionary organization, STEGAC faced war, not conflict, with a state that upheld the labor law on the same day that it threatened to murder every worker at Coca-Cola.

Meanwhile, the violence had continued to keep IUF and Atlanta Coca-Cola in motion. In April, when the twenty-eight EGSA workers were fired, the IUF affiliate, Australian Federated Liquor and Allied Industries Employees' Union, held work stoppages in several Coca-Cola bottling plants. In addition, hundreds of protest letters from European unions arrived in Atlanta. Afraid of an international consumer boycott and of solidarity strikes, Atlanta Coca-Cola sought—four days after Gómez and García were killed on May 1— a buyer for the EGSA franchise over Trotter's objections. When John Kirby, head of the Mexican Coca-Cola franchise, expressed an interest, Ted Circuit, Atlanta Coca-Cola's sales representative in Latin America, started negotiations in Costa Rica between Kirby and Israel Márquez, STEGAC's representative.

Apparently Trotter used the escalation of violence as a form of price negotiation or as a way of preventing the plant's sale, or both. The faster Atlanta Coca-Cola wanted to sell, the more Trotter demanded and the harder it was to find a buyer. After the May 1 deaths and the growth of the consumer boycott initiated by IUF affiliates, Trotter demanded $10 million, far more than Circuit felt the plant was worth. After the May 14 murder of Efraín Zamora, Kirby withdrew a bid out of fear, and Circuit could find no new potential buyer. Alarmed,

Circuit called a meeting with representatives of IUF and Marta Gloria Torres, STEGAC's legal adviser in exile, to bargain for time. But IUF would not call off the growing boycott. By the end of May, hotel and restaurant workers in Spain were refusing to serve Coca-Cola. At the end of June, after the murder of René Aldana and the kidnapping of the twenty-seven workers from CNT, and during the nine-day strike, Circuit flew to Guatemala to make a proposal directly to STEGAC. He checked into the luxurious Camino Real Hotel on the Avenida de la Reforma in Zone 10 and telephoned the plant. Hugo Aparicio remembered this well:

He telephoned ten times the first day. He wanted me to go over to the Camino Real but I didn't want to meet with him at his hotel because the problem was not in the Camino Real, it was in the plant. I told him to come here, which he would not do.

The second day he called and said that he couldn't come to the plant because he was afraid he'd be killed, which you can see is absurd because the workers here are very well behaved, very civilized.

The third day he sent a taxicab to the plant but we let the taxi go without getting in. We met again, however, and decided to go to the hotel but not in his taxi. We went. He was sitting by the swimming pool wearing a false mustache, a wig and sunglasses. Maybe he thought Trotter was going to kill him.

He made this offer to buy a piece of land and all the Coke workers could go over there and build a building and he would put machines in it. Then when Trotter's contract ended, Coke would cut him off and sell the formula to the new plant.

This sounded strange and without guarantee, so we said no on the spot. He said he would be in Guatemala, at the Camino Real, for six more hours and we could call him or we could call at any time collect in Mexico. And he gave us this little card with his name and telephone number and his secretary's name and telephone number.

We went back to the plant, met with the members, and everyone said no. We called him at the Camino Real and told him the base's reaction, and he left the country in despair because he had come to resolve the situation in a way which suited him and he couldn't.[38]

However small and battered, STEGAC was astoundingly firm and effective. Although only a minority of the work force belonged to it, it had won the re-hiring of the fired workers, led a nine-day illegal plantwide strike, and gained potent international support. Furthermore, the Employees' Association had been unable to supplant it or command a following: when management tried to capitalize on the rehiring of the twenty-eight fired employees by asking workers to sign a statement saying that the problems at EGSA were over, all workers, including association members, declined.

Gómez, González, and Aparicio nevertheless felt demoralized by the different levels of commitment within the union. They thought that everything rested on their shoulders, and that if the union depended only on them, it was not worth holding together; "no real group consists of three leaders," said Gómez. The three men made a pact that they would resign and effectively end the union's "active" status with the Labor Ministry if more people were not willing to serve on the executive committee.

The evening the nine-day strike ended they called a General Assembly to inform the membership that the case of the fired workers had been solved, that they personally would continue to search for the missing twenty-seven trade unionists kidnapped from CNT, "even if it took us to the secret cells," and that more workers must be prepared to join the executive committee at the next meeting, which they scheduled for July 5. According to Gómez:

> The saddest thing for us was the July 5 meeting because no one wanted to be on the executive committee. There were sixty there. We said that we'd continue if others joined us. We said that we wouldn't be martyrs or heroes and we'd give up if that's what the membership wanted. People said things like, "Oh, I have a child, I can't," or, "I love my wife so. She's young. I can't do that to her."
>
> We said, "What do you think we are, *mules*? Didn't we have wives and

Crucial to the Coca-Cola union's survival in 1980, Gregorio González (*left*) and Mercedes Gómez choose to be photographed in 1993 in front of a mural of assassinated union executive committee members (*left to right*) Pedro Quevedo, Manuel López Balam, and Marlon Mendizábal. (Photograph by the author)

children?" So three finally accepted but one resigned the next day. He said, "My wife." They all thought that we were cadavers. As you can see, I am not.

Another finally agreed. These three were new, young. They didn't even know how to read and write but they accepted.[39]

The Change in Franchise Ownership

At this moment, when STEGAC would have died legally if three new, young, illiterate production workers had not accepted leadership posts, Atlanta Coca-Cola, under tremendous strain, sold the plant. By then, over seven hundred newspapers around the world had covered some aspect of the STEGAC-EGSA conflict. The slogan that STEGAC had invented in 1979, "Coca-Cola has the flavor of blood," appeared in dozens of languages on stickers and posters urging consumers not to buy the soft drink. In July 1980 the world's largest trade union body, the International Conference of Federated Trade Unions (ICFTU), to which the AFL-CIO, ORIT, and IUF belonged, issued a statement supporting a tourism boycott and requested that the International Labor Organization, the United Nations, and the Organization of American States pressure the Guatemalan government. AFL-CIO head Lane Kirkland stated at a press conference in Sweden that U.S. workers were being asked not to drink Coca-Cola, and Douglas Frazier, of the United Auto Workers, wrote letters to congressmen. Letters and telegrams flooded the National Palace in Guatemala City. By late July, IUF affiliates in Australia, Belgium, Denmark, Finland, Holland, New Zealand, the Philippines, and Sweden were boycotting Coca-Cola and planning work stoppages. Non-IUF and IUF unions in Argentina, Bermuda, Canada, Colombia, West Germany, Honduras, Iceland, Israel, Italy, Japan, Mexico, Peru, Singapore, Sri Lanka, and the United Kingdom were calling for a consumer boycott. Venezuelan food and hotel workers struck for fifteen minutes in solidarity, hotel workers in France banned Coca-Cola in workers' canteens, and beverage workers in Mexico staged a support demonstration.[40] The sale of the plant was achieved by the international labor movement and sixty-three Guatemalan workers.

By August, Circuit had found two buyers, Anthony Zash and Roberto Méndez y Méndez. Zash had worked for both Pepsi-Cola and Coca-Cola in Latin America and had managed the Central American Division of Pepsi International with offices in Guatemala City. Méndez had replaced Zash in that job, later moving on to oversee the twenty-three Coca-Cola franchises and five company-owned plants in Bolivia, Brazil, and Peru. Both were experienced soft drink businessmen and personal friends of Ted Circuit. In September representatives of Atlanta Coca-Cola, Zash, and Méndez met with officials of IUF, with which STEGAC now affiliated, in Mexico City. There it was agreed that (1) Atlanta Coca-Cola would oversee the operations and the new managers for five years, (2) EGSA would guarantee STEGAC's union rights and dissolve the Employees' Association, (3) EGSA would establish a fund for the "martyrs' widows and children," (4) communication would be maintained between the four parties, EGSA, Atlanta Coca-Cola, IUF, and STEGAC, and (5) the new owners would intervene with Guatemalan authorities to ensure peace in the plant and with this aim visit the president and the labor minister.

The most important issue for both the union and Zash and Méndez in further negotiations, which began in November, was the dismissal of over seventy workers. Trotter had overstaffed the plant with nonunion workers at a time when sales were dropping, as a result of the spontaneous boycott of Coca-Cola in EGSA's primary market, the city. Zash and Méndez wanted the excess number dismissed, and STEGAC wanted antiunion workers out. Mercedes Gómez explained that this was "our vengeance, our way of punishing those who had been first in the union, and then later the Association, and hence were to blame for the deaths of so many. We were responsible for over seventy workers losing their jobs. We told the company who to fire. We tried to pick the seventy worst."[41]

In December STEGAC signed a three-year contract that granted a 56 percent wage increase and reestablished rights won in the 1978 contract. Among new items were a checkoff of union dues, time off for union work, bulletin boards, and a one-room union office on the premises. The Lucas García government was relieved: selling the plant and recognizing the union ended an international uproar. For STEGAC, the growth of an international movement gave the union the support it needed to successfully challenge the multinational's power and protected it from the effects of the national labor movement's demise.

Just as EGSA was being sold in August 1980, the second of the two mass kidnappings of urban trade unionists had taken place in Escuintla. One STEGAC member stated that the sale of the plant to resolve the crisis at Coca-Cola had been the union's "only alternative to going into the mountains [joining the guerrillas]. We were completely marked by then. We would never have found work elsewhere. We had held the union together up to a point beyond which I don't know what would have happened if the new owners had not come."[42]

STEGAC's Resurrection

After the plant changed ownership, mistrust and anger continued to poison relations among workers. STEGAC's leaders and members were furious with workers who had joined the Employees' Association, even if they did participate in the June nine-day strike, and STEGAC's leaders were enraged at union members for not having been more forthcoming. Mercedes Gómez realized that STEGAC needed to grow ("after all, that was what a union was all about"), but he also feared that the entry of "sell-out" workers would ruin the union.[43] Gregorio González recalled that he had felt paralyzed by wanting to keep ex-association members out and yet hoping to win them over. With the association gone, many workers were eager to join STEGAC, among other reasons because union membership suddenly appeared as the only route to job security. A bitter González explained that "workers who wouldn't talk to STEGAC in 1979 were ass-kissing us after the sale."[44]

What STEGAC leaders decided to do was to make membership conditional on both a period of probation and an oral examination. A Committee on Honor and Justice administered the test, asking each candidate questions such as "Have you ever engaged in antiunion activities?" and "Would you be willing to leaflet in the streets?" However, the union's leadership supervised the test and probation period in a disorganized and inconsistent manner. Thus, despite the concerns of Gómez, González, and Hugo Aparicio, the union increased to over one hundred without rigorous demands being made on the membership. After the job situation seemed stabilized, STEGAC stopped growing and remained motionless. The union no longer waged a battle to defend its dead and its life, and it pressed no new demands in dread of being "materialistic." As Gómez explained, "We did not want to end up like the Association after all those lives and years of sacrifice."[45]

In the bizarre circumstances of relative peace within the factory and ongoing civil war outside, fear complicated STEGAC's hesitancy to define itself. John Trotter was gone and because of international pressure the state was no longer attacking the union, but the national situation worsened daily. Workers who visited the countryside returned with bloodcurdling reports of army massacres (one man told of his brother-in-law being "chopped into 1,000 bits" in the Indian village of Joyabaj), Guatemala City lived under a state of siege, the university barely functioned, the army constantly dragnetted, and urban trade unionists continued to be kidnapped even if they were not currently active. Now, with no worker, high school, or university student groups, no CNT and no CNUS, no marches, leaflets, or public gatherings, in the city silence surrounded the massacres and disappearances.

A slate composed mainly of salesmen won the 1981 union elections. Over the next two years STEGAC seemed mild enough, and no more fiery declarations appeared. The small degree of conflict was routine and without ideological drama: a brief, successful strike was held when overtime pay was taken away. In late 1981 the Labor Ministry even sponsored a STEGAC member's trip to an International Labor Organization conference in Geneva. An IUF representative who met the STEGAC delegate was astonished by his apoliticism and wondered if the famous STEGAC had become a company union.[46] Worse than apoliticism in the eyes of some STEGAC members, decadence set in. Theft, always something of a problem, started to flourish in the sales department and a black market in soft drinks appeared in the city.

By late 1982, however, a renewed sense of the importance of the union became apparent among rank-and-file workers, one that would yield a change in leadership. The consciousness of the absolute necessity of the union that had led the majority of workers to join STEGAC from 1975 to 1978 not only still existed, it had been reinforced by the experiences of 1979–80. This was also true for workers who had retired from the struggle at times or had left STEGAC for the Employees' Association only to see the union triumph, materially and morally. After all, Trotter had never succeeded in making any worker really antiunion. Now for the first time STEGAC was allowed to exist; after years of accumulated blows hundreds of workers had the chance to breathe more life into their union.

One sign of revival was the organization of a caucus by a group of salesmen in response to the robbery of produce. They perceived stealing from EGSA as a selfish act that hurt the union's reputation and the company and ruined, for individual gain, a workplace on which many relied. As caucus member

Rodolfo Robles explained, "We thought this corruption damaged the union, and we asked the union leadership to authorize us to form a committee of worker vigilance, not to denounce workers to the management, but to speak with workers who were stealing the soft drinks, and stop the practice, which we did, by talking to people one by one, and raising their consciousness as to the effects of their actions."[47] The workers in the caucus worried about the ascendancy of Pepsi-Cola in the urban market as a result of the spontaneous boycott of the late 1970s and argued against a minority who countered that stealing "hurt the boss." Now most Coca-Cola workers did indeed want to increase sales, which did not mean that they had become procompany. They were dependent on Coca-Cola: the plant and the union were all they had in a presently almost nonunion city, a city with an effective blacklisting system, growing unemployment, and no promise of revolution. To have any power within the context of this dependency workers knew that they needed a strong countervailing force.

The salesmen who had initiated the antistealing caucus joined with Evert Soto, Guillermo Romero, Carlos Escobar, Marcos Alvarado, and others to form a slate that won the biennial union elections in 1983, and that in its totality represented all departments. The new executive committee was comprised of old-time STEGAC base members, such as Guillermo Romero, who had been in STEGAC since 1975, and former association members relatively new to EGSA, such as Evert Soto and Rodolfo Robles, the union's new secretary general. Like the majority of Coca-Cola workers, all of these men had participated in aspects of the citywide protest movement of the 1970s, some as STEGAC members, two as activist bus drivers, another as a member of a high school student association, and so forth.

With the union seemingly secure, the new executive committee members—born of the rank and file of either STEGAC or the Employees' Association—analyzed their years in STEGAC and in the broader urban movement that they had seen flourish and then die. They decided that the union had been too small and too unprepared for the tasks it set for itself, which in turn were unclear and seemed to them too vaguely "revolutionist." These new leaders made a respectful ("It was the times, it had to be that way") and private critique of their union's past: it was "too dependent on a few people, too leadership oriented." What they now wanted were "workers to participate, workers to know each other and identify with one another, and to overcome the division between sales and production." Unlike Gómez, González, and Aparicio, they were not braked by fury with the work force for abandoning the union; they even dubbed the new period "a democratic opening."[48]

They made their analysis in a city that had changed since 1979: by 1983 political parties barely operated, and the revolutionary groups had withdrawn from the shattered urban labor movement. Left to themselves, the rank and file turned to each other and chose leaders who were willing to draw some critical lessons from the past, in part because they had been around in the 1970s but had not been in charge and they had no personal stake in the criticism. Several workers thought that the epoch of trade unionism that began in the 1960s with the rise of CNT had ended in 1980, and they felt that a new era could start if they started it.

Reversing a tendency of the executive committee members of the late 1970s to be absorbed in building a radical urban and national movement, the newly elected leaders of STEGAC became singularly interested in the problem of expanding and strengthening union membership. It is important to underline that it was rank-and-file workers who promoted what was essentially a revitalization campaign: in order to create or rekindle trade union consciousness and activism, members of the rank and file proposed dramatizing aspects of the union's eight-year history. Coca-Cola workers began to construct a self-portrait based on the best parts of their past. The union's history was drawn up as a completely heroic story into which all workers could now write themselves if they so chose.

A salesman named Montenegro proposed building, and then designed, a Plaza of the Martyrs on one side of EGSA's new soccer field. Workers from every department contributed their time and labor to plant grass on the field, landscape the area, construct a small platform, and paint on the wall behind it a mural of workers with their fists raised and slogans such as "Everything Man Makes Is Culture." They named the field the Pedro Quevedo Sports Center and placed on the platform a stone plaque cut with the words: "In memory of Pedro

Quevedo. Your dauntless struggle took you to death, but your ideal of justice lives in our minds; praise to the martyrs fallen in the pro-worker struggle."

A production worker suggested that a history of the union be written, which Gregorio González and Hugo Aparicio were then commissioned to set down. The two wrote a four-page account structured around violence and the martyrs, whose self-sacrifice they presented as generating historical record; hundreds of mimeographed copies were distributed. Another worker thought that pictures of the martyrs should be displayed, and subsequently enlarged photographs of each murdered worker were mounted on the wall of the cafeteria to overlook workers as they ate and socialized. A second room was added to the union office, and the two rooms were each dedicated with the name of a martyr. Workers carefully lettered new signs for the walls such as "United forever in hope and sorrow!" and "May 1, 1886, dawn and tragedy of the proletariat."

A large celebration was planned to celebrate STEGAC's eighth anniversary in August 1983, and a contest to choose a union anthem received enthusiastic attention from workers. The winning entry, written by an assistant in the sales department, read:

> Forward, compañeros,
> this is your song, your song of Truth;
> with great courage we established our foundations
> and today our emblem is the sign of Unity.
> To the memory of our compañeros
> we must dedicate our respect;
> they fought, they sacrificed, and thus
> achieved their grand Ideal.
> Today we raise our fists, compañeros,
> and walk united with love;
> our victories, our union
> we will defend with faith and courage.

STEGAC paid a professional composer to write the music, and a newly formed union chorus rehearsed for weeks before presenting the anthem during the

Coca-Cola workers eat lunch in the plant's cafeteria, 1984. On the wall are the photographs of eight Coca-Cola union members who were assassinated between 1978 and 1980. (Photograph by Patricia Goudvis)

elaborate anniversary party. In the months that followed, STEGAC bustled internally. It started literacy, English, and music classes and revived the Committee on Honor and Justice to deal with such problems as drinking and stealing. By the beginning of 1984 union membership had grown to 220, and relations between workers took on a new or renewed sense of camaraderie based on shared struggle and victory.

On the walls, in song, in leaflets, and at union gatherings the workers constructed a memory of STEGAC as an organization of resistance and generosity developed by courageous workers. This representation gave union members what was due them, and it had healing powers for former members of the Employees' Association. The union's history could have been told with more dimensions: certainly the power of the state, the importance of international solidarity, or the divisionist Employees' Association, which signified the vacillation and not the constant valor of the majority of workers, could have been highlighted. But the focus of the reconstruction was on workers' capacities, and not on those of the state or IUF, and the Employees' Association was suddenly downplayed. There was nothing irrational about this semimythmaking, which told as whole truths, important partial ones: this was a narrative of the past as a means to the future, one that praised workers' tenacity and moral convictions, qualities on which the union had depended, even if all workers had not always displayed them.

This image of Coca-Cola's work force and of the union's past nevertheless denied workers access to many of their own problems, such as fear. By idealizing Coca-Cola workers, by claiming that they were united instead of divided, it obscured the illuminating history of how a small group of workers managed to persist and win in 1979–80. It diminished bravery by ignoring the power fear held over people, and it masked the obstacles to building a democratic union by portraying dead leaders as if they were flawless. Not wanting to repeat the past, indeed trying to promote a larger, more participatory union, the executive committee enclosed the past in a halo.

At the same time the hyperbole of this narrative communicated realities that would have been otherwise hard to express. The honoring of the dead as having died necessarily and gloriously, the anthem's stanzas, and signs such as "May 1, 1886 dawn and tragedy of the proletariat" and "United forever in hope and sorrow" made transparent and majestic difficult truths of working-class life in Guatemala. There had been and would be no gain except at the cost of enormous loss and suffering, no new life without harrowing deaths, no dawn without tragedies in the violent, unequal battle for workers' rights.

Without this post-1980 combination of affiliation with an international and the internal revitalization campaign that made history an explicit subject, it is impossible to imagine how STEGAC could have pressed on in February 1984, when the new franchise owners Zash and Méndez claimed bankruptcy and suddenly shut down the plant. With this sudden development STEGAC faced its greatest challenge, at a time when the army openly ruled the nation under General Oscar Mejía Víctores. No open urban organization existed beyond a few isolated unions, and no labor lawyers were available. In spite of this, when Zash and Méndez terminated operations in February 1984, well over four hundred workers voted up the simple resolution, "We all stay here together or we all get pulled out of here together."

As it happened, the plant reopened under new owners after the workers had occupied it for one year, and during the occupation STEGAC received support from international unions and human rights and solidarity groups. But for most of that year workers believed in the redeeming value of the fight *and* they doubted victory. In May 1984, a few months after the occupation began, representatives from STEGAC, IUF, and Atlanta Coca-Cola met in Costa Rica. There they signed an agreement requiring Atlanta Coca-Cola to find a new buyer who would reopen the plant and respect the union. At first seen as a victory, the May accord was soon perceived as a stalling device. Absolutely nothing happened in the subsequent months. With little in their stomachs or pockets, a few hundred workers sat inside an eight-acre compound under heavy surveillance in a country governed by a military dictatorship.

In November, after almost ten months of waiting, with no end in sight, a group of eighteen workers proposed giving Atlanta Coca-Cola the opportunity to simply pay them to leave the plant. They argued, reasonably enough, that the "plant will not open" and "we might as well get something out of it." But the union's executive committee strongly rejected the idea: "What we voted in February was, 'we all stay here together or we all get pulled out of here together' . . . we have a commitment to the martyrs, the existing national unions, to the international supporters. We would be selling out ourselves and the world. . . . It is very possible we will lose, but the only way to lose is with our heads up, with dignity." The proposal to leave was voted down more than 300 to 18. One worker recalled: "We did not have any money then, and we knew deep down we had only ourselves to rely on. Most were willing to go with that. It would have been a terrible defeat if we had lost the battle through our own decision. It would have contradicted everything STEGAC stood for."[49]

The 1984–85 occupation vindicated the 1983 revitalization campaign. A union member proudly related the story of Alejandro Hernández Simón, a former member of the Employees' Association, who became mortally ill during the occupation:

He had never been in the union in his eleven years at Coke. At first people did not trust him. But because of the democratic opening [in 1983] in the union, people like him started to join. He was very moved by the occupation, and worked intensely during it, almost like a kind of penance, doing vigilance shifts in the cold, which people felt did not help his poor health, and we urged him not to. Before he died he made a public statement at a meeting that he had been an insignificant person for not having joined the union [previously]. He was in agony, and when he died he was alive with faith in the union.[50]

The Occupation, 1984–1985

From 1980 to 1984, Antonio Zash and Roberto Méndez y Méndez undermined the Guatemala City plant by handling their finances carelessly and by first shifting distribution and then production away from it. Atlanta Coca-Cola loaned them $6.5 million to be paid over five years at 6 percent yearly interest, but the franchise owners neither met the payments to Atlanta nor invested the money in EGSA. What Atlanta Coca-Cola knew, and IUF and STEGAC did not, was that, in violation of the buyer's agreement, Zash and Méndez had bought and incorporated into EGSA's financial and legal structure six previously independent beverage distribution companies outside of Guatemala City. Instead of investing in promoting soft drinks within the territory that the city plant supplied (the departments of Guatemala, Santa Rosa, and El Progreso), they financed the expansion of the six distributorships located outside those areas with funds earmarked for increasing sales in Guatemala City. They also supplied the six distributors with soft drinks produced in the Guatemala City plant for 40 percent less than they charged other customers. Zash and Méndez then allowed the other two Coca-Cola bottling franchises operating in Guatemala—one of which, Sharp SA of Retalhuleu, was partly owned by Atlanta Coca-Cola—to sell in EGSA territory. Shortly afterward, they stipulated that EGSA bottles be sold to these plants instead of resold to EGSA. Finally, they permitted their distributors to sell soft drinks bottled at the other two plants.[51]

By Christmas of 1983, the peak sales time, EGSA suffered a bottle shortage and the company claimed it had no money to buy concentrate. In early January 1984 STEGAC learned that EGSA had authorized its distributors to handle soft drinks produced in other bottling plants. The union informed IUF, which in turn telexed Ted Circuit. Circuit acknowledged receiving the message and no more. Alarmed because managers were absent, paychecks were bouncing, and advertisements appeared saying that Sharp SA was the authorized bottler of Coca-Cola in the capital, STEGAC again called IUF at the end of January. Two weeks later, early on the afternoon of February 17, a sympathetic supervisor warned union secretary general Rodolfo Robles to be careful because "something was about to happen."[52]

Late that evening, when all the delivery trucks but one were in and the grounds were deserted except for four security guards at the front gate and four union representatives working in the little two-room office inside the compound, Zash and Méndez arrived with an armed bodyguard to inform the union members that, as Robles recalled Méndez's words, "Starting tomorrow this piece of shit is closed." An argument ensued about sales, market conditions, and the possibility of getting loans. Méndez insisted that the operation was "impossible, over, finished." He then offered each of the four union representatives $60,000. All they had to do was tell the workers who came in the next morning that the plant had been closed and they could collect their severance pay at the Labor Ministry. Robles said that the union leaders refused: "How could we have four workers loaded with money and hundreds out in the street with nothing?" He described what followed:

> We asked them why they didn't invest that money in the plant, and we asked them how they could be closing the plant without going through the legal procedures [whereby a factory had to give a month's notice to the Labor Ministry]?
>
> He [Zash] and Méndez invited us to go out, have dinner and chat at leisure elsewhere until dawn. We asked them why they were inviting us to go out to dinner? Here they were as if in their home because the factory belonged to them.
>
> We were very decided in that moment. We would have done whatever

was necessary to stay inside because we knew there were only two possible motives for getting us out of the plant. One was that they had armed
people outside who would grab us as we left. The other was that after we
left, they would send in people to destroy machinery, blame us, and justify the plant closing. We said if they wanted to take us out of there, they
would have to take us bound, gagged, dead, whatever.

Méndez started to cry. They warned us that we would have problems
for which they claimed no responsibility. They said people would jump
over the wall, commit "vandalism" and take us out. Then they called in
the security guards from the gate. Zash shook their hands, patted them
on the backs and informed them in a friendly voice that the plant had
shut. This was a shock of cold water and they stood there in silence.

We explained [to the guards] that they could leave or not but that we
had decided to stay in the plant because we did not accept the owners'
decision. After a moment they said they would stay with us. Then we were
eight. It would have been hard to have shot eight. Méndez told us we had
made our choice. And with that they left.

We started to mobilize. We turned on all the lights in the compound,
we filled up some bottles with gasoline in case of an attack, we took the
papers out of the administration [office] and sent them somewhere safe.
While we were doing this one of the security guards, a young guy, got
frightened and fled. But about then the one delivery truck that was still
out came in. We told them what had happened. "Will you stay or leave?"
we asked. "We'll stay," they replied.

We were a fairly large group, twelve or so, and we spread out over
the compound in groups. We telephoned the *Prensa Libre*, IUF in Geneva
and Pila [Evert Soto, one of the few workers with a telephone]. He came
down, mobilizing about ten people on the way, and we found some more
workers in the bar across the street, so by dawn we were thirty.

At dawn we saw these cars, some parked, some circling the plant, and
we could see men with masks on in one of them. It was a very disquieting
moment. But they did not fire or make any move to get into the plant—

there appeared to be so much movement in the plant. We had about eight guys up on the roof, very visible, with pipes. At about 5:00 A.M. some children showed up with leaflets from the owners explaining the plant was closed, and thanking the work force for their services. We thanked the children and destroyed the leaflets.

The next morning, Saturday, there was a front-page headline in the *Prensa Libre*: "Coca-Cola Closes!" So the rest of the work force, even people who didn't work Saturday—administrative people, some supervisors, people on vacation, family, over 500 people—arrived to see what was happening. We had a big meeting, recounting that a group of us had decided to stay inside and that people could leave and collect their severance pay if they wanted or they could stay and not collect their severance pay. Almost everyone decided to stay. I think most people thought the whole thing would be settled pretty quickly.[53]

At 10:00 A.M. an inspector from the Labor Ministry, who had no idea what was taking place, appeared because of the *Prensa Libre* headline. As he was filling out a report, a battalion of the antiriot squad surrounded the compound. One worker reflected that if the labor inspector had not acted appropriately, there would have been a massacre. The inspector convinced the commanding officer that nothing extraordinary was happening, and the men left. So did the inspector, after scheduling a meeting with the union on Monday at the ministry.[54]

Several meetings were held at the Labor Ministry over the next week. The STEGAC negotiating team included workers from the executive committee, from the union rank and file, and from among the large group of non-STEGAC members occupying the compound. The union responded to the emergency that the shutdown created by encouraging all workers to share leadership instead of by closing its ranks. Any participant in the occupation could attend the meetings if he or she wished, and this system created trust. "The word" about what went on at these meetings came from several sources.

Going to the Labor Ministry, located in the National Palace, was an elaborate operation. Fifty workers arrived in a convoy of Coca-Cola trucks. Fifteen went inside and the remainder stationed themselves in groups of five to forestall kidnapping attempts. "A tremendous security apparatus," explained one worker, "We had people not only around the palace, but in the entire plaza in front, and on all the street corners which touch it."[55] The workers were extremely tense. Twelve members of other unions had been kidnapped in the preceding months, and on the first day of the EGSA occupation union leader Fernando García was kidnapped from the nearby CAVISA factory. With each passing day the number of menacing phone calls to the plant increased. After armed men went to Hugo Aparicio's daughter's school searching for her (they did not find her), several workers sent their families out of the city.

The sessions at the ministry brought no solution. Workers raised the issue of the legality of the closure without success. The minister, Carlos Padilla Natareno, and EGSA's lawyer proposed workers' self-management. The delegates refused. As one worker explained, "You can't be a union and a cooperative at the same time, so we told them they could have the cooperative; what we wanted was the union." After this, the meetings degenerated: "The lawyer insulted us continually in front of the Minister and even took a camera out of his briefcase and started photographing us. Someone told him to go photograph his mother."[56] Finally, irritated that EGSA had closed without warning, the Labor Ministry paid to have three Coca-Cola workers go to Atlanta and meet with the parent company. Atlanta Coca-Cola simply disclaimed responsibility.

In mid-February most workers thought that the occupation would end quickly, but by the end of the month there was some doubt. In early March a company announcement that workers must immediately collect their severance checks at a local bank panicked workers because it meant that from EGSA's perspective, the issue was settled; moreover, if STEGAC lost the fight to keep EGSA open, would the checks still be there? A member of the union had a friend who worked in a bank explain to a newly formed General Assembly of Workers that the money would remain; if the plant did not reopen, they could still pick up their checks. With workers thus assured, the assembly voted that no one who took the money had the right to stay. Any worker who picked up a severance check and lied about it in order to eat at the plant would be ejected. To enforce this, a vigilance committee went daily to the bank where EGSA kept its account.

March passed with the plant still occupied. IUF tried to arrange meetings with representatives of Atlanta Coca-Cola but received vague responses. By the end of the month, most of the administrative personnel had collected their severance pay and gone home, usually apologetically. Of the remaining four hundred workers, only fifty left the occupation in the eleven months that followed. The struggle against the plant closing united more workers than had any other at Coca-Cola despite threats of violence, memories of the kidnappings and murders, and economic and physical hardships. During the year the occupiers never received more than Q600 each from the international funds sent to support the occupation; they lived on rice and beans, and many became ill, especially after the rains began in late April.

During the first few months all the occupiers slept, ate, and bathed inside the eight-acre compound. Surrounded by a high wall, the compound was divided between open space (a parking lot, the Pedro Quevedo Sports Complex, and several areas overgrown with weeds) and buildings housing the production line, cafeteria, warehouse, laboratory, mechanics' workshop, locker room, administrative offices, and STEGAC's two-room office. A few workers slept indoors on straw mats, but most improvised with little shacks made out of Coca-Cola crates and plastic sheets in the outdoor space. They gathered wood for fuel and made fires outside their shacks, where they kept pots and cups with which to prepare and drink their morning coffee. In shifts they ate the small meals prepared by crews of occupiers and four women cafeteria workers who supported the occupation and stayed without pay.[57] In June, as funds dwindled, the General Assembly of Workers decided that because feeding over 350 people a day was so expensive, one-half of the workers would take turns occupying the plant in twenty-four-hour shifts. Even so, some workers, who called themselves "Los Internos," stayed inside Coca-Cola the entire year in order to avoid burdening their families.[58] Thus, twenty-four hours a day, shifts of hundreds of workers lived inside the compound, patrolling the roofs and grounds day and night to ensure that assassins and provocateurs did not slip inside.

Workers stand around talking inside the Coca-Cola compound during the 1984 occupation. The volcano Agua forms the background. (Photograph by Patricia Goudvis)

What was the perspective of a rank-and-file occupier? Why did he or she remain? The most obvious reason was that Coca-Cola was a source of income and finding comparable work would have been nearly impossible. No employer wanted an ex–Coca-Cola worker. But more than a job was involved. As of 1984 Esperanza Jiménez had worked in the personnel department doing the payroll for twenty-five years. A religious woman and the daughter of middle-class professionals, she had never joined the union but she admired it. She had never attended a demonstration in her life, but she went to all the funerals of assassinated Coca-Cola workers. "I have to be here," she explained during the occupation, "This is my job, this is my home, these are my people. These are noble men, I have to support them. I have something to give, I'm not just a piece of decoration in life."[59] Angel Castellanos, a supervisor, felt that he stayed for his job and "*los muchachos*": "I'm on the side of the boys here because I don't want to be with the owners. I have seen the manipulations, I have seen how many lives this union movement has cost right here in this one plant in Guatemala. I'm here because everyone else is and I'll stay until everyone leaves together."[60] Veteran union member Guillermo Romero explained that "*compañerismo* is everything to me! The ambiance of trade unionism attracts me, the milieu of the occupation. We are all here together, finally, in struggle. It would be hard to leave. How could I leave?"[61]

The manner in which the occupation was conducted conveyed confidence in workers and built a sense of a community. The occupation was a participatory democracy. STEGAC deemed the General Assembly of Workers a collective decision-making body, with voice and vote for all workers, overseeing the occupation. By officially designating it, not the executive committee, the ultimate authority, the union avoided the suspicions that any other form of governing might well have created. Money, for example, a potential source of many difficulties, was accounted for by the assembly. As funds started to arrive from IUF and foreign unions, a wide majority voted up a proposal that donations be first apportioned for food and then divided equally, with a percentage going to the widows of the martyrs. The General Assembly rejected a suggestion that money be given proportionally according to what each worker normally earned.

Committees of workers, rather than the executive committee, managed the occupation's internal life because "the more responsibility people have, the more they understand."[62] Committees organized shopping brigades, helped the female cafeteria workers cook and clean, and patrolled the large compound. The Committee on Honor and Justice administered internal discipline, including the General Assembly's prohibition on alcohol. Committee members used gentle methods, such as benign ridicule or long conversations, "until I bored them with it," recalled one committee member, mechanic Pablo Telón. He thought that if discipline had not been handled with humor, and if the rules were not occasionally allowed to be broken, many occupiers would have left. As he explained: "We did not stress that people were 'bad' if they broke discipline in some way, like drinking. We gave the sense that they were involved in something more important and we needed them not to drink. It was always done with affection."[63]

A sports committee organized a soccer competition with neighborhood

STEGAC secretary general Rodolfo Robles addresses a General Assembly during the 1984 occupation. (Photograph by Patricia Goudvis)

teams. Carlos Rodas, Oscar Orellano, and Ricardo Samayoa formed a cultural committee. Enjoying the astonishing novelty of time and space on their hands, they wrote and produced a two-act play entitled "El Gran Robo," which recounted how franchise owners Zash and Méndez had faked bankruptcy in a suicidal foray that they anticipated would destroy STEGAC. Presented in bawdy language and in costume on an expansive loading platform, "El Gran Robo" delighted workers and eased tensions. By means of these and other activities, the more dedicated workers labored to maintain all workers' spirit and self-confidence. Good at improvising—whether they were creating theater or putting together housing—the Coca-Cola workers drew upon skills that they had already acquired handling everyday life in an environment where the state paid scant attention to building the material or cultural infrastructure of civil society. When Pablo Telón explained the occupation's practical philosophy, he could have been expounding the common sense of daily life in the city's neighborhoods: "If you are in charge of something, you have to do it. If you want to see something done, you have to do it. If you suggest something, you have to do it."[64]

Although various aspects of a "workers' utopia" emerged—participatory democracy, pay according to need, a flowering of workers' creativity—the occupation was not a new world. Many fundamental ways of being and thinking remained unchanged despite the incentive for questioning them that the occupation provided. Male workers' conception of trade unionism as masculine is one important example. The occupiers needed collaborators but the union rejected a foreign trade unionist's suggestion to form a wives' support committee because, in the words of one STEGAC leader, "we decided if the wives were brought into the plant, there would be all kinds of flirting and jealousy, and this would lead to conflicts among workers."[65] However proletarian in fact and however much they helped materially and emotionally, wives were perceived as dangerous objects of rivalry and sources of betrayal. The overwhelmingly male union welcomed the presence of four women cafeteria workers and a few women administrative workers in the occupation, and they appreciated the efforts of the women trade unionists from the ACRICASA textile factory who regularly donated food, time, and a little money. But views of female relatives and above all of wives had a specificity within the ideology about gender. In any case, men could not conceive of trade unionism as a feminine activity or commitment, no matter how many women had been trade unionists over the years. To maintain trade unionism as masculine, but not necessarily male in body, and to draw a line between activist women and women as they imagined them and fought for them to be, the Coca-Cola workers did what Guatemalan men trade unionists usually did when faced with militant women workers: they masculinized them. The Coca-Cola workers commonly complimented the women from ACRICASA with the remark, "So and so has helped us so much. . . . *She* has more pants than some *men* I know." Female relatives and especially wives could not assume the role of a double-gendered female more male than male without disrupting every code governing personal relationships between men and women. Throughout the occupation, wives remained a resource invisible from within the plant, as they worried themselves sick, cooked at home and sent the food to the plant, raised children, and often worked outside the home to compensate for the loss of their husbands' full wages.

Isolation inside the plant made it difficult to find sources of food, funds, and protection in the outside community. The few trade unionists who remained active in the city gave what they could: for example, the ACRICASA union held a fund-raising party and a union of rural workers supplied produce. Friends and a few customers lent what they could. Several times a week Doña Flory, owner of a seviche bar frequented by workers, arrived in a taxi late at night with tamales and coffee. A sympathetic doctor and pharmacist gave their services on credit; by the end of the year the union owed them Q2,000 because workers' health declined over the course of the occupation as a result of a meager diet, exposure to the cold during the rainy season, and tension.

National press coverage ended after the first days of the occupation. Without citywide or national structures to build support and to inform the public, STEGAC had to take on those tasks alone. After the General Assembly formed a University Committee, small bands of Coca-Cola workers went to the University of San Carlos, where they made speeches and collected money in simple disguises, "simple because the guerrillas used heavy ones and we didn't want to be confused with them, so we stuck to sunglasses and caps."[66] Someone suggested that brigades travel to workers' hometowns to rally support. The idea was accepted, and in consideration of the civil war, the assembly sent workers in groups for no longer than three days and no farther, for safety, than 100 kilometers. STEGAC wrote a "letter of presentation to the competent authorities." Workers fanned out into the towns near the city; in one town, the mayor collected food for the occupation.

As Holy Week, Guatemala's most important holiday, approached at the end of March, a worker proposed that union members carry a processional float. He convinced an old friend who was a parish priest to allow Coca-Cola workers to lead off the procession from his church without paying the customary fee for the right to perform the penance of hauling on their shoulders the heavy floats decorated with scenes of Christ's calvary. The Coca-Cola worker

A Coca-Cola worker at Mass in the warehouse during the 1984 occupation. (Photograph by Jean-Marie Simon)

remembered that "we made a big impression, in our Coke uniforms, instead of the usual purple robes. One hundred of us went to 'get rid of our sins.' Everyone watched, murmuring, 'Oh it's the Coke workers, poor things.' We got press coverage."[67] Orchestrating a major and unusual working-class battle in the shadow of a recently destroyed urban labor movement and in full view of a military state required inventive means of communication and a new style of self-reliance.

At the same time that Coca-Cola workers reached out to friends, acquaintances, and strangers, the occupation attracted affiliates of isolated unions that had once been part of the destroyed centrals and federations, such as the National Central of Workers. The compound became a center of more than its own activity in an otherwise silenced city. Workers from other companies sought advice and even shelter. After two of the three remaining leaders of the Pantaleón Sugar Workers' Union were kidnapped, the third came to live inside the Coca-Cola compound. Over eight hundred workers from plantations and other factories attended a May First 1984 mass and march inside the occupied plant, the first held since the massacre in 1980. Many workers felt that the occupation could revive trade unionism in Guatemala, and STEGAC made a short-lived attempt to form a new national confederation.

All of these activities animated the occupiers, as did the arrival of delegations of trade unionists and journalists from abroad, a sociologist, a graduate student in history, and above all an IUF-financed camera crew from New York City. The Coca-Cola workers thought that the nation and world were watching. They felt that they had to win not only for the seviche bar owner and the plantation workers who traveled for two days to bring them bananas, but as well for the millions whom they thought watched the movie *The Real Thing*, produced by the New York crew (and in fact, not widely distributed). Workers increasingly believed that, because of the IUF tie, the delegations that arrived from abroad, and the production of the film, the occupation was an international symbol of organized labor's power. As we sat in the cafeteria cleaning black beans in early August, a worker told me: "We think that if our union wins it will be an example to all unions, as much in Guatemala as on the international level. We want victory for ourselves, for others in the country, and

Coca-Cola workers sing the union anthem at a General Assembly meeting in the plant's warehouse, 1984. (Photograph by Patricia Goudvis)

for workers all over the world, and I want to be here to see how this all turns out."[68]

This consciousness of themselves as the makers of international working-class history helped sustain workers in the face of terrible anxieties. Many feared an army massacre or a sudden rash of kidnappings and eventual defeat. One worker was "arranging papers proving my death because you have to prove it when it happens . . . widows and children of the disappeared get nothing."[69] By late August everything—incessant soccer games, occasional literacy classes, the repair of motor vehicles, small talk and important conversations—had become tiresome, and to combat tension workers chain-smoked and often took tranquilizers. By September many felt demoralized and the more resolute occupiers spent much of their time huddled in discussion with the less convinced ones. When Marco Tulio Loza's friends said that they could no longer afford the occupation, Loza made "little deals" with them: "Come on, don't desert us, stay just one more week." Then a week later he would make the same deal again.[70] Activists' desire to defend the occupation overwhelmed fear and despair. It is noteworthy that when the proposal to leave in exchange for money—one that provided a way to get out safely and to get something in the bargain—was made in early November, none but its eighteen authors supported it. The overwhelming majority concurred with the executive committee's argument that "it is very possible we will lose, but the only way to lose is with our hands up, with dignity."

By that time a few businessmen who were unsuitable to the occupiers had expressed an interest in the plant. A Texan arrived in October but the workers thought that he was a "criminal of some kind." Subsequently the General Assembly also rejected a Nicaraguan, a former member of Somoza's National Guard, who had arrived at the factory with armed bodyguards. In late November union members began talking with a group of Guatemalan investors headed by economist Carlos Porras and capitalist Antonio Batres Arriola, who described themselves as "not antiunion" and "not doing you a favor. We think it's a profitable business." STEGAC thought that this group belonged to a "new" post–civil war bourgeoisie and agreed to discuss its bid.[71] Negotiations began in January 1985. For STEGAC the two key issues were state and company recognition of the union and the number of workers rehired. The Porras group, the Labor Ministry, and the military dictator Mejía Víctores agreed to recognize the union's continued legal status. By 1985 the triumphant military was already planning a return to civilian rule, and it was eager to improve its miserable international image. Opposing the recognition of STEGAC would have meant more adverse publicity. Accepting this one union, with the urban mass movement nonexistent and the guerrillas by now defeated nationally, seemed to pose little threat. Besides, as in 1954, the military had no intention of legally opposing trade unionism.

The negotiations over numbers lasted a month. Because EGSA had no sales, Porras wanted a work force of 150, plus administrative personnel, not 350, the number of workers occupying the plant. The figure of 265 (not counting administrative personnel) was finally agreed to on the union's condition that the remaining 85 workers would be the first rehired as sales increased. The General Assembly unanimously accepted the proposal and voted that the 85 "left out temporarily" would include the 18 workers who had suggested leaving in

Coca-Cola workers sing the union anthem on the roof of the plant the day that the agreement to reopen Coca-Cola was signed in 1985. (Photograph by Patricia Goudvis)

November—thus punishing them for violating the spirit of the struggle—and volunteers. The necessary number of workers volunteered and they became STEGAC's new heroes of sacrifice and generosity.

On February 1, Porras bought the franchise. A month later the plant opened under a new name, Embotelladora Central SA, with STEGAC dissolved and re-formed as the Union of Workers at Embotelladora Central SA (STECSA), a legal formality. Hundreds attended the dedication ceremony, including General Mejía Víctores and the labor attaché from the U.S. embassy. For a moment, the opening appeared as if it was the product of a joint effort between states, but it was a victory won by one democratic, mobilized union and by international solidarity. At the conclusion of the ceremony, the Coca-Cola workers climbed up onto the roof of the plant and sang the union's anthem as a small crowd of family, friends, and supporters stood in silence in the street below, breaking into cheers as the singing ended. A few Coca-Cola workers wept. One explained through his tears that they "had accomplished the impossible."[72]

The strength of the occupation lay in the ability of the more committed workers to recognize and handle internal and external problems. The occupation did not collapse because some workers made it their business to bring problems to the surface instead of hiding them, to urge all to take responsibility for reality, and to insist on the struggle's broader meaning. Intervention to shape a particular course of action, whether it came from elected leaders or members, was essential. To say that the practice of leading was vital to the occupation is not to dismiss the rank and file: leaders and leadership came from the rank and file, and leaders' talents resided in their ability to mobilize and rely on all the workers inside EGSA and make them central. The operating principles of the occupation were that the occupiers, not STEGAC, made and enforced decisions, issues had to be taken up openly and resolved immediately by the General Assembly, and nothing or no one was accepted on faith or word, that is, trust had to be constantly won. Over the course of the 376 days inside the plant, most of the occupiers joined STEGAC.

STEGAC, now STECSA, had changed since the 21 workers had met in the CNT office in 1975. Between its inception and 1978, a majority of workers belonged to the union. This majority was the critical mass but not the critical decision-making power. The union was led by upper-strata workers who worked in partnership with lawyers and advanced the union by developing ties of solidarity in ever-widening circles—first nationally through CNUS and then internationally through IUF. Trade unionism in Guatemala City peaked in this period, attaining its height in late 1977 and early 1978 and thereafter declining. From early 1979 to 1980, when violence reached a new zenith, the union diminished in numbers (as did the urban mass movement generally), and leadership passed to production workers. The production workers held together a small, intensely active group, a courageous minority united by their commitment to their murdered dead as the embodiment of what was important in life. By keeping their hands in the fire, they enabled IUF to force out John Trotter. By the time of the sale, almost all progressive lawyers had fled the country and the more prominent urban trade union leaders were dead or gone. Between the sale in 1980 and 1983, the union grew a bit but activity ebbed. And then from 1983 until the plant reopened in 1985, the union gained a more democratic dimension as more workers became its heart and head.

By 1985 union militants did not mention revolution. Leaders such as Pablo

Telón, Samuel Estrada, Evert Soto, Rodolfo Robles, and Joaquín Rosales advocated resolving conflicts through negotiation and they opposed sharp confrontation. This is not to say that the union had become politically complacent; resistance and accommodation were not mutually exclusive. Union members supported a day-care center in a nearby shantytown, assisted in the rebuilding of the citywide union movement after the return to constitutional rule in 1986, and aided other workers, peasant groups, and the new organizations of relatives of the disappeared. The union continued to sponsor its theater group, which toured the country presenting a worker-authored drama condemning the Guatemalan military for massacring Maya Indian and ladino workers and peasants until one of its cast was tortured to death and the group dissolved.

From STEGAC's inception, individual workers made history because they grasped that class organization was a project and not simply an automatic or semiautomatic consequence of class exploitation. If, for example, Mercedes Gómez, Gregorio González, and Hugo Aparicio had flagged in 1980, the union would have died, and if in 1983 some workers had not found ways to incorporate more workers into a union whose genesis and maintenance they proclaimed lay within workers' provenance, the union would have ceased the day the plant shut down in 1984 or shortly thereafter.

The union had not overcome, once and for all, its internal problems by 1985, when the plant reopened under yet another set of franchise owners. Plantwide solidarity and union democracy had been hammered out in the hard-fought context of the occupation, but these were fragile qualities. After the occupation ended, the union was stronger than it had ever been, and, simultaneously, old troubles such as drinking, stealing, mistrust, fear, dependency on a few leaders, and antagonisms between sales and production reemerged. Several workers who had been important to the union became inactive. Many strong friendships had been forged, though everyone was not, in the words of the union's anthem, "united with love." In 1987 one old-timer pointed out that "there is always some compañerismo and always the opposite."[73] The affirmation of new identities did not equate or impel completely new ways of being. As the union would argue, its future depends on workers' values and capacities in the face of what arises.

Conclusion:
The Unexpected

The heart of the Guatemalan labor movement was not in mining, steel, ports, or auto, but in a bottling and distribution plant. The entrepreneurs of the global economy, such as the Korean and U.S. businessmen who since 1986 have rushed into Guatemala with their *maquiladora* finishing plants, count on having a tame work force, one that is poverty-stricken and eager for any employment.[1] They may be in for a surprise. "You! You think we are poor," a Coca-Cola worker said to me. Pointing to his head, he continued, "We are not poor, we are rich."[2]

Guatemalan urban trade unionism since 1954 has not confirmed various images of the genesis of working-class political consciousness. Although workers utilized socialist and liberal thought, religion was the language of resistance. Working-class activists recast the notions of the conservative Catholic Action, and more generally of Christian doctrine, to construct their own views. They also gathered strength from their local urban neighborhoods, but not explicitly from ethnic identity or from the solidarity of a long-standing community, as scholars argue occurred in other cases.[3] Instead, there was a modernity about their solidarity, one based on a willingness to take risks and on new relationships and identities new in their synthesis, even if these drew upon old themes and images.

This study has underscored the importance of historical specificity. The state under which workers live, the structures workers experience, the unique values by which they gauge their experiences, their working conditions, their craft, and so forth make groups of workers distinct from one another. Trade unionism in Guatemala City shared characteristics with labor movements in Latin America and elsewhere in the world. However, it was different in ways that call into question varied generalizations about Latin American trade unions: Guatemalan urban trade unionism was not the product of corporatism, it was not managed by the state, it never became institutionalized or bureaucratized, Communist and Socialist parties did not have hegemony within it, and it was not strictly secular; moreover, it was not started by, nor did it become the base of or lead to the formation of, a political party, mass, populist, or otherwise.

Even though in one case trade unionists managed by the skin of their teeth to cultivate the international support that made it possible to win concessions from the sort of multinationals responsible for Guatemala's honky-tonk industrial growth, Guatemalan trade unionists were on their own. By means of their intense focus on the power of will, they nurtured the sense that they could handle that condition of their existence. In 1987, years after the demise of the Young Catholic Worker and the National Central of Workers, a line from a union play, in which unarmed workers who are cornered by soldiers continue to fight, reads, "At least, we have what's essential—*will*!" Will was not enough, but perhaps, as Antonio Gramsci argued, only people "who will something strongly can identify the elements which are necessary to the realization of [their] will."[4]

One needs to understand the particular social context in which labor militants acted and thought, and one must decode the way in which they understood that context. In Guatemala City, the "order of things" was understood as psychopathic and untenable. The collective conceptual achievement of an activist and social consciousness was elaborated in the name of humanity, not only class, and trade unionists thought they reached toward a new humane society, not the inauguration of proletarian rule. The pace of the urban labor movement was breathtaking. Its members did not seek a place in the order of things. They raced beyond it, as if against time, as if to reach the millennium before that too was disappeared as a possibility. In Guatemala City unions were the vanguard of a struggle, not for socialism, but for the survival of every-thing workers understood to be human.

Labor historians often seem to be trying to sort out whether a labor move-ment is "good" (class conscious, smart, brave, basically revolutionary, an "old mole" always at work with its own class strategy, a strong historical force) or "bad" (easily seduced by the state and political parties, bourgeois in its interest in money, docile, narrow-minded, a weak historical force). But looking at the Guatemalan labor movement, it is clear that labels such as revolutionary, re-formist, accommodationist, or economist clarify little. What was an important (however inconstant) strength of Guatemalan urban trade unionism was not its "purity" or lack of internal problems, but an ability dependent on internal democracy: to acknowledge its own problems; not to not have problems, but to endeavor to discern them. This ability, perhaps more than its political "line" at a given moment, was liberating.

I have argued that the Guatemalan labor movement is explained in part by the social identity activists fashioned for themselves, as they did within JOC and the Coca-Cola workers' union. Activism required that workers per-ceive themselves, subjectively, in ways that made action possible in the specific situation that was theirs. An important element of this self-identity was the notion that trade unionists could make history. Were they right? On the one hand, they accomplished very little: The labor movement never achieved sta-bility; it did not change the standard of living for the urban majority, generate a progressive political party, or alter the state. On the other hand, activists organized a number of vigorous unions without which no sense of alternative and no hope would have remained within the working class in those years of political, economic, and psychological misery. Trade unionists denied victim-ization, even if they died in the process. They chose to take on the making of their own destinies. Their power to spurn the places assigned them allowed a trade unionism whose development was unpredicted. By keeping alive a few unions, they "accomplished the impossible" and kept trade unionism alive. The history of the urban labor movement suggests two insights into the in-escapable twin truths that workers can make history but that their ability to do so is limited. The first is that workers' confidence in their own historical power does not call that capacity into existence, but that power cannot flourish unless workers believe in it. The second is that unless workers recognize the real limits on their power, they cannot wield it effectively or expand it beyond those bounds.

The urban labor movement left both a rich and an ambiguous legacy. Some of the qualities that propelled it onward at one point harmed it at another. Faith in the power of the will is one important example. At times, it was not combined with a shrewd recognition of the real barriers ahead and thus tended to turn into voluntarism, the belief that will by itself is enough. Voluntarism helped workers organize against near impossible odds, but it rested on a certain blindness to the state's powers and to the unions' vulnerabilities. It nourished trade unionism and then led to a disastrous triumphalism, with workers heralding victory just as they were on the verge of defeat. Another example is machismo. In the face of state violence, male workers' perception of themselves as courageous and protective no doubt helped them to defend themselves and others, but it undermined the ability of workers to unite and it made the path women trade unionists had to cut a doubly perilous one. A final example is the exaltation of Christ or David as figures to emulate. The reverence accorded these biblical heroes encouraged workers in their struggle, but it also made trade unionism appear to be the inaccessible province of an elect group. It should be a relief to know that Guatemalan trade unionists, tough as they were, were not saints: they had to grapple with problems such as alcohol and fear, some left the movement, some even turned traitor. As inspiring as the story of Christ or David has been for many oppressed people, fortunately no one has to be David or Christ to make history.

Appendix

Three Life Stories: Constructing Protagonists

Efraín Alonso
Rural worker, student, city worker, trade unionist, Christian
Democrat, supporter of the revolutionary movement, immigrant

My family was ambulant. I was born in El Niño near Palo Gordo, in San Antonio Suchitepéquez, in 1940 but because of poverty my family had to migrate to Tiquisate, where the banana company [the United Fruit Company] was at its height in its business of exporting bananas.

My father was a campesino. He grew up in Palo Gordo and he died there. He could not read or write, none of that. He worked picking coffee on the fincas and rented some land to grow corn. We lived in such poverty that my parents had to separate, and my brothers and sisters and I wandered with my mother to find work. When I was eight we found work cutting bananas in Tiquisate. My mother died there; she died young too, very young, and now I realize why she died. She died from the same poverty my father died from.

I cut bananas and cleaned bananas and all that from the time I was eight. I lived with my sister and her husband. He treated me well. I paid for my food with bananas and he let me go to elementary school, but he kept me out of school a lot too. This was in the time of the 1950 elections and the arrival of Arbenz. There had been a period of good government under Arévalo, but when Arbenz came he made change more profound. He wanted people to have the

United Fruit's land, and in this zone of Escuintla, Arbenz was very popular. And this was the first area where he did give land. My brother-in-law and my brothers and sisters were very happy. A lot of United Fruit workers had their little piece of land all picked out. They knew that United Fruit exploited them, sending huge quantities of bananas to the exterior, and they saw a chance to improve their lives. I remember my brother-in-law taking me to meetings. It was very exciting! Ninety-nine percent of the campesinos were Arbenzcistas. . . . I saw a lot of things. Arbenz gave land but no orientation whatsoever and he gave money for whatever—seeds, fertilizers. After the coup [in 1954] people did not know what to do with it. Some people didn't invest their money, they drank it. My brother-in-law's father preferred to die drinking this money; he died in the street, he lost his land and much else besides. Many took this decision, others were more cautious.

I remember that after Arbenz's overthrow a lot of people had to flee the area because they had taken very radical positions against United Fruit. I remember very well. The River Nagualate is in this zone, and dead bodies constantly appeared in the river. They were campesino leaders who had been shot and thrown into the river. I saw this one, two, three, four times, their bodies riddled with bullets.

I was 16. I went to the capital because I wanted to study. I lived with my aunt, she fed me. She lived in a palomar [a one-story building of rooms built around and opening onto an open space]. Everyone was very poor. About twelve families shared one waterspout, and there were problems because there was always someone who didn't agree with the way things were, and I didn't feel very good there.

I remember I worked in road construction. And I started in school [at night] but I couldn't finish because I got involved with some of the students in the Central Institute for Boys. This was 1960, 1961, something like that, when the thing about Cuba was very hot. There were so many movements that I couldn't study. It was a dramatic era, because I belonged to FUEGO [an anti-imperialist high school student group]. I learned a lot from those boys, from Edgar Ibarra and Oscar Arturo Pérez. I was enthralled that they wanted to deal with the problems that existed in Guatemala. I left that school because I wasn't getting any studying done, and went to the Commercial high school, but it was the same thing, all over again, the student movement. I was very proud that the boys I went to school with became distinguished revolutionary leaders. Oscar Arturo Pérez and Ibarra were in the Commercial high when the first anniversary of the Cuban Revolution was celebrated, and they were among the most important guests whom Fidel invited. They went there. After they came back, they were put in prison. It was different then than it is now. Before they just tortured people and let them go, now no, they kill you. But Arturo and Ibarra managed to get out of jail because there was a big fuss. They told us about jail, about how they had to sit nude on a block of ice for a half hour, and they put a hood over them so they couldn't breathe. This made us angry because there was no reason for this. In any case, we all used to meet after school, and they would tell us about Cuba, and we would settle our doubts about Cuba and what all that meant.

I went to yet another school to study but it was the same thing, dedicated compañeros, and I didn't get anything done. It was about that time that I felt frustrated because I wasn't getting anything accomplished in terms of studying, and I had no money. I left road construction and school because my cousin found me a job in a textile factory, CIDASA. I worked there and the first thing we did was start to form a union. I didn't know much about unions, but I knew what I learned in Tiquisate, that there could be unions. Maybe because we were not experienced and talked too much, the managers heard about us and we were fired, one by one. From that I felt a greater desire to do something. Losing the job was a big problem. My aunt was mad that I had gotten involved, and I was eight months without work because I was blacklisted. I went to factories and they would hire me and then the next day say no, sorry, it was a mistake.

After I left CIDASA, there wasn't much control in the factory. They tried to control the workers so that another union would not start, but they couldn't control them and it did. This is one of the things I am happy about. Despite the fact that we couldn't do it, the people who stayed WERE interested, because later they unionized. So we had interested the people. So you can see that there were smart people who recognized what was good for them. So even if we failed, there was someone else staying on and pushing forward.

I only found work because I was a good soccer player. I started to play with a team from the Kern's factory and the manager of the team, who was the plant manager, hired me without a security check because he wanted me on the team. I started out during the tomato season, canning. To tell you the truth, I still wanted to unionize workers, but I was afraid, after what happened last time! I was really frightened because I had spent eight months without work. So I was quiet for about a year when I started a little friendship with a worker named Lavarreda, who was a schoolteacher. And so I asked him if he was a schoolteacher why was he working in a factory and he explained there were no jobs for teachers, and I asked him if he liked the work in the factory and he didn't and we started to talk more.

Well, the point is that I remember that there were these managers, these middle-class young guys with their cute little cars. And when the harvest came they needed a lot of extra women to work so they always picked the prettiest ones, and what they did afterwards [the managers], they took them to drink on Fridays, on the weekend, I don't know what they did, and these poor women had to give in to what they wanted because they needed the job. This was incredible and the teacher and I discussed it thoroughly, and this was how the whole thing started. He had contacts and we got in touch with FECETRAG [a Christian federation organized in the 1960s by ex-members of the Young Catholic Worker]. We met with Julio Celso de León, and he was delighted! We were the third or fourth union to join FECETRAG.

We went about convincing people in the plant one by one, very secretly, until we had the number we needed, and we invited them to a championship soccer game between Guatemala City and Quetzaltenango. I remember it was a Saturday or Sunday, and inviting them to the game was the way of getting them all together. It was the only way. And then after the game we took them to the FECETRAG office, and Julio explained everything. Well, we got an injunction against the company so that no one could be fired, and then looked for a way to win people to the union, which we did by talking about the truck that they used to transport workers. It was an open truck and very dangerous, and right as we were trying to organize it crashed right in front of the social security institute. We finally got the union and a contract, in about 1963 or 1964, and we won the right to hire temporary workers. That was very important to us because the managers could not take advantage of women.

[Alonso left Kern's in 1965.]

Some priests from Caritas invited me to an institute in Miami, at Opa Locka, to learn about the union movement in the United States, and I went. At Opa Locka there were about 600 or something children who were refugees from Cuba and I was taken to talk with these children two or three times. The way they talked was very interesting. They had them there and were educating them with the hope that they would be rebels against Fidel, but the children said that this was a lie; they were there because they had to be, and when they grew up they were just going to look after their individual lives.

I was there with these priests who had this very frank look on their faces, but I spent the whole time very disoriented because I didn't have a penny of my own—for all they gave you—and the whole thing was garbage. They talked on and on about the union movement in the United States, but no one understood anything. There were workers there from all over Latin America— from Venezuela, Colombia, Mexico. A lot of them were Dominicans. I returned to Guatemala in July and I didn't have a job.

I knew all those people through FECETRAG like Enrique Torres and Gabriel Aguilera. They had a student front of the Christian Democrats called Frente Estudiantil Cristiano, and I went to this center they had out in Mixco. And then Julio recommended me for a job in the federation, and in the party—the Christian Democratic party—dealing with the peasants who came in from the countryside with problems about land.

This job was very important for me because I learned a lot about people in the countryside. Sometimes I had to go into the countryside to deal with peasant groups affiliated with the party, to see cooperatives or schools, and I had the opportunity to really talk with people, to encourage them to organize, which is why I always understood the position of the people who were the left of the Christian Democrats. People like René de León [Schlotter] were caciques who manipulated a lot of the young leaders in the party, and who became very important in government, and who were not so concerned with popular organization, really, although they said they were. And there were working-class people in the party then because it was the only place to go. The federation [FASGUA] was completely burnt, completely involved in politics, and the left controlled it. Not only that but there was a state of siege in Guatemala then, so if there was any problem [in the city], they just arrested the people from the federation [FASGUA], so a lot of people joined FECETRAG instead or the party [the Christian Democrats], because FECETRAG was not so militant politically.

It was about then that I went to some courses in Venezuela run by a federation that the Christian Democrats supported. What was very interesting to me was that even though this was supposed to be a course for workers, there was only one worker besides myself, and he was a guy from Panama who wasn't really a worker because he was a deputy. The rest were professionals. I remember a guy from Nicaragua who was very left-wing, but another class of person, almost with a doctorate. There was a guy from Paraguay who had just been in a conference in Europe. This was my first experience with this sort of thing, I was really just in diapers. I didn't talk or anything. I learned a lot, and I came away with the idea that union federations should not be utilized or manipulated by political parties. Well, I came back to FECETRAG with this idea and it was very difficult because the person who predominated in FECETRAG was Julio Celso de León who ran it like a dictator, and he was also the director of CLAT [the Christian Democrat–supported continentwide organization]. A lot of young workers were interested in FECETRAG but Julio Celso frustrated them. He frustrated me; he used to threaten me and accuse me of being a leftist and a Communist. He wanted to control everything, and that couldn't work. Well, after I came back from Venezuela I said that the workers in the unions and the peasants in the cooperatives should make their own choices about if they wanted to support a political candidate or not—in other words, that the party we supported had to make a commitment to us, the workers, and not vice versa. Julio Celso didn't like that because he wanted to be a deputy, and he became one, from Escuintla. After that the federation split and CNT was born, I think in 1968. I don't know about that because I was not living in Guatemala by then.

The people from the Christian Democrats, the right, like Danielo Barillas, fired me from FECETRAG. They came with a letter firing me, just like they were bosses! And I said, OK, if I was just a worker to them, they had to pay me indemnification, like to any worker who is fired, and I had been there 4 years! They said they didn't have any money. I said if you really are a party for the workers, how can you just leave me without work like that? So I fought for indemnification, and I went to the Labor Ministry, and there was a guy there I knew—he was killed later—and he sent Barillas a citation and he was furious. So finally the Christian Democrats just settled with me, out of court. They gave me a sum of money, maybe 300 quetzales, and with this money I eventually came to New York.

I lived in a neighborhood in Guatemala City which had a lot of problems, no drains, no water, no school. And we organized a betterment association there in that neighborhood. Well, it seems that this land wasn't owned by anyone. We started investigating because people wanted to have title to their lots. And they had started to buy them, they started making payments, but it turned out that the guy who was selling the lots didn't even own the land! And some older people had already bought lots from him, but their titles were canceled. Well, a whole investigation started about this because he had been selling land he didn't own, and someone came from the government to intervene the land. I was part of this committee, I was still in the Christian Democrats then. I used to go to the party whenever the committee in the neighborhood needed leaflets made up. We started to have a lot of activities, we got the municipality to put up a school. It was about then that someone who sympathized with the FAR started to make contact with us. They were very interested in us, in seeing if we wanted to work at the political level with them. We had a really strong committee, understand? We moved a lot of things in that neighborhood, for the school, for water, a health center, so they wanted to work with us. So they called us. They made an appointment with us, and a man came and asked us—two of us went to talk to them—if we wanted to work at "another level." And we said, "whatever helps the community." And he said, "Well, yes, for the community and for more, for what we are concerned about politically."

After awhile I agreed to participate, and more than anything I delivered leaflets and passed their newspaper around. But I had a lot of problems with the woman with whom I lived. She was very nervous, and sometimes my work with the Christian Democrats took me away from the house. If I had not had a wife, I would not be here talking to you. I would have joined the guerrillas because my parents were very poor people, and I suffered all the real problems of poverty. I would have been more decided, and do you know why I would have been more decided? Because I understood the situation of my family, of my parents. I'm not ashamed to say that I am poor. All my family is poor, and because of that my desire to understand more and to involve myself in something was born. I was very proud they asked me to work with them. I had known some of those boys from high school [who led FAR] and people in the Christian Democrats who they said were in FAR and were murdered.

But after I was fired from the Christian Democrats and FECETRAG, I felt frustrated. There were so many pressures. I felt disappointed with everything, above all with myself, and I left Guatemala and came to the United States.

Sonia Oliva
Student, factory worker, leader of the ACRICASA
textile workers' union, an exile

I'm from a small village in Zacapa, where I was born in 1953, and my father is a peasant. My mother did not live with us because my parents had separated and so, since I was the only woman in the house, I did all that kind of women's work—cooking, cleaning, washing, ironing. I finished elementary school when I was thirteen because I made a big effort. I had to walk six kilometers daily but I did it! There was no high school in the area and I wanted to keep studying so I came to live with an aunt in Guatemala City. She found me a job in a supermarket as a cashier, but I couldn't go to school because she made me stay in the house cleaning in the evening. She treated me badly and even hit me. I admired the young women who went to school every day, they were so lucky. . . . Oh, how I wanted to study! But she wouldn't let me because of all the work in the house.

I befriended a girl and I used to cry and tell her my problems. Since she lived alone in a boardinghouse, she said, "Look, you're working. You can leave the house, you don't have to put up with this." My father came to the city a few days later. I explained my situation, and he said I was right, and he gave me the money to buy the things one needs to live alone, like a bed, so off I went to live with my friend, alone where she lived. Everything went beautifully after that. I studied at night at the Normal Central and worked in the day. I joined the school basketball team that was part of a student association which held protests about more desks and electricity and so forth. But after I left the supermarket and got involved with the union at ACRICASA, the students would seek me out because I was a trade unionist, which was something important, well thought of. But you know the reason I've told you this tale is to explain how I could get involved in the union. There was no one at home to stop me . . . no husband, mother, father, mother-in-law, father-in-law. I was alone.

The very first thing that amazed me about ACRICASA was the kind of treatment the machines got. The machines, which are *machines*, got medical attention 24 hours a day. Who were their doctors? The mechanics. What were their medicines? New parts, grease, repairs. They got everything they needed to function 24 hours a day without hitches or failures, but we did not. A machine breaks and a mechanic comes running in seconds. Do you realize the difference? The machines had all, the people nothing. And the machines had no safety devices for the people! For example, there was no warning light on the machinery, and one day a mechanic was working on a machine and a compañera who did not see him turned on the machine and he lost all his fingers. She felt terribly guilty forever but it wasn't her fault. And then there were these tanks of boiling water and one broke and water spilled on a guy. We grabbed him and threw cold water on him. I felt desperate and helpless and screamed at the Japanese, "Do something!" And he said, "I'll call an ambulance," and I said, "No, that will take forever!" First you have to get a line—phones don't really work in Guatemala—and then chances are if you reach the hospital, no ambulance is available. So I told him to take the guy *immediately* in the company car, which he did eventually but not immediately.

There was great fear of protesting, walking into the manager's office and saying, "Look, I want this, I want that." But the rumor started to make the rounds—a *union*. There had been some meetings before I went to one—I was not especially trusted because by then I had been trained as a machine instructor and was considered an "employee in the company's confidence." But I heard the rumor, and someone told me a friend of mine was involved, so I went over to her and said, "You are incredible. Why didn't you tell me about this?" "Shut up," she said, "someone will hear you!" She was very agitated and I was very enthusiastic and yelling. I said I wanted to go to the secret meetings which, like a lot of secret meetings in Guatemala, turn out to be not so secret, and she said no because I might tell the Japanese. I fought with her about my right to go to the meetings and finally they let me in. We didn't have a very clear idea of what we were doing. From what I knew about unions, it seemed very daring to me. I had heard my father talk about railroad workers getting killed in the 1950s. Anyway, we proceeded.

One of the workers had a father who was a railroad worker so we arranged through her father to meet someone in FASGUA, but the person didn't show up the day he was supposed to, and there we were just standing out in the street and one of the girls says, "Hey, I saw a sign for a workers' group downtown." So we went over there, and it was CNT. We walked in very humble, eyes down, and said in these small voices, "We're workers and we have all these problems." Miguel Angel Albizures was sitting there, all smiles: "Oh, sit down." We started to explain how things were, and Miguel Angel talked about a union, and he said, "You have to think about it and decide, but we will give you all the information you need to have one." And that's how it started.

[Although there had been a spy in the original group and several male organizers were fired, with the help of CNT lawyers the workers at ACRICASA won a union. Busy with the union, Oliva dropped out of school and after the initial male leaders were fired, she and other women became officers in a union that was, like the work force, mainly composed of women.]

After we got the union, the issue was a *pact*! The company did not want to talk about anything. They would just not show up at the meetings at the Labor Ministry, so the Labor Minister would make another appointment and they would not show up at the next one! *We always* showed up, but they did not. The Labor Minister kept throwing paper around, making more appointments.

We started work stoppages, lowering production, working like turtles, and then they would call a Labor Inspector, saying we had abandoned work. The minute the inspector came we would start working fast, and when he left, very slowly. We had about 100 items we wanted to discuss, like a bus to go into the neighborhoods to take us back and forth, day-care, bathrooms, pay, [dust] masks, vacations, [medical] treatment. We really had to pressure them, and it took almost two years of work stoppages, or suddenly a whole shift on its way out the door would take over management's offices, and we would walk out and everyone would yell, "Strike! Strike!" We were very animated, what with slowdowns, taking over offices, painting on the walls inside the plant, "We Want an Increase," "We Want Bus Service," things like that, and they didn't like to have the walls painted. Once a compañera painted a manager's car, she painted Union of ACRICASA on it. He was furious.

I was pregnant when the company finally started negotiating [in late 1976], and we kept up the stoppages during the negotiations—I don't even remember why. To pressure on some point, I guess. One night the night shift made a little strike . . . I was about six months pregnant. I went rushing over to the factory—I was on the day shift—and I had to come over the wall, and there was a huge spotlight to illuminate the yard. It was like a prison. I had to wait until it had moved to jump into the yard and run into the factory. The wall was very high; something could have happened to me, but nothing did.

After the pact was finally signed, the company violated most of the agreements, including about day-care. Pavel [Sonia's son] had just been born and when I got home from the maternity ward, someone comes over to where I lived saying the factory was on strike. "A strike?," I said, "why a strike?" So I grabbed Pavel—he was about two days old or something—and we rushed over. Everyone cheered when we showed up. The strike [in March 1977] was about company noncompliance with the agreements in the pact. The strike lasted 15 days; for 15 days we slept inside the plant compound. The Riot Police came the first night and I was afraid they would do something like throw gas bombs, and Pavel was there inside with me, he could die of the gases. I didn't know what to do, confront the police or take care of Pavel. Someone from CNT came down to take out Pavel, but the Riot Police circled very tightly and prevented anyone from entering. Then one of the *compas*, the guy who took care of the boiler, said, "I have the boiler on. If the Riot Police enter, I'm going to blow up this whole factory." This was quite something, because the whole block would have blown up, so the Chinese [the owners] said, "No, no, no," and we said "Yes, yes, yes. Either the Riot Police go or we all die together." Well, the Chinese told the Riot Police to go. It was dramatic.

We got a lot of support from other unions during those 15 days, baskets of food, and from the revolutionary groups as well; they would send a basket of fruit and under the fruit were leaflets. The leaflets from the revolutionary groups didn't shock us or surprise us. It seemed sort of normal, so the boxes of food would come and then some reading material. Food and reading material. We ate and read. We studied those leaflets, people grabbed them and started reading and analyzing them.

Finally the company agreed to implement the pact and we ended the strike. But some things took even more pressure, like day-care. Now that's interesting.

It's important to have day-care and it's part of the Labor Code, which says day-care must be provided in all factories where the majority of the workers are female. It should be mandatory in *all* factories because men and women should share child care, but few people see it that way, so it is only mandatory in factories where most workers are women, like ACRICASA. Day-care was in the Labor Code and in the pact but it wasn't in the factory. So, when Pavel was 40 days old I took him to work to make a point.

Pavel and I showed up at work one day, me with diapers, bottles and so forth, and everyone was astonished. At that time I worked in the laboratory with chemicals so the manager says, "You have to work, you can't have a child here with these chemicals." "Right," I said. There was supposed to be a day-care center and if they wanted to, they could give me a paid holiday until they built one, but until that time I would come with Pavel. They said they'd call a

Labor Inspector. I said, "Great! because according to the pact there was supposed to be day-care." I got a box and fixed it up for Pavel, I put the box on
my desk. The day was wild. I got up all the time to prepare his bottles. Every
time he cried, I'd say, "Ah, my little son," and stopped working to take care
of him. I always made him my priority. After a few days of this, the company
took a worker off a machine, placed her in a small room and brought cribs
and supplies. This was the day-care center. We never got what we really had
envisioned, a new little building with not someone watching children—just
feeding them and making sure they don't have accidents. We wanted someone
who knew how to develop children's capacities. I think Pavel's crib is still in
that room.

Another problem was that management didn't want to run the day-care center during the night, something the Labor Code is not specific about, so one
night I left Pavel there all night. Poor thing! I felt awful but these are the things
one must do. I didn't pick him up and there he stayed. I knew they wouldn't
leave him alone, that they would have to do something. Next day they came
and bawled me out. They had had to keep the girl there all night and pay her.
Finally they gave in.

Starting in late 1978 and early 1979 men were watching our homes, all of
the leaders in unions and in CNT. They would come to the door and ask for
you. They would call you on the phone at the CNT office and just breathe into
the phone. I got calls like that at the CNT office. I insulted them on the phone.

I really felt fear. I would go out with my son and feel like they were watching.

I was kidnapped on March 15, 1979. The secretary general of our union's
name had appeared on a death list and he had resigned. No one wanted the
job, everyone was so frightened. We couldn't be without a secretary general
so I took the position. Several positions were empty on the executive committee that month. On March 15 I realized that my house was being watched.
These men, so typical of that type, with wool caps or straw hats, were waiting,
and waiting, and watching, and watching. They had a manner that was very
middle-class.

That day I went to work. I got off the bus near work and went into a store
with Pavel because I always bought something for him on the way to work. I

saw this white car without license plates and one, two guys inside. I thought to myself, who could they be waiting for? Someone from our leadership? I left the store and turned and looked and saw this guy talking on a radio. I kept walking with Pavel. Nobody was in the street. I walked and a microbus without plates crossed in front of me, and masked men got out. They hit me and in the fight I pulled one of the masks down, and I haven't forgotten that face. Fat. Awful. They pulled me in the van and grabbed Pavel. I fainted. When I woke up I saw I was in a van with the seats out in back and about twelve men in back and two in front. I thought I was going to die so I asked them to leave Pavel in the street where someone could take him. One of them was carrying him. My hands and feet were tied. The van went on and on until we got to some place in the countryside, in the afternoon, but by then they had covered my eyes so I didn't know where I was. They started interrogating me, and they had a tape recorder on and they asked about the union and why it was formed, by whom, from where. Unfortunately I had a list of affiliates with me. They asked about our relations with the guerrillas. That interested them. One was very friendly and said he wanted to help me, and another one hit me. I was trembling with fright and with the cold. I told them I wasn't in the guerrillas. They said that wasn't true, and that all the union leaders were. They asked about a lot of people. They knew everyone.

Finally one came and said, "Look, I talked to the boss and it looks like we will set you free because of the child." One guy with the big voice said that they had decided that they would give me my life on the condition that I leave the country in 48 hours and never come back because the day I came back they would kill me because I was dangerous. They said they would leave me near my house, blindfolded, and when I heard a shot I could remove the blindfold. I was sure that meant they would kill me.

They threw me and Pavel out of the van somewhere, not near my house, but very far away. I heard frogs, and what time could it be? Silence and the highway. I almost fainted. I walked. I didn't know where I was going. I finally saw a light, and it was a gas station. There was this guy there with a wool cap over his face sleeping and suddenly I was frightened, but it was a worker there. He was startled when he woke up and saw me and the child . . . my pants were stained with blood and I looked like I was in shock. He said I could stay there, and I said no. He said a bus would pass and take me, and it did. The driver didn't ask me for money or say anything; he just took me because of my appearance, and the child's. I got home and the compañera who I lived with got sick when she saw me. I didn't know what to do. She said I had to leave. I went to the factory. The managers—I think they knew—were very solicitous. "What happened?," they asked. I said, "Nothing. I'm leaving. I want my indemnity." They had this friendly attitude. "Oh, of course," they said. Then I went to see the little day-care center, and something happened. I started to cry. I could not go into the plant. I felt ashamed. The compas came in and said, "You have to leave, they will kill you."

I left. I went to the Canadian embassy, but they said no, they couldn't give me a visa. And then I went to the Costa Rican embassy, and they did. Pavel and I left.

Marco Tulio Loza
City youth, worker, member of the Coca-Cola workers' union

[The fourth of eight children, Marco Tulio Loza was born in 1960 in Guatemala City.]

I've lived in the same neighborhood all my life. I loved growing up there and I had many friends when I was young. We did the things young people do: we made theater and circuses on the street, we played soccer. We were poor and we stole, but only from the fruit trees that belonged to a rich family who lived nearby and never from the poor. We were a good-natured crowd. We brought justice to the bad-tempered neighbors and joy to the good-humored ones every year during the Burning of Judas [the annual holiday when effigies of Judas are burned in the street]. We listed the names of bad neighbors and their deeds—like who had not returned a borrowed shovel—on the Judas and left it there all day before we burned it at night. We kept accounts in our heads all year about how people treated each other.

I remember during the earthquake in 1976, we, the youngsters, organized the area. We had a vigilance committee against thieves. We mobilized the fathers to participate but they proved unreliable. We took over a bakery on the block, and baked and distributed bread until the flour ran out. When the relief-aid trucks started showing up, we refused to let them in the street because we wanted to avoid chaos and fights. We told the drivers exactly how much we wanted and we distributed it. We rationed water, we took care of everything and everybody. Most of those friends are gone now, I don't even know where they live.

Once a friend disappeared and no one knew where he went. So of course his mother thought he had been kidnapped and she went looking for him in prisons, hospitals, morgues. One day a neighbor went up to the morgue checking for her and saw a body, all mangled from tortures, but with a mark on the right hand like my friend had, although you couldn't see the face. The mother talked to a psychologist who lived in the neighborhood and he said, yes, he knew in his heart it was her son. I suppose he just wanted her to stop looking. My father went up to the morgue and said it wasn't him and the mother asked me to go up, but I didn't, I knew it wasn't him. She decided it was him, and she went and got the body and we waked it or what was left of it and buried it. A year later the family prayed for nine days, which is the tradition here, and next day, there was my friend, sitting on the side of the road, afraid to go in his house. He had gone to Mexico to work. We called him Lazarus after that.

I remember my father kept a gun. One night soldiers came and started searching the area. My father quickly thrust the gun in a plastic bag, and shoved the bag deep into a big pile of river sand he kept for making bricks. The soldiers came and went through everything but they didn't find it, and it had taken us two minutes to hide it. Three of them even sat down to rest on the sandpile! We all sat around laughing after they left.

My father made bricks for a living and he made out OK. But he drank the money and spent it on other women. I was ashamed of him and refused to let him buy me anything. When I was ten I left, and lived with an uncle, who was a shoemaker, as his apprentice, but he only paid me two quetzales a week and when it finally hit me that this was not right, I left. I worked with my father for a while, and then made furniture in a carpentry shop, but I quit that too because they paid unfairly. Once my father left us entirely and with no money, nothing. Since I had a general idea about how to make bricks, I got together my friends and asked them to help me. We made bricks for a week and sold them to his customers and I gave the money to my mother. When my father came back, he was astonished. This repeated itself several times; he'd go off, and I'd run the business, keep up the customers and turn the money over to my mother. One day, I realized this wasn't right, that I was abetting his behavior and getting nothing for myself, and the next time he left I didn't make bricks. I explained to my mother and she said, "You're right. I understand." But the situation with my family worsened, he basically stopped providing. For a while I made miniature marimbas, real works of art which I could sell for 30 quetzales, but there was a limit to how many people would buy something like that.

Finally, I decided to go the United States. In that way I could send money home and make a life for myself. But I didn't get farther than Oaxaca [Mexico] where I was jailed along with many Salvadorans and a few Mexicans in a huge cell. One of the Mexicans kept challenging me to fight and finally I did. I beat him by myself. He couldn't believe I was only sixteen and after that he treated me with respect and told his family to bring me food. I remember there was a huge image of a devil painted on the wall. The jail was near a train station and every time a train passed, even in the middle of the night, one of the Salvadorans would jump up, yell "May another fall!" and hit the painted devil with all his might. I didn't understand this but what I found out was that the jail keepers would ship the Salvadorans home if they had twenty-five of them, so the Salvadorans were encouraging the devil to have more arrested. To wish ill on others in order to save oneself seemed wrong to me, but I started to get the idea that if you didn't find some good way out of bad situations, you found bad ways. In any case, you found a way and that was the whole idea.

When I got out of there and returned to Guatemala, I went to the technical high school for a year. I remember there was a student strike in 1977 and a few of us didn't strike, we locked ourselves in a workshop and kept working on a project. But some students came in and explained in a firm and polite way what the issues were . . . I think it was after some students had been killed. I thought they were going to beat us up and I was so impressed by their reasonable manner that I joined them. I was one of the last the cops pulled out of the courtyard.

I quit school soon after that because an uncle at Coca-Cola found me a job there as a helper on a delivery truck. I didn't understand what was going on and my uncle didn't say much. The atmosphere was tense. One day a manager asked me if I played soccer and if I didn't want to be on the EGSA team. I was a good player and said yes. My uncle gets word and comes over: "What are you doing? That's the company team!" He explained that they had a union team, STEGAC, and that EGSA had been started to draw people away from the STEGAC team and the union. I had no idea what a union was, but my uncle explained some and I joined the STEGAC team. We played EGSA and I made the three goals which won the game and broke my ankle. Marlon [Marlon Mendizábal, one of the leaders killed in 1980] took me to the hospital and we became friends and that's how I got involved. I was here when Aldana [René Aldana] was killed and when the rest were killed. I stayed.

I still support my family, and working at Coca-Cola I can give my brothers and sister opportunities I didn't have. I talk to them about the importance of finishing high school all the time. I never stop encouraging them to study. A few years ago when they were getting bad grades, I tied my two brothers to their chairs at the kitchen table to force them to study.

Notes

Introduction

1. Interview with Marco Tulio Loza (pseudonym), Guatemala City, January 1986.

2. Between 1954 and 1991 some 200,000 people were killed and/or disappeared according to Susanne Jonas, *The Battle for Guatemala: Rebels, Death Squads, and U.S. Power* (Boulder, Colo.: Westview, 1991). At least 60,000 of these deaths or disappearances took place between 1980 and 1986; precise figures are not known. "Unofficial" violence exceeded the official in the 1954–80 period. For example, between 1966 and 1968 the army waged a war against a guerrilla movement in the eastern part of the country in which an estimated 3,000 people died. During the same period, 7,000 were disappeared or found dead from torture, "the majority so mutilated their bodies were beyond identification." *Amnesty International Report* (London: Amnesty International, 1974). As of 1986 there were 35,000 Guatemalans reported as disappeared. That number represents more than 40 percent of all the reported disappeared in Latin America. The Guatemalan population comprises less than 3 percent of the total population of Latin America.

3. Allen Nairn, "To Defend Our Way of Life: An Interview with a U.S. Businessman," in Jonathan Fried, Marvin Gettleman, Deborah Levenson, and Nancy Peckenham, eds., *Guatemala in Rebellion: Unfinished History* (New York: Grove Press, 1983), 89.

4. Interview, name withheld upon request, Guatemala City, August 1984.

5. Interview, name withheld upon request, Guatemala City, August 1984.

6. Interview with Rodolfo Robles, Guatemala City, August 1984.

7. Interview with Julio Arriaza, Guatemala City, November 1985.

8. Carlos Figueroa Ibarra, "Contenido de clase y participación obrera en el movimiento anti-dictatorial de 1920," *Política y Sociedad* 4 (July–December 1977): 5–51; Mario López

Larrave, *Breve historia del movimiento sindical guatemalteco* (Guatemala: Editorial Universitaria, 1979); Guadalupe Navas, *El movimiento sindical como manifestación de la lucha de clase* (Guatemala: Editorial Universitaria, 1979); Miguel Angel Albizures, *Tiempo de sudor y lucha* (Mexico: N.p., 1987).

9. Walter Benjamin, *Illuminations* (New York: Schocken Books, 1969), 262.

10. This debate was lively for thirty years and continued into the early 1990s. See Danielo Rodríguez, *El 21 de Junio de 1980* (Mexico: Equipo de Apoyo Sindical, 1990). He writes: "Historicamente el elemento consciente siempre llega a las masa desde afuera ya que la dinámica espontánea de estas, la lucha reinvindicativa inmediata solo puede generar el económicismo, es decir, la lucha por aumentos salariales y mejoras económicas" (p. 10). Rodríguez, a lawyer, was an adviser to the National Central of Workers (CNT) and a member of the Rebel Armed Forces (FAR) in the 1970s; in the 1980s he joined a group of exiles who attempted to influence trade unionism within Guatemala. In March 1992 he left FAR and returned to Guatemala, where he signed an amnesty promoted by the army as part of its continuing pacification strategy.

11. A Leninist position implicitly delineates workers as having class "instinct" and middle-class intellectuals as capable of knowing and teaching progressive proletarian "culture." Under the right managers the workers become true to themselves as a class and can act upon their essential "natural" need to overthrow capitalism.

12. James Scott, *Weapons of the Weak: Everyday Forms of Peasant Resistance* (New Haven: Yale University Press, 1985), 27.

13. Pablo Pozzi, *Oposición obrera a la dictadura* (Buenos Aires: Contrapunto, 1988); Manuel Barrera and Gonzalo Falabella, *Sindicatos bajo regímenes militares: Argentina, Chile, Brazil* (Santiago: Centro de Estudios, 1990).

14. John Weeks, *The Economies of Central America* (New York: Holmes and Meier, 1985); Victor Bulmer-Thomas, *The Political Economy of Central America since 1920* (Cambridge: Cambridge University Press, 1987); Robert G. Williams, *Export Agriculture and the Crisis in Central America* (Chapel Hill: University of North Carolina Press, 1986).

15. The National Central of Workers, which divided into two factions, CNT and CNT-21, and the Autonomous Federation of Guatemalan Unions (FASGUA) continued for a brief period after the 1980 kidnappings as underground organizations that had voice through publications, almost no activities, and few members.

16. To understand the character of this war, see Ricardo Falla, *Masacres de la selva* (Guatemala: Editorial Universitaria, 1992).

17. Henry J. Frundt's book, *Refreshing Pauses: Coca-Cola and Human Rights in Guatemala* (New York: Praeger, 1987) and my book complement one another. Frundt's deals primarily with the international campaign and mine with the local union.

18. For inspirational discussions of the problems and uses of oral testimony, see Daphne Patai, "U.S. Academics and Third World Women: Is Ethical Research Possible?," in Sherna Berger Gluck and Daphne Patai, *Women's Words: The Feminist Practice of Oral History* (New York: Routledge, 1991), 137–53; Daphne Patai, *Brazilian Women Speak: Contemporary Life Stories* (New Brunswick, N.J.: Rutgers University Press, 1988), 3–35; Michael Frisch, *A Shared Authority: Essays on the Craft and Meaning of Oral and Public History* (Albany: State University of New York Press, 1990); and Alejandro Portelli, *The Death of Luigi Trastulli* (Albany: State University of New York Press, 1991).

Chapter 1

1. Pedro Cortés y Larraz, *Descripción geográphico-moral de la diócesis de Goathemala* (Guatemala: Sociedad de Geografía e Historia de Guatemala, 1958); Murdo MacLeod, *Spanish Central America: A Socioeconomic History, 1520–1720* (Berkeley: University of California Press, 1973). I use the term *Maya Indians* or *Mayas* or *Indians* to refer to the descendants of the pre-Conquest population, the Maya of Guatemala, whom the Spanish misnamed as Indian, a name that over the centuries became commonly used. In the 1990s the use of the term *Maya* has started to spread in tandem with a revival of ethnic consciousness, and in some arenas it has partially replaced or joined *Indian* as well as other common identifications: *campesino*, the name of a village (a San Juanero to identify a person from the town of San Juan Sacatepéque), and the name of a language such as Mam or Quiché. All of the names applied to the Maya of Guatemala are charged with political, social, historical, and cultural implications. The term *Maya* was not generally used in the city from 1954 to 1985. My informants used *indio* (Indian), *natural* (a natural or native person), and *indígena* (an indigenous person).

2. David McCreery, "An Odious Feudalism," *Latin American Perspectives* 13, no. 48 (Winter 1986): 99–115, and "Debt Servitude in Rural Guatemala, 1876–1936," *Hispanic American Historical Review* 63 (November 1976): 735–59; Julio Castellanos Cambranes, *Café y campesinos en Guatemala, 1853–1897* (Guatemala: Universidad de San Carlos, 1985).

3. Ricardo Falla, "Juan el Gordo: Visión indígena de su explotación," *Estudios Centroamericanos* 268 (1971): 98–107. Examples of such urban tales are the well-known "Viernes del diablo" and "La carbonera ambiciosa," which appear in Celso A. Lara Figueroa, *Por los viejos barrios de la ciudad de Guatemala* (Guatemala: Artemis y Edinter, 1984).

4. Alfredo Guerra Borges, *Compendio de geografía económica y humana de Guatemala* (Guatemala City: Instituto de Investigaciónes Económicas y Sociales Universidad de San Carlos de Guatemala, 1981), 2:283–96.

5. Apparently in the colonial period the term *ladino* referred to a Spanish-speaking Maya

Indian. In contemporary usage, ladino means "non-Indian." For generations many upper-class families have used adjectives that in their eyes have a far more positive value, such as German (many are of German origin), Spanish, or white. See Marta Casaus Arzu, *Guatemala: Linaje y racismo* (Costa Rica: FLACSO, 1992), 191–305.

6. *Primer Congreso Pedagógico Centroamericano* (Guatemala: N.p., 1893), 164–203; Carlos González Orellano, *Historia de la educación en Guatemala* (Guatemala: Editorial Universitaria, 1980), 267–344.

7. Renate Witzel de Ciudad, *Más de 100 años del movimiento obrero urbano en Guatemala: Artesanos y obreros en el período liberal, 1877–1944* (Guatemala: Asociación de Investigación y Estudios Sociales en Guatemala, 1991), 1–70.

8. On the Workers' League and events in 1920, see Carlos Figueroa Ibarra, "Contenido de clase y participación obrera en el movimiento anti-dictatorial de 1920," *Política y Sociedad* 4 (July–December 1977): 5–51, and "La Insurrección Armada de 1920 en Guatemala," *Política y Sociedad* 8 (July–December 1979): 91–146; and Rafael Arévalo Martínez, *Ecce Pericles: La tiranía de Manuel Estrada Cabrera en Guatemala* (San José, Costa Rica: EDUCA, 1982).

9. Antonio Obando Sánchez, *Memorias: La historia del movimiento obrero* (Guatemala: Editorial Universitaria, 1978); Luis Cardoza y Aragón, *La Revolución Guatemalteca* (Mexico: Cuadernos Americanos, 1955).

10. *Claridad*, August 3, 1945. For the impact of the Atlantic Charter on labor activists, see Medardo Mejía, *El movimiento obrero en la Revolución de Octubre* (Guatemala: N.p., 1949). On the coalition that forced out Jorge Ubico in July 1944 and overthrew his appointed successor, Frederico Ponce, in October 1944, see Alfonso Solórzano, "Factores económicos y corrientes ideológicas en el movimiento de Octubre de 1944," *Alero* 8, no. 3 (September–October 1974), 23–31, and Manuel Galich, *Del pánico al ataque* (Guatemala: Editorial Universitaria, 1985).

11. Jim Handy, *Gift of the Devil: A History of Guatemala* (Boston: South End Press, 1984), 123–47, and "'The Most Precious Fruit of the Revolution': The Guatemalan Agrarian Land Reform, 1952–1954," *Hispanic American Historical Review* 68, no. 4 (1985): 675–705; Victor Bulmer-Thomas, *The Political Economy of Central America since 1920* (Cambridge: Cambridge University Press, 1987), 105–29.

12. Obando Sánchez, *Memorias*; Mario López Larrave, *Breve historia del movimiento sindical guatemalteco* (Guatemala: Editorial Universitaria, 1979); Edwin Bishop, "The Guatemalan Labor Movement, 1944–1959" (Ph.D. dissertation, University of Wisconsin, 1959); Archer Bush, "Organized Labor in Guatemala, 1944–1949" (M.A. thesis, Colgate University, 1950); María Eugenia Ramos Guzmán de Schmook, "El movimiento sindical en el decenio revolucionario, 1944–1954" (thesis, Universidad de San Carlos, 1978); Arcadio Ruiz

Franco, *Hambre y miseria* (Guatemala: Tipografía Nacional, 1950); Arturo Morales, *Movimiento sindical ferroviario* (Guatemala: N.p., 1950).

13. *Vanguardia*, December 14, 1946.

14. López Larrave, *Breve historia*, 25–44. Tens of thousands belonged to the rural National Confederation of Guatemalan Peasants, a part of CGTG after 1952.

15. Bishop, "The Guatemalan Labor Movement," 130–50.

16. The founding party congress was clandestine because Arévalo attacked the left by closing a Marxist school, Escuela Claridad de Henri Barbusse, and exiling Salvadoran Communists. It adopted the name Guatemalan Communist party and elected a central committee of nine. The party remained underground until its second congress in 1952, which changed the party's name to the Guatemalan Labor party. Carlos Cáceres, *Aproximación a Guatemala* (Mexico: Universidad Autónoma de Sinola, 1980); Víctor Manuel Gutiérrez, *Apuntes para la historia del partido comunista de Guatemala* (Guatemala: N.p., 1965); Rina Villars, *Porque quiero seguir viviendo . . . habla Graciela García* (Tegucigalpa: Editorial Guaymuras, 1991), 208–41.

17. *Octubre*, August 7, 1952.

18. The union press included weekly newspapers of craft and rail workers such as *La Voz de Obrera, Adelante, Alerta, STTN, Vanguardia Gráfica, Periódico Acción, Revista Social Fraternal de Barbero, El Sindicalista, Unidad, Unificación Obrera y Campesina, Tribuna Ferrocarrilera, SAG,* and *Vanguardia,* as well as the Communist *Octubre.*

19. Piero Gleijeses argues the importance of PGT under Arbenz in his *Shattered Hope: The Guatemalan Revolution and the United States, 1944–1954* (Princeton: Princeton University Press, 1991); see also Bishop, "The Guatemalan Labor Movement," in addition to the union press, which leaves little doubt of PGT's enormous ideological influence, despite its small size. The U.S. State Department justified the 1954 coup on the grounds of the "Communist menace." The Communist menace consisted of national capitalist development, a moderate land reform, and labor laws that curbed U.S. companies' free hand in Guatemala.

20. Huberto Alvarado, *Por un arte nacional, democrático y realista* (Guatemala: N.p., 1953). Saker-Ti formed in 1946 and its distinguished members included writers Luis Cardoza y Aragón and Rafael Sosa, artists Carlos Mérida and Juan Antonio Franco, and musician Ricardo Castillo as well as almost all of the players in the new National Symphony Orchestra. Saker-Ti published a magazine and promoted national culture and world left-wing culture, from Enrique Gómez Carrillo to Bertolt Brecht and Nizam Hikmet.

21. Quoted from Graciela García, *Las luchas revoluciónarias de la nueva Guatemala* (Mexico, 1952), 76.

22. *Unificación Obrera y Campesina*, March 9, 1946.

23. Roque Dalton, *Miguel Mármol* (Costa Rica: EDUCA, 1982), 508.

24. *El Sindicalista*, November 1946.

25. *Tribuna Obrera*, June 2, 1952.

26. Ruth Berins Collier and David Collier, *Shaping the Political Arena* (Princeton: Princeton University Press, 1991), is one recent example of the attention scholars have paid to corporativism in Latin America. To whatever degree the state may have subtly dominated labor movements in other Latin American countries, it did not do so in Guatemala under Arévalo and Arbenz. The history of Guatemalan trade unionism between 1944 and 1954 is not one of incorporation but of persistent worker mobilization.

27. Dalton, *Miguel Mármol*, 517–18.

28. *Tribuna Ferrocarrilera*, November 6, 1949; *Unidad*, August 15, 1953; *Unificación Obrera y Campesina*, May 1, 1953; *SAG*, February 1, 1954.

29. Comité de Acción Político, "Manifesto" (leaflet), July 22, 1950, Archivo General de Centroamérica (AGCA).

30. José Alberto Cardoza, "A treinta años de la Revolución de Octubre de 1944," *Alero* 8 (September–October 1974): 97.

31. Miguel Valdés, "Memorias de un militante obrero," *Alero* 1 (May–June 1979): 133.

32. Guillermo Toriello, *La batalla de Guatemala* (Mexico City: Editorial América Nueva, 1956); Steven Schlesinger and Stephen Kinzer, *Bitter Fruit: The Untold Story of the American Coup in Guatemala* (Garden City, N.Y.: Doubleday, 1982); Richard Immerman, *The CIA in Guatemala: The Foreign Policy of Intervention* (Austin: University of Texas Press, 1982).

33. *La Hora*, July 31, August 5, 13, 18, 1954. By August 18, 800 of the 7,000 jailed had been charged. Of these 800, over 70 percent were peasants accused of violating private property.

34. *La Hora*, August 12, 1954.

35. Interview with Carlos Escobar, Guatemala City, August 1984.

36. *La Hora*, July 1, 5, 7, 1954.

37. Ibid., July 14, 1954.

38. Ibid., July 18, 1954.

39. Ibid., June 3, 1955. See also Nathan Whetten, *Land and Labor in Guatemala* (New Haven: Yale University Press, 1961).

40. Calculated from the registers, Guatemala, Archivo, Dirección Administrativo de Trabajo (A-DAT).

41. Carlos Figueroa Ibarra, *El recurso del miedo: Ensayo sobre el estado y terror en Guatemala* (Costa Rica: EDUCA, 1991), 98–103. For an explanation of the ideology of Guatemalan elites, see Edelberto Torres Rivas, "Vida y muerte en Guatemala: Reflexiónes sobre la crisis y la violencia política," *Alero* 5 (January–February 1980): 85–103.

42. *La Hora*, July 8, 1954.

43. Ibid., July 20, 1954.

44. *El Imparcial*, September 20, 1954; Serafino Romualdi, *Presidents and Peons* (New York: Funk and Wagnalls, 1967).

45. *La Hora*, September 23, 1954.

46. Ibid., September 24, 1954.

47. Ibid., February 5, 1955.

48. Bishop, *The Guatemalan Labor Movement*, 230.

49. *El Imparcial*, July 8, 1956.

50. *La Hora*, January 20–28, 1957. ORIT raised this issue after workers fled José Luis Arenas Barrera's plantation, La Perla, in the isolated Ixcán and went to the city to give testimony to the effect that they had been enslaved and beaten. Ministry of Labor officials flew up to La Perla in a small plane and later reported that all the accusations were true but that "there is nothing we can do to make the *finqueros* comply with the labor laws." *La Hora*, January 15, 1957.

51. *Organo de Información del Sindicato de Acción y Mejoramiento Ferrocarrilero*, June 15, 1956.

52. *La Hora*, June 1, 1955.

53. Interview with Leticia Najarro, Guatemala City, July 1984.

54. *Prensa Libre*, March 9–10, 1967. By then one death squad specialized in trade unionists.

55. *Prensa Libre*, October 14, 1968; *La Hora*, June 19, 1968.

56. Actas, 1954–68, expediente SAMF, A-DAT. The pro-Liberation leader whom the railroad workers rejected, Luis Padilla, later established the progovernment Federation of Guatemalan Workers (FTG), which did little until it was taken over by militants in the 1970s.

57. See letters and articles in *SAMF*, May 15, July 15, 1956, November 1962, April, May 1965, January 1966. In 1963 the minister of interior refused to recognize SAMF because its new leaders had been leaders, though anti-PGT ones, in the 1944–54 era; in 1967 SAMF's executive committee members who were in the Revolutionary party (PR) were investigated by the governing PR's minister of defense. Actas, March 1963, September 1967, expediente SAMF, A-DAT.

58. *La Hora*, August 14, 1969; Interview, name withheld upon request, San José, Costa Rica, March 1985.

59. *El Gráfico*, September 9, 1973; *Diario Impacto*, January 6, 1974; *Diario La Tarde*, August 27, 1974; *La Nación*, September 13, 1974.

60. *AIFLD Report*, December 3, 1965, July 4, 1966, June 6, May 19, 1969. On AIFLD in Central America, see Daniel Cantor and Juliet Schor, *Tunnel Vision: Labor, the World Econ-*

omy, and Central America (Boston: South End Press, 1987), and Tom Barry and Deb Preusch, *AIFLD in Central America: Agents as Organizers* (Albuquerque, N.Mex.: Inter-Hemispheric Education Resource Center, 1986).

61. *La Hora*, December 16, 1955.

62. Ibid., July 27, 1954. FASGUA was originally known by the acronym FAS.

63. See José García Bauer, "El Concepto de justicia social cristiana" and "Proyecto para la creación de una escuela sobre cuestiones sociales," expediente CEDAC, Archivo de Arquidiocesano, Palacio Arzobispal, Guatemala City; and Hubert J. Miller, "Catholic Leaders and Spiritual Socialism during the Arévalo Administration in Guatemala, 1945–1951," in Ralph Lee Woodward, Jr., *Central America: Historical Perspectives on the Contemporary Crises* (Westport, Conn.: Greenwood Press, 1988), 85–104.

64. *La Hora*, May 2, 1955.

65. Committee for the National Defense Against Communism to Ministry of Labor, December 23, 1954, expediente 10, A-DAT.

66. President of Graphic Arts Committee of the General Association of Industrialists to Ministry of Labor, January 1955, and CNDCC to Ministry of Labor, January 1955, expediente 10, A-DAT.

67. Actas, January 1957, expediente FASGUA, A-DAT.

68. Actas, expediente 10, A-DAT.

69. Valdés, "Memorias de un militante obrero."

70. *El Estudiante*, May 3, 1956; *La Hora*, May 2, 1956.

71. *La Hora*, May 2, 7, 1957.

72. Ibid., May 2, 1959, May 2, 1960; *Diario Impacto*, May 3, 1961.

73. *Prensa Libre*, February 18, 1963, May 2, 1966.

74. Expediente FASGUA, A-DAT.

75. Actas, June 1968, expediente 133, A-DAT; *La Hora*, May 28, 1968; Sindicato de CAVISA, "18 años de lucha," Guatemala City, 1984; *El Gráfico*, September 13, 1968; Actas, September 1968, expediente FASGUA, A-DAT.

76. Interview, name withheld upon request, San José, Costa Rica, March 1986.

77. Actas, July 12, 1965, expediente FASGUA, A-DAT.

78. "Manifesto de la Democracia Cristiana," *Acción Social Cristiana*, November 24, 1955.

79. North American Congress on Latin America, *Guatemala* (New York: NACLA, 1974): 179.

80. Partido Guatemalteco de los Trabajadores, "Táctica general, desarrollo y formas de lucha de la revolución guatemalteca," Guatemala, 1961.

81. *Diario Impacto*, March 3–10, 1962; *Prensa Libre*, March 10, 1962; Manuel Colón Ar-

gueta, "Guatemala: El significado de las jornadas de Marzo y April," Centro de Estudios Regionales y Urbanos, Guatemala, April 1969.

82. Eduardo Galeano, *Guatemala: Occupied Country* (New York: Monthly Review, 1967), 133–43.

83. For descriptions of the guerrilla movement during this period, see Galeano, *Guatemala: Occupied Country*; Ricardo Ramírez, *Lettres du front guatemalteque* (Paris: Maspero, 1970); and Adolfo Gilly, "The Guerrilla Movement in Guatemala," *Monthly Review* (May and June 1965): 7–41.

84. *Prensa Libre*, March 25, 1968; Gabriel Aguilera Peralta, *La dialéctica del terror en Guatemala* (San José, Costa Rica: EDUCA, 1981).

85. Carlos Figueroa Ibarra makes this argument in *El recurso del miedo*. On the continuing violence in Guatemala, see Americas Watch, *Getting Away with Murder* (New York: Americas Watch, 1991). The growing literature on the culture of fear in Guatemala and elsewhere includes Kay Warren, ed., *The Violence Within: Cultural and Political Opposition in Divided Nations* (Boulder, Colo.: Westview, 1993); Michael Taussig, *Shamanism, Colonialism, and the Wild Man: A Study in Terror and Healing* (Chicago: University of Chicago Press, 1987); Benjamin D. Paul and William J. Demarest, "The Operation of a Death Squad in San Pedro de La Laguna," in Robert M. Carmack, ed., *Harvest of Violence: The Maya Indians and the Guatemalan Crisis* (Norman: University of Oklahoma Press, 1988), 119–55; Ignacio Martin-Baro, *Acción y ideologia: Psicología social desde Centroamérica* (El Salvador: UCA Editores, 1983); Elaine Scary, *The Body in Pain: The Making and the Unmaking of the World* (Oxford: Oxford University Press, 1985); Elizabeth Lira and María Isabel Castillo, *Psicología de la amenaza política y del miedo* (Santiago: Ediciónes Chile América, 1991); and Juan E. Corradi, Patricia Weiss Fagen, and Manuel Antonio Garretón, *Fear at the Edge: State Terror and Resistance in Latin America* (Berkeley: University of California Press, 1992).

Chapter 2

1. Interview with Rodolfo Robles, Guatemala City, August 1984.

2. *Diario Impacto*, May 3, 1963.

3. On industrial development, see René Poitevin, *El proceso de industrialización en Guatemala* (San José, Costa Rica: EDUCA, 1977), 97–142; Edelberto Torres Rivas, "Aspectos generales de la economía centroamericana," *Alero* 14, no. 1 (May–June 1979): 37–58; Roman Mayorga Quirós, *El crecimiento desigual en Centroamérica* (Mexico: N.p., 1983); and Victor Bulmer-Thomas, *The Political Economy of Central America since 1920* (Cambridge: Cambridge University Press, 1987), 175–99.

4. Luis Alvarado, "El desarrollo capitalista de Guatemala y la cuestion urbana," *Cuadernos Universitarios* (October 1979): 6.

5. Interview with Miguel Cifuentes, New York City, March 1984.

6. Interview with Sonia Oliva, Costa Rica, March 1986.

7. *La Hora*, December 14, 1962.

8. Julio Alfonso Figueroa Gálvez, *Estructura y grado de desarrollo en la industria manufacturera en Guatemala* (Guatemala: Universidad de San Carlos, 1978).

9. Interview with Eduardo Baptista, Guatemala City, August 1984.

10. Jonathan Fried, Marvin Gettleman, Deborah Levenson, and Nancy Peckenham, eds., *Guatemala in Rebellion: Unfinished History* (New York: Grove Press, 1983), 114.

11. Per capita industrial output in Guatemala in 1973 was $90, as compared with the Latin American average of $161.55. Figueroa Gálvez, *Estructura y grado de desarrollo en la industria*.

12. Figueroa Gálvez, *Estructura y grado de desarrollo en la industria*, 28; *Encuestra Industrial*, 1965, 1974; Santiago López Aguilar, *La clases sociales en Guatemala* (Guatemala: Editorial Universitaria, 1984), 33–43.

13. Alfredo Guerra Borges, *Compendio de geografía económica y humana de Guatemala* (Guatemala City: Instituto de Investigaciónes Económicas y Sociales Universidad de San Carlos, 1981), 2:283–92.

14. James Dunkerley, *Power in the Isthmus* (London: Verso, 1988), 207.

15. *Encuestra Industrial*, 1975. In 1946 factories in the city with more than twenty workers accounted for 42 percent of the industrial work force. Guatemala, Dirección de Estadísticas, *Censo Industrial*, 1946.

16. Alvan O. Zarate, *Principales patrones de migración interna en Guatemala, 1964* (Guatemala: Estudios Centroamericanos, no. 3, 1967); René Arturo Orellano González, *Guatemala: Migraciónes internas de población* (Guatemala: University of San Carlos, 1978).

17. According to the 1973 National Census, the percentage of women in manufacturing was 17 percent; traders and vendors, 27 percent; office workers, 36 percent; professionals, 39 percent; and service workers (including domestics), 74 percent. The high number of women in the professions is explained primarily by the fact that 73 percent of the city's schoolteachers were women. Guatemala, Dirección de Estadísticas, *Censo Poblacional*, 1973. See also Norma S. Chinchilla, "Industrialization, Monopoly Capitalism, and Women's Work in Guatemala," *Signs: Journal of Women in Culture and Society* 3, no. 1 (1977): 39–55.

18. According to the 1973 National Census, 12 percent of the city's population was Indian, but this figure is unreliable for want of a definition of the term *Indian* in the urban context. The ethnicity of the urban working class is a charged issue. Two scholars, Carlos

Guzmán Bockler and Jean-Loup Herbert, whose work has had an impact on intellectuals, students, and guerrilla groups, argue that the basic national contradiction is an ethnic one—between Maya Indians and ladinos—and not also a class one. They imply that the struggle for liberation has to take place between the ladino city (and its ladino working class) and the nonladino countryside, and they assume an oppositional relationship between ladinos and Maya Indians. Carlos Guzmán Bockler and Jean-Loup Herbert, *Guatemala: Una interpretación histórico-social* (Mexico City: Siglo Veintiuno, 1970).

19. Santiago Bastos and Manuela Camus, *Indígenas en la Ciudad de Guatemala: Subsistencia y cambio étnico* (Guatemala: FLACSO, 1990).

20. In his book, *Thanks to God and the Revolution* (New York: Columbia University Press, 1988), Roger Lancester argues that in the same period Managua, Nicaragua, was a "city of peasants." The population of Guatemala City was not so homogeneous in the 1960s and the 1970s, and the countryside from which the city drew population was not composed only, or even necessarily mainly, of peasants. On the complexities of the Guatemalan countryside, see Huberto Alvarado, *Proletarización del campesino de Guatemala* (Guatemala: Piedrasanta, 1981); Carlos Figueroa Ibarra, *El proletariado rural en el agro* (Guatemala: Editorial Universitaria, 1979); and Carol Smith, "Local History in a Global Context: Social and Economic Transitions in Western Guatemala" (Paper presented at the American Anthropological Association, Los Angeles, April 1983).

21. Orellano González, *Guatemala: Migraciónes internas*. It is suggestive of the composition of the urban working class that 60 percent of the union officers of the 1950s were city born and most of the remainder were from the southern coast. The weight of the city born decreased with time but it remained significant. Archivo, Dirección Administrativo de Trabajo.

22. Interview with Efraín Alonso, New York City, April 1984.

23. Luis Alvarado, "El desarrollo capitalista."

24. In the 1970s urban transportation was described by one city official as "true anarchy." *Diario Impacto*, July 7, 1978. By the late 1970s, literally hundreds of companies ran 857 buses in this metropolis of one million. Companies competed for riders along heavily traveled routes, leaving large areas of the city without services.

25. Bryan Roberts, *Organizing Strangers* (Austin: University of Texas, 1973).

26. René Arturo Orellano González, *La realidad de la infancia y la juventud en Guatemala* (Guatemala: Universidad de San Carlos, 1979).

27. For example, see Manuel Salguero B., *Estudios sociales* (Guatemala: Ministerio de Educación, 1969) or Fredy Sandoval, *Estudios sociales* (Guatemala: Ministerio de Educación, 1969).

28. Richard Adams, *Crucifixion by Power* (Austin: University of Texas Press, 1970), 279–317; Luis Samandu, Hans Siebers, and Oscar Sierra, *Guatemala retos de la iglesia católica en una sociedad en crisis* (Costa Rica: Editorial DEI, 1990), 19–36.

29. Torcuato di Tella, *Sindicato y communidad: Dos tipos de estructura sindical latinoamericana* (Buenos Aires: Editorial del Instituto, 1967).

30. Brian Ford, "Hegemony and Its Inverse: Ethnicity and Terror in Guatemala" (Paper presented at The MacArthur Peace and Security Seminar, February 3, 1993, Columbia University).

31. *El Gráfico*, October 10, 1978; Speech, May First, 1978.

32. Cristobal Monzón Lemus, *Camino de adolescente: La vida de Ramón en el barrio El Gallito* (Guatemala: N.p., 1991).

33. Interview with Marco Tulio Loza, Guatemala City, January 1986.

34. Interview with Rodolfo Robles, Guatemala City, January 1986.

35. Interview with Marco Tulio Loza, Guatemala City, January 1986.

36. Guatemalan folklorist Celso A. Lara Figueroa has collected many of these stories and published them in *Leyendas y casos de la tradición oral de la ciudad de Guatemala* (Guatemala: Editorial Universitaria, 1973).

37. Interview with Pedro López, Guatemala City, February 1986.

38. Deborah Levenson-Estrada, *El futuro debería haber estado en frente de ellos* (Guatemala: AVANCSO, forthcoming).

39. Interview with Marco Tulio Loza, Guatemala City, January 1986.

40. Interview with Rodolfo Robles, Guatemala City, January 1986.

41. Interview with Rafael Méndez, Guatemala City, October 1984.

42. Interview with Mercedes Gómez, Guatemala City, August 1984.

43. Interview with Sonia Oliva, Costa Rica, March 1986.

44. Ibid.

45. Interview with Luis Colocho, Guatemala City, November 1985.

46. Leticia Najarro, who worked with the AFL-CIO in the 1960s, commented that it was "impossible for a woman to be a trade unionist and married." Interview with Leticia Najarro, Guatemala City, July 1984.

47. Interviews with Luis Colocho (Guatemala City, November 1985) and Efraín Alonso (New York City, April 1984).

48. Interview with Lorena Ibarra, Guatemala City, October 1984.

Chapter 3

1. Renate Witzel de Ciudad, *Más de 100 años del movimiento obrero urbano en Guatemala: Artesanos y obreros en el período liberal, 1877–1944* (Guatemala: Asociación de Investigación y Estudios Sociales en Guatemala, 1991), 74.

2. Joseph Cardijn quoted from *Avance Juvenil*, no. 5 (September 1947), no. 14 (October 1950), no. 22 (August 1955), no. 34 (June 1956).

3. Scott Mainwaring, *The Catholic Church and Politics in Brazil, 1916–1985* (Stanford: Stanford University Press, 1986), 116–41. On the many intellectual sources for Catholic Action, see Yves M. J. Congar, *Lay People in the Church* (Westminster, Md.: Newman Press, 1965), and Emmanuel de Kadt, "JUC and the AP: The Rise of Catholic Radicalism in Brazil," in *The Church and Social Change in Latin America*, ed. Henry A. Lansberger (Notre Dame, Ind.: University of Notre Dame Press, 1970), 191–219.

4. Reports from the Conferences of Central American and Panamian Bishops (CEDAC), expediente CEDAC, Archivo de Arquidiocesano, Palacio Arzobispal, Guatemala City.

5. Conferencia de los Exsmos, Prelados de Centro América, Seminario de San José, December 1953, expediente CEDAC; *Estatutos generales de la acción católica de la Arquidiócesis de Santiago de Guatemala* (Guatemala: Tipografía Sánchez y de Guise, n.d.).

6. Interview with Julio Celso de León, Guatemala City, January 1991; *Avance Juvenil*, no. 37 (September 1956).

7. Luis Samandu et al., *Guatemala retos de la iglesia católica en una sociedad en crisis* (San José, Costa Rica: Editorial DEI, 1990), 19–36; Phillip Berryman, *The Religious Roots of Rebellion: Christians in Central American Revolutions* (New York: Orbis Books, 1984), 163–19.

8. *Avance Juvenil*, no. 14 (October 1950).

9. Interview with Miguel Angel Albizures, Mexico City, November 1984.

10. Interview with Julio Celso de León, Guatemala City, January 1991.

11. *Avance Juvenil*, no. 32 (April 1956).

12. Interview with Miguel Angel Albizures, Mexico City, November 1984.

13. Interview with Alberto Colorado, New York City, April 1984.

14. *Avance Juvenil*, no. 29 (September 1954), no. 43 (May 1957), no. 44 (July 1957), no. 47 (December 1957), no. 48 (May 1958).

15. Interview with Julio Celso de León, Guatemala City, January 1991.

16. Ibid.

17. Interview with Miguel Angel Albizures, Mexico City, November 1984.

18. Ibid.

19. *Prensa Libre*, May 1, 1962.

20. CNT, "Boletín," Guatemala City, 1973, Centro de Documentación, Inforpress Centroamérica (CDIC), expediente CNT.

21. CNT, "Formación," 1974, CDIC, expediente CNT.

22. *Acción Popular*, October 1974.

23. Comité de Trabajadores de la Elegante, Untitled leaflet, March 1975, CDIC, expediente Trabajadores.

24. Antonio Malouf to his employees, March 13, 1975, CDIC, expediente Trabajadores.

25. Comité de Trabajadores de la Elegante, Untitled leaflet, March 1975, CDIC, expediente Trabajadores.

26. *El Gráfico*, November 5, 1975; *La Nación*, November 7, 1975.

27. Interview with Enrique Torres, Mexico City, November 1984.

28. Luis Alberto López Sánchez, *Derecho de trabajo para el trabajador* (Guatemala: Impreso Industriales, 1985).

29. Interview, name withheld upon request, Guatemala City, September 1984.

30. Interview with Efraín Alonso, New York City, April 1984, May 1993.

31. Ibid.

32. Jim Handy, *Gift of the Devil: A History of Guatemala* (Boston: South End Press), 167.

33. Arana Osorio quoted from *Inforpress*, March 5, 1986. For suggestive discussions on the evolution of the Guatemalan bourgeoisie and its relationship to governing parties and to the military, see Edelberto Torres Rivas, "Authoritarianism and Transition to Democracy in Central America," in Jan Flora and Edelberto Torres Rivas, *Sociology of Developing Societies: Central America* (New York: Monthly Review, 1989); and Gabriel Aguilera Peralta, "El proceso de militarización en el estado guatemalteco," *Polémica* 19 (January–April 1986): 13–26.

34. *El Gráfico*, November 5–25, 1972.

35. The teachers marched, fought police in the streets, and occupied schools. By the end of the four-month strike, the capital was a combat zone, with shuttered stores, tear gas drifting through the streets, and hovering army helicopters showering leaflets that superimposed photos of strike leaders with those of Che Guevara and Karl Marx. *Prensa Libre*, *El Imparcial*, and *La Hora*, April–August 1973.

36. *Acción Popular*, February 1974; Miguel Angel Albizures, *Tiempo de sudor y lucha* (Mexico: N.p., 1987), 32.

37. CNT, Untitled leaflet, October 1974, CDIC, expediente Trabajadores.

38. CNT, "El Sindicato," Guatemala City, 1975, CDIC, expediente Trabajadores.

39. Interview with Miguel Angel Albizures, Mexico City, November 1984.

Chapter 4

1. Interview with Miguel Cifuentes, New York City, March 1984.

2. Interview with Roberto Lemus, Mexico City, November 1984; Danielo Rodríguez, *El 21 de Junio de 1980* (Mexico: Equipo de Apoyo Sindical, 1990).

3. Interview with Sonia Oliva, Costa Rica, March 1986.

4. Archivo, Dirección Administrativo de Trabajo.

5. The law students belonged to Legal Aid for Workers and Peasants (COJUCO). Among the COJUCO students were the soon-to-be-prominent CNT lawyers Rosa María Wantland, Yolanda Urízar, and Frank Larrue. Urízar was disappeared in 1983. Others live in exile.

6. *Diario Impacto*, June 22, 1975; *La Nación*, June 23, 1975. Interview with Frank Larrue, Washington, D.C., March 1984.

7. Interview with Marta Gloria Torres, New York City, December 1984. The legal staff included Marta Gloria Torres and her husband Enrique, as well as Danielo Rodríguez, Leónel Luna, and Roberto Lemus. It soon recruited law students Yolanda Urízar, Rosa María Wantland, and Frank Larrue.

8. Interview with Joaquín Rosales, Guatemala City, December 1985.

9. Interview with Mercedes Gómez, Guatemala City, December 1985.

10. Ibid.

11. Interview with Joaquín Rosales, Guatemala City, December 1985.

12. Interviews with Guillermo Romero, Pablo Telón, and Joaquín Rosales, Guatemala City, August 1984, December 1985.

13. Interviews with Guillermo Romero, Domingo Pérez, Luis Quevedo, Giovanni Quevedo, María Quevedo, Joaquín Rosales, and Pablo Telón, Guatemala City, August 1984, December 1985.

14. Interview with Mercedes Gómez, Guatemala City, August 1984.

15. Interview with Pablo Telón, Guatemala City, December 1985.

16. Ibid.

17. Interview with Mercedes Gómez, Guatemala City, November 1985.

18. Interview with Guillermo Romero, Guatemala City, August 1984.

19. Interview with Joaquín Rosales, Guatemala City, December 1985.

20. Interview with Pablo Telón, Guatemala City, December 1985.

21. Interview with Mercedes Gómez, Guatemala City, November 1985.

22. Ibid.

23. Interviews with the widows Carmen López Balam and María Quevedo, Guatemala City, August 1984.

24. *Prensa Libre*, March 26, 1976.

25. *La Nación*, March 30, 1976.

26. CNUS press release, April 15, 1975, Centro de Documentación, Inforpress Centroamérica (CDIC), expediente CNUS.

27. See Roger Plant, *Guatemala: Unnatural Disaster* (London: Latin American Bureau, 1978).

28. CNUS leaflet, April 3, 1976, CDIC, expediente CNUS.

29. *Diario Impacto*, April 26, 1976.

30. Ibid., May 18–28, 1976; Various authors, "La huelga de Pantaleón," *Revista de la Facultad de Ciencias Jurídicas y Sociales de Guatemala* 4 (June–October 1977): 34–53; Interview with a former Pantaleón worker, name withheld upon request, Guatemala City, August 1984.

31. *Prensa Libre*, May 26, 1976; *La Nación*, May 27, 1976.

32. AVANCSO, *La política de desarrollo del estado guatemalteco, 1986–1987* (Guatemala: AVANCSO, 1988).

33. Interview with Roberto Lemus, Mexico City, November 1984.

34. *Diario Impacto*, March 11, 1977; *Prensa Libre*, March 13, 1977; Interviews with Marta Gloria Torres (New York City, December 1984) and Sonia Oliva (Costa Rica, March 1986).

35. Minas de Guatemala, owned by the Abularach family, had opened in the 1960s, transforming Mam peasants into miners. When the union organized in 1974, it represented 320 workers and was headed by Luis Federico Castillo Mauricio, who was murdered in the early 1980s.

36. Luis Federico Castillo Mauricio, unpublished diary, author's possession.

37. *Prensa Libre*, November 15, 1977; *Diario Impacto*, November 16, 1977.

38. *Gente Seminario* 12 (November 1977): 9.

39. *El Gráfico*, November 17, 1977.

40. Interview, name withheld upon request, Guatemala City, December 1985.

41. Inspired by the miners' march, 1,500 workers constructing a hydroelectric dam in Aguacapa on the southern coast struck against the Mexican firm Associated Civil Engineers (ICA) in early 1978 and marched to Guatemala City to gather support for their demands for higher pay and better treatment without receiving a large welcome. They won an agreement but within a year ICA had hired Mexican workers and had reduced the union to nothing. Interview with Miguel Angel Albizures, November 1984, Mexico City.

Workers on a second state hydroelectric project were more successful, but in the regional and not the national context. In April 800 workers on an ICA hydroelectric project in Alta Verapaz demanding higher wages marched to Cobán, where the local population supported them. A representative of the Labor Ministry flew up and some concessions were granted. Luis Raul Salvado C., "Crónica de una huelga," *Política y Sociedad* 14 (June 1978): 103–21.

42. *Diario Impacto*, April 13, 1977; CNT press release, February 1977, CDIC, expediente CNT.

43. *El Gráfico*, March 13–22, 1977; *Diario Impacto*, April 13, 1977.

44. Interview with Miguel Angel Albizures, Mexico City, November 1984. For an English-language discussion of Guatemalan revolutionary groups, see Susanne Jonas, *The Battle for Guatemala: Rebels, Death Squads, and U.S. Power* (Boulder, Colo.: Westview, 1991).

45. Interview with Sonia Oliva, Costa Rica, March 1986.

46. CNUS, October 22, 1977, CDIC, expediente CNUS.

47. CNT, "Un crisis relevadora," April 1978, CDIC, expediente CLAT.

48. CNUS, January 1978, CDIC, expediente CNUS.

49. "Third Extraordinary National Congress," April 30, 1978, CDIC, expediente CNT.

50. Interview with Miguel Cifuentes, New York City, March 1984.

51. Ibid.

52. Ibid.

Chapter 5

1. The epigraph is quoted from Roque Dalton, *Miguel Mármol* (Costa Rica: EDUCA, 1982), 387. For the 1978 slaughter of Indians in Panzós, see Gabriel Aguilera Peralta, "The Massacre at Panzós and Capitalist Development in Guatemala," *Monthly Review* 31 (December 1979): 26–32.

2. Interview, name withheld upon request, Guatemala City, March 1986.

3. *Adelante*, August 1979.

4. *Diálogo*, July 1978.

5. Interview with Marcos Antonio Figueroa, Costa Rica, March 1986.

6. *El Gráfico, El Imparcial*, and *La Nación*, February 24, 1978; *Diario La Tarde* and *La Hora*, February 28, 1978; *La Nación, Diario La Tarde, Diario Impacto*, and *La Hora*, March 4, 1978; Interview with Marcos Antonio Figueroa, Costa Rica, March 1986.

7. One story illustrates the impossibility of gaining union recognition at this time. Bus drivers at the Eureka Bus Company had asked for legal recognition from the Labor Ministry in early 1977. They heard nothing until the time of the July–August 1978 strike, when they received an obscure reply: since Eureka's owners had established a cooperative, the ministry needed to know "whether the cooperativists are the same people forming a union and whether cooperativists can legally organize a union." The workers responded that none of them, or any other worker at Eureka, belonged to the owners' cooperative. A year later the ministry communicated to the union that it remained "unclear who is a cooperativist and who is a worker, who is in the cooperative and who is in the union." The workers re-

plied that a year had passed since they answered this query, but they would explain again, which they did at great length. But after receiving this communication, the ministry in September 1979, when several Eureka drivers trying to unionize were fired, solicited from the National Institute of Cooperatives a definition of cooperatives and a judgment as to whether the workers could unionize. The institute explained that no controversy existed "in the case of the workers in a cooperative organizing a union if the workers did not belong to the cooperative." One year later, in August 1980, the union gained legal status. By that time, two key leaders were dead and others had been forced into inactivity; the union remained on the books, "legal" and "inactive." Dirección Administrativo de Trabajo, expediente 635.

8. *Diario Impacto*, July 14, 1978; *Nuevo Diario*, July 15, 1978.

9. *La Hora*, July 15, 1978.

10. *Nuevo Diario*, July 15, 1978.

11. Interview, name withheld upon request, Mexico City, November 1984.

12. *Diario Impacto*, August 1, 1978; *La Nación*, August 2, 1978.

13. FENOT, "Al pueblo de Guatemala," August 10, 1978, Centro de Documentación, Inforpress Centroamérica (CDIC), expediente Trabajadores; *Nuevo Diario*, August 11, 1978.

14. Interview with Carlos Escobar, Guatemala City, August 1984.

15. *Diario La Tarde*, August 17, 1978; *Nuevo Diario*, August 30, 1978; *El Imparcial*, September 8, 1978; Carlos González Quezada, *Analisis político Guatemala 1978 y sus implicaciónes para el 79* (Guatemala: Instituto de Ciencias Políticas y Sociales Universidad Rafael Landivar, 1978), 33–50.

16. *La Nación*, September 28, 1978.

17. Interviews with Marcos Antonio Figueroa (Costa Rica, March 1986), Israel Márquez (Mexico City, November 1984), and Miguel Angel Albizures (Mexico City, November 1984).

18. Interview, name withheld upon request, Guatemala City, September 1984.

19. *Noticias de Guatemala*, October 11, 1978.

20. Interview with Edgar Gutiérrez, Mexico City, November 1984.

21. CNUS press release, October 10, 1978, CDIC, expediente CNUS.

22. Interview with Marcos Antonio Figueroa, Costa Rica, March 1986.

23. CNUS, CETE, AEU, MONAP, CEEM, and FERG press release, October 1978, CDIC, expediente CNUS.

24. *La Nación*, October 14, 1978.

25. Gabriel Aguilera Peralta, "Luchas sociales en Guatemala: La huelga de Octubre de 1978" (paper presented at four meetings of Latin American and Caribbean historians, 1983).

26. Phillip Berryman, *The Religious Roots of Revolution: Christians in Central American Revolutions* (New York: Orbis Books, 1984), 192.

27. Interview with Miguel Cifuentes, New York City, March 1984.

28. Danielo Rodríguez, *El 21 de Junio de 1980* (Mexico: Equipo de Apoyo Sindical, 1990), 72; Interview, name withheld upon request, Mexico City, November 1984.

29. CNUS press release, October 20, 1979, CDIC, expediente CNUS.

30. *Diario Impacto*, July 1, 1979.

31. Unions of El Izotal and Tejidos San Antonio, "Carta de los 25 trabajadores" (leaflet), October 1979, CDIC, expediente Trabajadores.

32. CNT press release, October 1979, CDIC, expediente CNUS.

33. Interview with Rosa María Wantland, Mexico City, November 1984.

34. Interview with Domingo Pérez, Guatemala City, August 1984.

35. *Adelante*, July 1978.

36. *La Nación*, October 8, 1978.

37. Interview with CAVISA worker, name withheld upon request, Guatemala City, October 1984.

38. Leaflet, Union of Private Guards (VIP), February 1980, CDIC, expediente Trabajadores.

39. Interview with Marcos Antonio Figueroa, Costa Rica, March 1986.

40. For information about CUC, see Dina Jiménez, "El movimiento campesino en Guatemala, 1969–1980," and Arturo Aries, "El movimiento indígena en Guatemala, 1970–1983," in Daniel Camacho and Rafael Menjívar, *Movimiento populares en Centroamérica* (Costa Rica: EDUCA, 1985), 62–119, 293–342; Rigoberta Menchu with Elizabeth Debray, ed., *I. . . Rigoberta Menchu* (London: Verso, 1984); Arturo Arias, "Changing Indian Identity: Guatemala's Violent Transition to Modernity," in Carol Smith, *Guatemalan Indians and the State, 1540–1988* (Austin: University of Texas Press, 1990), 230–58; José Manuel Fernández Fernández, *El Comité de Unidad Campesina: Origin y desarrollo* (Guatemala: Cerca, 1988); and Rigoberta Menchu y Comité de Unidad Campesina, *Trenzando el futuro* (Mexico: Gaka, 1992).

41. *De Sol y Sol*, nos. 33–43, March–April 1980; *Diario Impacto*, March 2, 1980.

42. Gabriel Ixmata, "El pueblo de Guatemala: Su vida, su cultura, su revolución" (pamphlet), Guatemala, 1982.

43. Rodríguez, *El 21 de Junio*, 124–37; Miguel Angel Albizures, *Tiempo de sudor y lucha* (Mexico: N.p., 1987), 104–7.

44. *Diario Impacto*, March 1, 1980.

45. CNUS press release, May 1, 1980, CDIC, expediente CNUS.

46. *Diario Impacto*, May 4, 1980.

47. Rodríguez, *El 21 de Junio*; Albizures, *Tiempo de sudor y lucha*. CNUS stated that "historically this [responsibility] has been recorded and the political line of these two groups will never be cleansed of this." *Unidad*, August–September 1980.

48. *Unidad*, August–September 1980.

49. Ibid.

50. Miguel Angel Albizures, "La lucha de los trabajadores y el movimiento obrero guatemalteco" (manuscript), Mexico, 1985, 112–13 (courtesy of the author).

51. Romero Lucas García belonged to a group of army officers intent on becoming as wealthy as they could. Others, above all General Héctor Gramajo, criticized them for losing sight of the army's key political role in their rush for economic power. Gramajo and his allies in the military carried out a rectification campaign in the early 1980s, when they removed individualistic, myopic officers from important commands and imposed the discipline necessary to wage war against the civilian population. See AVANCSO, *La política de desarrollo del estado guatemalteco, 1986–1987* (Guatemala: AVANCSO, 1988).

52. See Mario Payeras, *El trueno en la ciudad: Episodios de la lucha armada urbana de 1981 en Guatemala* (Mexico, 1987).

Chapter 6

1. CNT Bulletin, no. 12, 1977; *Diario Impacto*, March 3, 1977; *El Gráfico*, March 16, 1977; Interview with Marta Gloria Torres, New York City, December 1984.

2. STEGAC, "Compañeros trabajadores en general," Guatemala, 1983.

3. Henry J. Frundt, *Refreshing Pauses: Coca-Cola and Human Rights in Guatemala* (New York: Praeger, 1987), 42–55.

4. *Diario de Centro América*, February 13, 1978.

5. Interview with Gregorio González, Guatemala City, August 1984.

6. Interviews with Pablo Telón and Mercedes Gómez, Guatemala City, November 1985.

7. *Voz y acción: Vocero popular de trabajadores de Coca-Cola*, September 1978.

8. Ibid.

9. *La Nación*, December 13, 1978.

10. Interview with Hugo Aparicio, Guatemala City, August 1984.

11. Interview with Pablo Telón, Guatemala City, November 1985.

12. *La Hora*, January 24, 1979; *El Gráfico*, January 24, 1979; Interview with Israel Márquez, Mexico City, November 1984.

13. Interview with Gregorio González, Guatemala City, August 1984.

14. Israel Márquez to STEGAC, *Diario Impacto*, February 9, 1979.

15. STEGAC to Israel Márquez, *El Gráfico*, February 16, 1979.

16. STEGAC press release, January 29, 1979, Centro de Documentación, Inforpress Centroamérica (CDIC), expediente Trabajadores.

17. Interview with Rodolfo Robles, Guatemala City, August 1984.

18. *Prensa Libre*, March 10, 1979.

19. Interview with Gregorio González, Guatemala City, August 1984.

20. *Nuevo Diario*, January 17, 1979.

21. Frundt, *Refreshing Pauses*, 83.

22. Interview with Joaquín Rosales, Guatemala City, November 1985.

23. In May, union member Silverio Vásquez was shot and survived and another was kidnapped, beaten, and released. At the end of June, guerrillas tried to shoot EGSA manager Alfonso Riege. They missed and killed his bodyguard, whose widow became part of the community to which STEGAC felt obligated and it assumed her support.

24. Ninety-eight percent of the shareholders voted against the resolution. Frundt, *Refreshing Pauses*, 73–90.

25. Congressman Donald Pease to President Jimmy Carter, September 20, 1979; IUF Bulletin, October 29, 1979; Allen Nairn, "Coca-Cola Backs Down in Guatemala Dispute," *Multinational Monitor*, July 1980; Walker Simon, "After Global Pressure, Things Go Better with Coke," *Food Monitor*, November–December 1980.

26. International Union of Food and Drug Workers, *The Coca-Cola Guatemala Campaign* (Geneva: IUF, 1983), 36.

27. Interview with Evert Soto, Guatemala City, August 1984.

28. Interview with Rodolfo Robles, Guatemala City, August 1984.

29. Interview with Marco Tulio Loza, Guatemala City, January 1986.

30. STEGAC, "Al pueblo de Guatemala," February 1980, CDIC, expediente Trabajadores.

31. Interview with Mercedes Gómez, Guatemala City, November 1985.

32. Ibid.

33. Interview with Pablo Telón, Guatemala City, November 1985.

34. Interview with Mercedes Gómez, Guatemala City, November 1985.

35. Interview with Evert Soto, Guatemala City, August 1984.

36. Interview with Mercedes Gómez, Guatemala City, November 1985.

37. Interviews with Gregorio González (Guatemala City, August 1984) and Marco Tulio Loza (Guatemala City, January 1986).

38. Interview with Hugo Aparicio, Guatemala City, August 1984.

39. Interview with Mercedes Gómez, Guatemala City, November 1985.

40. For more information on this campaign, see Miguel Angel Reyes Illescas, "La derrota de una transnacional," Costa Rica, July 1985 (mimeographed); Mike Gatehouse and Miguel Angel Reyes Illescas, *Soft Drink, Hard Labour* (London: Latin American Research Bureau, 1987); International Union of Food and Drug Workers, *The Coca-Cola Guatemala Cam-*

paign; and Frundt, *Refreshing Pauses*. IUF attributes much of its success to continuity (for example, writing letters over a period of time) and nonsectarianism (for example, its ability to ally itself with the AFL-CIO unions).

41. Interview with Mercedes Gómez, Guatemala City, November 1985.

42. Interview, name withheld upon request, Guatemala City, November 1985.

43. Interview with Mercedes Gómez, Guatemala City, August 1984.

44. Interviews with Gregorio González (Guatemala City, August 1984) and Mercedes Gómez (Guatemala City, November 1985).

45. Interview with Mercedes Gómez, Guatemala City, August 1984.

46. Interview with Sally Cornwall (IUF staff member), New York City, December 1984.

47. Interview with Rodolfo Robles, Guatemala City, August 1984.

48. Interviews with Marcos Alvarado (Guatemala City, August 1984, November 1985), Rodolfo Robles (Guatemala City, August 1984), Guillermo Romero (Guatemala City, August 1984), Joaquín Rosales (Guatemala City, November 1985), Pablo Telón (Guatemala City, November 1985), and Emilio Ortíz (Guatemala City, August 1984).

49. Interview with Pablo Telón, Guatemala City, November 1985.

50. Interview with Joaquín Rosales, Guatemala City, August 1984.

51. Reyes Illescas, "La derrota de una transnacional"; Interview with Hugo Barahona, New York City, December 1984.

52. Interview with Rodolfo Robles, Guatemala City, August 1984.

53. Ibid.

54. Interview with Carlos Escobar, Guatemala City, November 1985.

55. Interview with Emilio Ortíz, Guatemala City, August 1984.

56. Interview with Mauro Hernández, Guatemala City, August 1984.

57. Interview with Rosa Méndez, Guatemala City, August 1984.

58. Interview with Marco Tulio Loza, Guatemala City, August 1984.

59. Interview with Esperanza Jiménez, Guatemala City, August 1984. Jiménez died of cancer in 1992.

60. Interview with Angel Castellanos, Guatemala City, August 1984.

61. Interview with Guillermo Romero, Guatemala City, August 1984.

62. Interview with Rodolfo Robles, Guatemala City, August 1984.

63. Interview with Pablo Telón, Guatemala City, November 1985.

64. Ibid.

65. Interview with Rodolfo Robles, Guatemala City, August 1984.

66. Interview with Freddy Mack, Guatemala City, August 1984.

67. Interview with Guillermo Romero, Guatemala City, August 1984.

68. Interview with Hugo Ramírez, Guatemala City, August 1984.

69. Interview with Eduardo Bautista, Guatemala City, August 1984.

70. Interview with Marco Tulio Loza, Guatemala City, January 1986.

71. Interviews with Emilio Ortíz and Mauro Hernández, Guatemala City, November 1985.

72. Personal communication.

73. Interview with Joaquín Rosales, Guatemala City, February 1987.

Conclusion

1. Kurt Petersen, *The Maquiladora Revolution in Guatemala* (New Haven: Institute for International Human Rights, 1992).

2. Interview with Jorge Lemus, Guatemala City, August 1984.

3. Craig Calhoun, *The Question of Class Struggle: Social Foundations of Popular Radicalism during the Industrial Revolution* (Chicago: University of Chicago Press, 1982); June Nash, *We Eat the Mines and the Mines Eat Us* (New York: Columbia University Press, 1979); Jeffrey Gould, *To Lead as Equals: Rural Protest and Political Consciousness in Chinandega, Nicaragua, 1912–1979* (Chapel Hill: University of North Carolina Press, 1990); Douglas Kincaid, "Peasants into Rebels: Community and Class in Rural El Salvador," *Comparative Studies in Society and History* 29, no. 3 (July 1987): 466–94; Carol Smith, "Culture and Community: The Language of Class in Guatemala," in Mike Davis, ed., *The Year Left 2* (London: Verso, 1987): 197–217.

4. Quintin Hoare and Geoffrey Nowell Smith, eds., *Selections from the Prison Notebooks of Antonio Gramsci* (New York: International Publishers, 1971), 171.

Index

Ac Bín, Gonzalo, 58, 151
Acción Popular, 102
ACRICASA textile plant: union organization at, 10, 107, 244–45; working conditions in, 51–52, 57, 243–44; labor strikes, 127, 150, 245–46; and Coca-Cola plant occupation, 221, 222
Agriculture, 17, 19, 166; and rural migration, 8, 56, 57, 59–60; forced labor, 14
Aguilera Peralta, Gabriel, 98, 239
Alarcón Monsanto, Carlos, 147, 186
Albizures, Miguel Angel, 174 (ill.); exile of, 5–6, 154; training in JOC, 84–86, 90–91; as CNT union organizer, 94, 99, 106, 107, 111, 117, 127, 244; and U.S. unions, 103–4; and guerrilla organizations, 134; on failures of labor movement, 172–73
Aldana, René, 195, 196, 199, 252
Alliance for Progress, 33, 34
Alonso, Efraín, 60, 99–100, 235–42
Alvarado, Huberto, 18, 24
Alvarado, Marcos, 206
Alvarado Monzón, Bernardo, 18
Alvarez Ruiz, Donald, 186
American Federation of Labor-Congress of Industrial Organizations (AFL-CIO), 10, 29–30, 32, 33–34, 39, 121
American Friends Service Committee, 178
American Institute for Free Labor Development (AIFLD), 33–34
Amnesty International, 190, 191
Anticommunism, 29; in labor movement, 19, 30, 35, 88; of Guatemalan regimes, 26–27, 97
Aparicio, Hugo, 183; in Coca-Cola union leadership, 187, 195, 197, 216, 229; in Coca-Cola workers' strike, 198, 199–200; and rejuvenation of Coca-Cola union, 204, 207, 208
April 12 Movement, 43–44
Arana Osorio, Carlos, 34, 45, 52, 101, 102, 105, 135
Arbenz Guzmán, Jacobo: labor policies, 17, 19, 22–23, 235–36; overthrow of, 23–24, 26, 30, 236; Catholic church and, 35, 82
Archila, Miguel, 156
Arenas Barrera, José Luis, 259 (n. 50)
Arévalo, Juan José, 235, 257 (n. 16); labor policies, 17, 21, 22; Catholic church and, 35, 82
Army of Guatemala, 101, 272 (n. 51); war

and bus drivers' strikes, 145, 146; and repression of Coca-Cola union, 177, 193, 198, 205, 215–16, 226

Labor strikes, 9, 22–23, 32–33, 170; Labor Code restrictions on, 22, 28, 108; glass workers, 40; plantation workers, 52–53, 125, 167, 168–69; textile workers, 102, 127, 245–46; teachers, 103, 266 (n. 35); INCATECU shoe factory, 108–9, 110, 120, 121; state workers, 127, 144–45, 149, 150, 151–52; bus drivers, 145–46, 147–48, 152; Coca-Cola workers, 197–98, 200, 205

Labor unions, 6; violent repression of, 2, 30, 32, 37, 46–47, 66, 102, 157, 176; organization of, 2–3, 5, 17–18, 22, 40, 101–2, 105, 107–8, 127, 232; destroyed by state repression, 4, 8, 47–48; effects on working class, 7, 20, 31, 39–40, 93, 97, 172–73; revolutionary role of, 7, 155; worker participation rates, 8–9; number of legally recognized, 9, 28, 131; in Guatemala City, 9–10, 56, 106, 108, 126, 131, 231–32; legal abolition of, 16, 25, 34–35; Revolution of 1944 and, 17, 22–23, 136; communist influences in, 20, 35, 36–37, 47; the Liberation and, 25, 27, 34–35, 36; political activity forbidden to, 27; employer tactics for defeating, 27–28, 29, 98, 125–26; legal recognition process, 27–28, 31, 41, 96, 98, 116, 269–70 (n. 7); U.S. role in organizing, 29–34; Catholic activism and, 35–36, 80, 89–92; women activists and, 57, 73, 74–76, 233; Indian activists and, 58–59, 188; and sexual harassment, 75, 76, 100; in United States, 104; collective action by, 120–21, 122, 191; guerrilla influences in, 133, 134; declines in membership, 150, 157, 165

Ladinos, 15, 55, 229, 255–56 (n. 5), 262–63 (n. 18); in labor movement,

57–59, 166, 167; in guerrilla movement, 143

La Elegante shirt factory, 94–97, 99, 120

Land reform, 17, 19, 20–21, 29, 43, 45, 50

La Perla plantation, 259 (n. 50)

Larrue, Frank, 267 (n. 5)

Latin America: Communist parties in, 19, 133; labor law in, 28; industrialization in, 53–54, 55; Catholic organizations in, 82; Christian Democratic parties in, 97; trade unionism in, 231; disappearances in, 253 (n. 2)

Latin American Confederation of Workers (CLAT), 33, 82, 97, 99, 136, 191, 240

Laugerud, Kjell, 105–6, 129, 135; labor organization under, 107, 108, 122, 126, 142–43

Lawyers, 98, 106, 131–32, 228

Legal Aid for Workers and Peasants (COJUCO), 267 (n. 5)

Leninism, 138, 173, 254 (n. 11)

Leo XIII (pope), 35, 84

León Schlotter, René de, 98, 239–40

Liberal party, 14, 15–16, 64

Liberation, the, 25–27, 34–36, 37–38, 50

Liberation Theology, 82, 83, 88, 90, 144, 178, 182

López, Abel, 83, 90

López Balam, Manuel, 120; assassination of, 58, 154, 189–90, 193; in Coca-Cola union leadership, 185, 187

López Larrave, Mario, 5, 40, 108, 122, 128

Loza, Marco Tulio, 1–2, 68–69, 72, 73, 192, 225, 249–52

Lucas García, Romero, 67, 148, 203, 272 (n. 51); violent repression under, 46, 143, 167; elected president, 140, 142–43

McClellan, Andrew, 30–31, 32

Machado, Antonio, 66